Advancing Maths for AQA
STATISTICS 1

Roger Williamson, Gill Buqué, Jim Miller and Chris Worth

Series editors
Roger Williamson   Sam Boardman   Graham Eaton
Ted Graham   Keith Parramore

Heinemann Educational Publishers
a division of Heinemann Publishers (Oxford) Ltd,
Halley Court, Jordan Hill, Oxford OX2 8EJ

OXFORD   MELBOURNE   AUCKLAND   JOHANNESBURG
BLANTYRE   GABORONE   PORTSMOUTH NH (USA)   CHICAGO

New material © Roger Williamson, Gill Buqué, Jim Miller and Chris Worth 2000
Existing material © CIMT 1995

First published in 2000

02 01 10 9 8 7 6 5 4 3

ISBN 0 435 51312 5

Cover design by Miller, Craig and Cocking

Typeset and illustrated by Tech-Set Limited, Gateshead, Tyne & Wear

Printed and bound by Bath Press in the UK

Acknowledgements
The publishers and authors acknowledge the work of the writers, David Cassell,
Ian Hardwick, Mary Rouncefield, David Burghes, Ann Ault and Nigel Price of
the *AEB Mathematics for ASA A-Level Series*, from which some exercises and
examples have been taken.

The publishers' and authors' thanks are due to the AEB for permission to
reproduce questions from past examination papers.

The answers have been provided by the authors and are not the responsibility
of the examining board.

About this book

This book is one in a series of textbooks designed to provide you with exceptional preparation for AQA's new Advanced GCE Specification B. The series authors are all senior members of the examining team and have prepared the textbooks specifically to support you in studying this course.

Finding your way around

The following are there to help you find your way around when you are studying and revising:

- **edge marks** (shown on the front page) – these help you to get to the right chapter quickly;
- **contents list** – this identifies the individual sections dealing with key syllabus concepts so that you can go straight to the areas that you are looking for;
- **index** – a number in bold type indicates where to find the main entry for that topic.

Key points

Key points are not only summarised at the end of each chapter but are also boxed and highlighted within the text like this:

> A **parameter** is a numerical property of a **population** and a **statistic** is a numerical property of a **sample**.

Exercises and exam questions

Worked examples and carefully graded questions familiarise you with the specification and bring you up to exam standard. Each book contains:

- Worked examples and Worked exam questions to show you how to tackle typical questions; Examiner's tips will also provide guidance;
- Graded exercises, gradually increasing in difficulty up to exam-level questions, which are marked by an [A];
- Test-yourself sections for each chapter so that you can check your understanding of the key aspects of that chapter and identify any sections that you should review;
- Answers to the questions are included at the end of the book.

Contents

CHAPTER 1

Collection of data

Learning objectives

After studying this chapter, you should be able to:
- identify different types of variable and to distinguish between primary and secondary data
- understand the terms population, sample, parameter, statistic
- use random digits to select a random sample.

1.1 What is statistics?

> Statistics is about all aspects of dealing with data: how to collect it, how to summarise it numerically, how to present it pictorially and how to draw conclusions from it.

This chapter introduces some statistical terminology you will need to understand.

Statistics deals with events which have more than one possible outcome. If you buy a sandwich, in a canteen, priced at £1.20 and offer the cashier a £5 note you should receive £3.80 in change. This is not statistics as there is (or should be) only one amount of change possible.

If the canteen manager wishes to know how much customers spend when visiting the canteen, this is statistics because different customers spend different amounts.

The quantity which varies – in this case the amount of money – is called a **variable**.

Who uses statistics?
- Car manufacturers to ensure components meet specification.
- Doctors to compare the results of different treatments for the same condition.
- Government to plan provision of schools and health services.
- Scientists to test their theories.
- Opinion pollsters to find the public's opinion on local or national issues.

Types of variables

Qualitative variables

There are a number of different types of variables.

> **Qualitative variables** do not have a numerical value. Place of birth, sex of a baby and colour of car are all qualitative variables.

Quantitative variables

> **Quantitative variables** do have a numerical value. They can be **discrete** or **continuous**.

- **Discrete variables** take values which change in steps:

The number of eggs a hen lays in a week can only take whole number values. **Discrete** means separate – there are no possible values in between.

Variables which are counted, such as the number of cars crossing a bridge in a minute, are discrete but discrete variables are not limited to whole number values. For example, if a sample of five components are examined, the proportion which fail to meet the specifications is a discrete variable which can take the values 0, 0.2, 0.4, 0.6, 0.8 and 1.

- **Continuous variables** can take any value in an interval. For example, height of a child, length of a component or weight of an apple. Such variables are measured, not counted.

← 12.423 cm →

A lizard could be 12 cm long or 12.5 cm or any length in between. In practice length will be measured to a given accuracy, say the nearest millimetre. Only certain values will be possible, but in theory there is no limit to the number different possible lengths.

Sometimes variables which are strictly discrete may be treated as continuous. Money changes in steps of 1p and so is a discrete variable. However, if you are dealing with hundreds of pounds the steps are so small that it may be treated as continuous.

Primary and secondary data

A vast amount of data on a wide variety of topics is published by the government and other organisations. Much of it appears in publications such as *Monthly Digest of Statistics, Social Trends* and *Annual Abstract of Statistics*. These will provide useful data for many investigations. These data are known as **secondary** data as they were not collected specifically for the investigation. Data which are collected for a specific investigation are known as **primary** data.

There will be questions on secondary data in module S2. For this module all you need to know is the difference between primary and secondary data.

EXERCISE 1A

1 Classify each of the following variables as either qualitative, discrete quantitative or continuous quantitative

(a) Colours of roses

(b) Numbers of bicycles owned by families in Stockport

(c) Ages of students at a college

(d) Volumes of contents of vinegar bottles

(e) Countries of birth of British citizens

(f) Numbers of strokes to complete a round of golf

(g) Proportions of faulty valves in samples of size ten

(h) Diameters of cricket balls

(i) Prices, in £, of chocolate bars

(j) Makes of car in a carpark.

1.2 Populations and samples

What is the average height of women in the UK? To find out you could, in theory, measure them all. In practice this would be impossible. Fortunately you don't need to. Instead you can measure the heights of a sample. Provided the sample is carefully chosen you can obtain almost as much information from the sample as from measuring the height of every woman in the UK.

In statistics we distinguish between a **population** and a **sample**.

> A **population** is all the possible data and a **sample** is part of the data.

The **population** is **all** the possible data

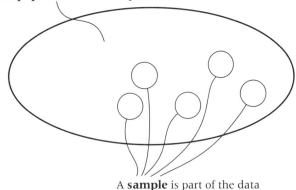

A **sample** is part of the data

The difference between a population and a sample is of great importance in later statistics modules.

Sampling is useful because it reduces the amount of data you need to collect and process. It also allows you to carry out a test without affecting all the population. For example the contents of a sample of tubs of margarine, from a large batch, might be weighed to ensure that the actual contents matched that claimed on the label. Emptying the tubs to weigh the margarine makes them unsaleable, so it would be ridiculous to weigh the contents of the whole population of tubs.

A numerical property of a population is called a **parameter**. A numerical property of a sample is called a **statistic**. For example, the proportion of tubs in the consignment containing more than 450 g of margarine is a parameter while the proportion in the sample is a statistic. Similarly the mean height of all adult females in the UK is a parameter while the mean height of the adult females in our sample is a statistic.

A **parameter** is a numerical property of a **population** and a **statistic** is a numerical property of a **sample**.

EXERCISE 1B

1 Read the following passage and identify an example of:

(a) a population

(b) a sample

(c) a parameter

(d) a statistic

(e) a qualitative variable

(f) a discrete variable

(g) a continuous variable

(h) primary data

(i) secondary data.

A South American sports journalist intends to write a book about football in his home country. He will analyse all first division matches in the season. He records for each match whether it is a home win, an away win or a draw. He also records for each match the total number of goals scored and the amount of time played before a goal is scored. Reference books showed that in the previous season the mean number of goals per game was 2.317. On the first Saturday of the season he recorded the number of goals scored in each match and calculated the mean number of goals per match as 2.412. For the whole season the mean number of goals per match was 2.219.

EXERCISE 1C

Read the following paragraph:

'All pupils at Gortincham High School undergo a medical examination during their first year at the school. The data recorded for each pupil include place of birth, sex, age (in years and months), height and weight. A summary of the data collected is available on request. A class of statistics students decides to collect data on the weight of second year pupils and compare them with the data on first year pupils. It is agreed that the data will be collected one lunchtime. Each member of the class will be provided with a set of bathroom scales and will weigh as many second year pupils as possible. At the end of the lunchtime they will each report the number of pupils weighed and the mean of the weights recorded.'

1 In the paragraph you have just read identify:
  (a) **two** qualitative variables
  (b) **two** continuous variables
  (c) **one** discrete quantitative variable
  (d) secondary data
  (e) primary data
  (f) a population
  (g) a sample
  (h) a statistic.

1.3 Sampling without bias

When you are selecting a sample you need to avoid **bias** – anything which makes the sample unrepresentative. For example, if you want to estimate how often residents of Manchester visit the cinema in a year it would be foolish to stand outside a cinema as the audience is coming out and ask people as they pass. This would give a biased sample as all the people you ask would have been to the cinema at least once that year. You can avoid bias by taking a random sample.

Sampling is a major topic in module S2. In this module you only need to know about random sampling

Random sampling

For a sample to be random every member of the population must have an equal chance of being selected. However, this alone is not sufficient. If the population consists of 10 000 heights and a random sample of size 20 is required then every possible set of 20 heights must have an equal chance of being chosen.

For example, suppose the population consists of the heights of 100 students in a college and you wish to take a sample of size 5. The students' names are arranged in alphabetical order and numbered 00 to 99. A number between 00 and 19 is selected by lottery methods. For example, place 20 equally sized balls numbered 00 to 19 in a bag and ask a blindfolded assistant to pick one out. This student and every 20th one thereafter are chosen and their heights measured. That is if the number 13 is selected then the students numbered 13, 33, 53, 73 and 93 are chosen. Every student would have an equal chance of being chosen. However a sister and brother who were next to each other in the alphabetical list could never both be included in the same sample, so this is **not** a random sample.

> Not every set of five students could be chosen.

Usually if you decide to choose five students at random you intend to choose five different students and would not consider choosing the same student twice. This is known as sampling without replacement.

A random sample chosen without replacement is called a **simple random sample**. If you did allow the possibility of a member of the population being chosen more than once this would be sampling with replacement. A random sample chosen with replacement is called an **unrestricted random sample**.

Random numbers

The previous section referred to numbers being selected by lottery methods. In practice it is much more convenient to use random numbers. These are numbers which have been generated so that each digit from 0 to 9 has an equal chance of appearing in each position. They may be obtained from your calculator or from tables. An extract from random number tables is shown on page 7.

> Your calculator may generate random numbers between 0 and 1, say 0.206. To turn these into random digits ignore 0. and use 206.

Worked example 1

Describe how random numbers could be used to select a simple random sample of size 7 from the 63 residents of Mandela Close who are on the electoral register.

Solution

First number the residents. This is easy as a list of names is already available in the electoral register.

You could place a number by each name, or simply decide that the top name will be 00, the next 01 and so on.

00	Chuzzlewit, M
01	Ngo, S
02	Sodiwala, V
03	Shah, D
04	O'Shea, M

Next choose any starting point in the random number tables:

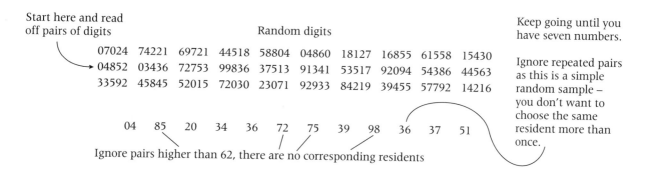

Start here and read off pairs of digits

Random digits

Keep going until you have seven numbers.

```
07024  74221  69721  44518  58804  04860  18127  16855  61558  15430
04852  03436  72753  99836  37513  91341  53517  92094  54386  44563
33592  45845  52015  72030  23071  92933  84219  39455  57792  14216
```

Ignore repeated pairs as this is a simple random sample – you don't want to choose the same resident more than once.

04   85   20   34   36   72   75   39   98   36   37   51

Ignore pairs higher than 62, there are no corresponding residents

When you have seven different numbers in the range 00 to 62, use them to choose the corresponding residents:

04   20   34   36   39   37   51

O'Shea

You could have numbered from 01 to 63. In this case you would have to ignore 00 and numbers greater than 63.

Worked example 2

A trade union wished to ask a sample of 100 members to answer a questionnaire about the services it provides. A list of all the 98 650 members of the union is obtained and numbered from 00 000 to 98 649.

Five digit random numbers are read from a table and any numbers over 98 649 are ignored. This continues until 100 five-digit numbers have been obtained. The corresponding union members are contacted with a request to complete the questionnaire.

(a) What is the name given to this method of sampling?

(b) How would this method of sampling be modified if a simple random sample was required?

(c) Which of these two methods of sampling would you recommend?

Solution

(a) This is an **unrestricted random sample**.

(b) The method would be the same except that any repeated random numbers would be ignored. This would prevent the same union member being selected twice.

(c) There is no purpose in asking the same union member to fill in a questionnaire twice and so a simple random sample would be preferred. (However, as the sample is small compared to the population it is, in this case, very unlikely that the same member would have been selected more than once.)

Worked example 3

Following a spell of particularly bad weather, an insurance company received 42 claims for storm damage on the same day. Sufficient staff were available to investigate only six of these claims. The others would be paid in full without investigation. The claims were numbered 00 to 41 and the following suggestions were made as to the method used to select the six. In each case six different claims are required, so any repeats would be ignored.

Method 1	Choose the six largest claims.
Method 2	Select two digit random numbers, ignoring any greater than 41. When six have been obtained, choose the corresponding claims.
Method 3	Select two digit random numbers. Divide each one by 42, take the remainder and choose the corresponding claims (e.g. if 44 is selected, claim number 02 would be chosen).
Method 4	As 3, but when selecting the random numbers ignore 84 and over.
Method 5	Select a single digit at random, ignoring 7 and over. Choose this and every seventh claim thereafter (e.g. if 3 is selected, choose claims numbered 03, 10, 17, 24, 31 and 38).

Comment on each of the methods including an explanation of whether it would yield a random sample or not.

Solution

Method 1. This would be a sensible policy for the insurance company to adopt but it would not be a random sample. The smaller claims have no chance of being chosen.

Method 2. This is exactly the method we have used in Mandela Close and would yield a random sample.

Method 3. This would not give all claims an equal chance of being chosen. For example, the claim numbered 01 would be included in the sample if 01, 43 or 85 were selected. However, the claim numbered 30 would only be included if 30 or 72 were selected.

> Some claims would have two chances of being included, others would have three chances.

Method 4. This would yield a random sample. All claims would have two numbers associated with them and so have an equal chance of being chosen. In the example on method 3 the claim numbered 01 is now only chosen if 01 or 43 were selected.

Method 5. Each claim would have an equal chance of being selected but this would not be a random sample as not all combinations of six claims could be chosen.

> This is an unnecessarily complicated method but has the advantage that less two-digit random numbers are rejected as too high than in method 2. It might be useful if there were, say, 1050 items in the population numbered 0000 to 1049. Four-digit random numbers would be needed but the great majority would be out of the required range.

EXERCISE ID

1 On a particular day there are 2125 books on the shelves in the fiction section of a library. Describe how random numbers could be used to select a random sample of size 20 (without replacement) from the 2125 books.   [A]

2 Describe how random numbers could be used to select a simple random sample of size 6 from the 712 employees of a large city centre store.   [A]

3 A gardener grew 28 tomato plants. Describe how you would use random numbers to take a simple random sample of size 8 from the population.   [A]

4 The ages in years of the students in a statistics class are given below.

```
19   20   23   21   21   20   20   19   19   20   19   24
20   19   20   22   21   25   20   33   19   19   19   20
24   36   27   33   26   38   43   24   41   30   27   49
```

Explaining fully the procedure you use take

(a) An unrestricted random sample (i.e. allow the same student to be chosen more than once) of size 6 from the population.

(b) a simple random sample (i.e. do not allow the same student to be chosen more than once) of size 6 from the population.   [A]

5 Describe how a simple random sample of 20 rods could be taken from a population of 500 rods.   [A]

6 In order to estimate the mean number of books borrowed by members of a public library, the librarian decides to record the number of books borrowed by a sample of 40 members. She chooses the first member of the sample by selecting a random integer, r, between 1 and 5 inclusive. She then includes in her sample the rth member to leave the library one morning and every 5th member to leave after that until her sample of 40 is complete. Thus if $r = 3$ she chooses the 3rd, 8th, 13th ... 198th members leaving the library as her sample.

   (a) Does the sample constitute a random sample of the first 200 people leaving the library? Give a reason.

   A list of the names of the 8950 members of the library is available.

   (b) Describe how random sampling numbers could be used to select a random sample (without replacement) of 40 of these names. [A]

7 In a particular parliamentary constituency there are 64 000 names on the electoral register. Of the electors, 32 000 live in property rented from the local authority, 21 000 live in owner-occupied property and 11 000 live in other types of property.

A total of 64 electors are selected at random from those living in property rented from the local authority, 42 electors are selected at random from those living in owner-occupied property and 22 electors are selected at random from those living in other types of property. State, giving a reason, whether a random sample of electors has been selected.

Key point summary

1 **Statistics** is about all aspects of dealing with data.   *p1*

2 **Qualitative variables** do not have a numerical value   *p2*

3 **Discrete quantitative variables** take values which change in steps.   *p2*

4 **Continuous quantitative variables** can take any value in an interval.   *p2*

5 A **population** is all the data.   *p3*

6 A **sample** is part of the data.   *p3*

7 A **parameter** is a numerical property of a population.   *p4*

8 A **statistic** is a numerical property of a sample.   *p4*

9 A **random sample** of size n is a sample selected so that all possible samples of size n have an equal chance of being selected.   *p6*

10 **Simple** random samples are selected without replacement, **unrestricted** random samples are selected with replacement.   *p6*

Test yourself	What to review
1 Explain the difference between a population and a sample.	*Section 1.1*

2 State the type of each of the following variables:
 	
  (a) time you have to wait to see a doctor in a casualty department
 	
  (b) colour of eyes
 	
  (c) proportion of rainy days in a given week.
	Section 1.1

3 Explain the difference between a statistic and a parameter.	*Section 1.2*
4 An inspector tests every 100th assembly coming off a production line. Explain why this is not a random sample of the assemblies.	*Section 1.3*
5 Explain the difference between primary and secondary data.	*Section 1.1*

Test yourself **ANSWERS**

1 A population is all the data a sample is part of the data.

2 (a) Continuous quantitative.

  (b) Qualitative.

  (c) Discrete quantitative.

3 A statistic is a numerical property of a sample, a parameter is a numerical property of a population.

4 Not all combinations of assemblies could be included in the sample. For example two adjacent assemblies could not both be sampled.

5 Primary data is data collected specifically for a particular investigation. Secondary data may be used in the investigation but was not collected specifically for this purpose.

CHAPTER 2

Numerical measures

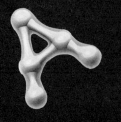

Learning objectives

After studying this chapter you should be able to:
- calculate various averages
- calculate measures of spread
- use these statistics to compare sets of data.

2.1 Measures of average

There are three main measures of the 'average' of a set of numerical data, which you may have met at GCSE, the mode, the median and the mean.

Low average High average

> These three measures of average tell us something that is typical of a set of data.

Mode

The mode is the most frequently occurring value (most popular), and is the easiest to obtain – just see which value occurs most often in the data.

> Sometimes the term 'modal value' is used.

Median

The median is the central value, when the data are arranged in order – easy to do, as data are often given in numerical order.

Mean

The mean is commonly called the 'average' value, and requires more calculation than either of the other two measures. You add all the values, then divide this total by the number of values that you have added up.

> Unlike the other 'averages' all observations contribute to the mean. For most purposes it is the most useful measure of average.

Worked example 1

The number of fish caught by each of 20 anglers is given in the table below.

$$4 \quad 7 \quad 12 \quad 13 \quad 0 \quad 5 \quad 21 \quad 13 \quad 10 \quad 6$$
$$6 \quad 8 \quad 15 \quad 9 \quad 6 \quad 0 \quad 14 \quad 12 \quad 6 \quad 8$$

Find

(a) the modal number of fish per angler

(b) the median number of fish per angler

(c) the mean number of fish per angler.

Solution

For both the mode and the median, it is clearer if the numbers are arranged in order:

$$0 \quad 0 \quad 4 \quad 5 \quad 6 \quad 6 \quad 6 \quad 6 \quad 7 \quad 8$$
$$8 \quad 9 \quad 10 \quad 12 \quad 12 \quad 13 \quad 13 \quad 14 \quad 15 \quad 21$$

> With an odd number of values, there is one central value. If there are an even number of values, the median is halfway between the two central values.

(a) The **modal** number of fish is **6**, as 6 occurs more frequently than any other value (it occurs four times).

(b) As there are an even number of values (20) you need to look at the 10th and 11th value in the ordered list. As both values are 8, then the **median** number of fish is **8**.

> If the two central values had been 8 and 9, say, then the median would be the mid-point:

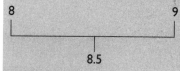

(c) The sum of the 20 values is 175. So the **mean** number of fish is $\frac{175}{20} = $ **8.75**.

When the data are given in a frequency table, the calculation of these three averages is made a little easier. The *frequency* is the number of times an observation occurs.

> It is often more convenient to write the frequency table in columns.

Worked example 2

A reunion was held 20 years after the members of Form 11 KQ had left the school. The number of children of each form member is given in the table.

Number of children	0	1	2	3	4	5	6
Number of members	9	4	6	5	2	0	1

Calculate **(a)** the mode, **(b)** the median and **(c)** the mean number of children per member of the form.

No. of children (x)	No. of class members (f)	(x × f)
0	9	0
1	4	4
2	6	12
3	5	15
4	2	8
5	0	0
6	1	6
Total	27	45

Solution

(a) As the most frequent number of children was 0 (nine members had no children) the **mode** is **0**.

(b) There were 27 members at the reunion. The median will be the number of children had by the 14th person, when put in order. Nine members had no children, the next four had one child (i.e. these 13 had no children or one child). Therefore, as there are six members in the next group, each having two children, the 14th member must be in this group. The **median** number of children is therefore **2**.

(c) The total number of children that these 27 members had is most easily calculated as follows.

$(0 \times 9) + (1 \times 4) + (2 \times 6) + (3 \times 5) + (4 \times 2) + (5 \times 0) + (6 \times 1) = 0 + 4 + 12 + 15 + 8 + 0 + 6 = 45$.

The **mean** number of children per member is $\frac{45}{27} = $ **1.67**.

If the data consists of the whole population the mean is usually denoted by μ. If the data is a sample from the population the mean is denoted $\bar{x}$.

Usually you will be dealing with a sample. In example 2 of exercise 1 the tomato plants are clearly a sample from a population of tomato plants. In this case you can calculate $\bar{x}$ the sample mean. This will almost certainly not be equal to μ, the population mean, but may be used as an estimate of μ. In later modules it will be very important for you to be clear about whether you are dealing with a population mean or a sample mean.

The 'Σ' symbol means 'sum of'. If you have a set of values $x_1, x_2, x_3, ..., x_n$, then

$$\sum_{i=1}^{n} x_i = x_1 + x_2 + x_3 ... + x_n$$

The mean value of a set of data $x_1, x_2, x_3 ... x_n$ is $\frac{\Sigma x_i}{n}$

EXERCISE 2A

1 Find the mode, median and mean of these numbers:

17, 4, 9, 19, 6, 11, 6, 8, 9, 15, 6

2 The number of usable tomatoes on 16 tomato plants is given below:

8 5 20 17 10 9 12 9
15 11 9 10 19 10 9 14

Find the mean, mode and median number of tomatoes per plant.

3 The weights of the eight members of a rowing crew, in kilograms, are: 107, 88, 90, 93, 110, 99, 86, 95, to the nearest kilogram.

Find the mean weight of a crew member.

4 The table shows the number of times my team scored 0, 1, 2, …, goals in their 51 games last season.

Number of goals	0	1	2	3	4	5	6	7
Number of games	7	16	13	7	4	2	0	2

Work out the mode, the median and the mean number of goals per game.

5 A die is thrown 40 times. The scores are shown in the table.

Score	1	2	3	4	5	6
Frequency	4	5	6	10	8	7

Work out **(a)** the mode, **(b)** the median and **(c)** the mean score on the die.

6 In the 24 homework exercises that Henry completed last term, his marks, out of 10 each time, are shown in the table.

Mark (out of 10)	0	1	2	3	4	5	6	7	8	9	10
Frequency	0	0	0	1	3	0	1	1	1	4	13

Work out **(a)** the mode, **(b)** the median, and **(c)** the mean homework mark. Which do you think gives the most realistic mark?

7 A set of five whole numbers has a mode, of 3, a median of 4 and a mean of 5. List all possible sets of five numbers having these measures of average.

Discrete and continuous data

The questions in the exercise above all used discrete data – goals in a game, or tomatoes on a plant. You could not have a score of 4.73 on a die, and your team cannot score 2.735 goals in a game. Discrete data can take only certain values (in many cases integers, as in the examples above). You can think of them as **countable** data. If, however, you were to weigh each tomato on a plant, you would not be restricted to whole number answers. Only the accuracy of the weighing scales would limit the number of decimal places you could have. You can think of continuous data as **measurable** – weights, lengths, times, etc. When calculating 'average' values for continuous data, you usually need to put them into suitable groups, or 'class intervals'.

> You have already met discrete and continuous variables in Chapter 1.

Worked example 3

The lengths of 50 metal rods are given in metres, correct to the nearest centimetre. Group the lengths into classes 1.00 m to 1.10 m, 1.10 m to 1.20 m, 1.20 m to 1.30 m, etc. and find the modal length, the median length and the mean length of a rod.

1.34	1.26	1.02	1.53	1.33	1.40	1.19	1.04	1.56	1.44
1.22	1.30	1.13	1.53	1.33	1.40	1.24	1.05	1.24	1.14
1.16	1.32	1.58	1.41	1.25	1.20	1.16	1.13	1.31	1.10
1.44	1.19	1.08	1.47	1.19	1.33	1.13	1.06	1.50	1.32
1.21	1.07	1.22	1.43	1.42	1.03	1.11	1.23	1.33	1.28

Solution

Although it seems straightforward to group the data as requested, we shall need to decide into which group to put a length of, say, 1.20 m. We can decide ourselves, but we need to be consistent. One way (possibly the more conventional way) is to **include** the **lower** boundary and **exclude** the **upper** boundary, in each class interval.

We can write this as '1.00–, 1.10–, 1.20–, …', or '$1.00 \leqslant x < 1.10$, $1.10 \leqslant x < 1.20$, $1.20 \leqslant x < 1.30$', etc.

Putting the lengths into a table will help.

Length of rod	1.00 m –	1.10 m –	1.20 m –	1.30 m –	1.40 m –	1.50 m –
Frequency	7	11	10	9	8	5

The **mode** is **1.33 m**, as it occurs more times (4) than any other length. However, with many different possible lengths, and low frequencies, this is not a useful measure of average. With only small changes you would get a completely different result. For example, if two of the 1.33 m were replaced by 1.32 m and 1.34 m and 1.41 m by 1.44 m, the mode would now be 1.44 m.

The 25th and 26th rod, when put in order, are 1.24 m and 1.25 m. The **median length** is therefore **1.245 m**.

The **mean length** is

$$\frac{(1.34 + 1.26 + 1.02 + \ldots + 1.28)}{50} = \frac{63.35}{50} = \mathbf{1.267\ m}.$$

Grouped data

If we had not been given individual lengths of rods in Example 3 above, but *only* the grouped frequency table, we could not give exact values of the three averages.

> Your calculator is highly likely to have statistical functions where a set of data can be entered, and then the facility of the calculator can give you the mean, variance, standard deviation, and other statistics.
> Some graphical calculators can draw histograms, pie charts, box and whisker plot, scatter diagrams, etc.
> It is important, however, to be aware of the meaning of the various attributes of a set of data and how they are calculated.

> As the data is given to two decimal places, the grouping asked for in the question cannot be used. This is the nearest you can achieve.

Instead of the mode, we could use the **modal class**, which is the '**1.10**–' class, as it has the greatest frequency (11). Compared to the mode in Example 3 above, this *is* a useful measure, as it will not be affected by small changes in the data.

To estimate the mean, we will need to assume that *each* length in a class is equal to the central value of that class – *the mid-interval* length. As the rods were measured to the nearest centimetre, any *true* length greater than 0.995 m and smaller than 1.095 m would go into the '1.00 m–' class. The mid-interval value of this class is therefore 1.045. Similarly, for the other classes, the mid-interval values are 1.145, 1.245, etc. A table makes it clearer.

Length of rod	1.00 m –	1.10 m –	1.20 m –	1.30 m –	1.40 m –	1.50 m –
Mid value	1.045 m	1.145 m	1.245 m	1.345 m	1.445 m	1.545 m
Frequency	7	11	10	9	8	5

The mean may be obtained directly from your calculator.

The best estimate of the **mean** is:

$$\frac{[(1.045 \times 7) + (1.145 \times 11) + (1.245 \times 10) + (1.345 \times 9) + (1.445 \times 8) + (1.545 \times 5)]}{50} = \textbf{1.275 m}$$

If it had been possible to measure the lengths *exactly*, then the mid-interval values would have been 1.05, 1.15, 1.25, etc., and the mean length would have been 1.28 m.

We could estimate the median like this:

There are 18 rods less than 1.20 m, and there are 10 rods in the next class interval. The 25th and 26th rods will therefore be in the 7th and 8th rods in the group, '1.20 m–'.

Our best **estimate of the median** will be $\frac{7\frac{1}{2}}{10}$ into this group,

i.e. $1.195 \text{ m} + \left(\frac{7\frac{1}{2}}{10} \times 0.10 \text{ m}\right) = \textbf{1.27 m}$

Worked example 4

The accuracy of the timing is not stated. In this case assume that the times are exact, so the class mid-values are 5, 15, 25, 35, 45 and 55.

Students were asked how long they had spent on solving a homework problem. The results are shown in the table.

Time (t min)	$0 \leqslant t < 10$	$10 \leqslant t < 20$	$20 \leqslant t < 30$	$30 \leqslant t < 40$	$40 \leqslant t < 50$	$50 \leqslant t < 60$
No. of students	6	17	20	8	4	0

Estimate the median time and the mean time spent on solving the problem.

Solution

There are 55 students, so the median will be the time spent by the 28th student. This is the 5th student in the $20 \leqslant t < 30$ group. Our estimate of the **median** is $20 + \left(\dfrac{5}{20} \times 10\right) = \mathbf{22.5}$ minutes.

Our estimate of the **mean** is:

$$\frac{[(5 \times 6) + (15 \times 17) + (25 \times 20) + (35 \times 8) + (45 \times 4) + (55 \times 0)]}{55}$$

$= 22.636363 \ldots$ or **22.6** minutes.

EXERCISE 2B

In the following questions assume all the measurements are exact.

1 The weights of a sample of 40 items taken at random from a production line are given in the table.

Weight (*g*)	88–	90–	92–	94–	96–	98–
Frequency	4	6	12	10	6	2

Calculate an estimate of (**a**) the median, and (**b**) the mean weight.

2 An athlete has kept a record of the times taken to win a number of 400 m races, over a period of 18 months.

Time (*t*, s)	58–	59–	60–	61–	62–	63–	64–	65–
Frequency	5	8	12	9	14	17	10	5

(**a**) In which period of 1 second does the median 400 m time lie?

(**b**) Estimate the median 400 m time.

(**c**) Calculate an estimate of the mean 400 m time.

3 A market gardener buys some canes. Their lengths are given in the table.

Length (m)	70–	80–	90–	100–	110–	120–	130–
Frequency	13	27	36	68	51	30	12

(**a**) What is the modal group?

(**b**) Estimate the median length.

(**c**) The mean length is supposed to be within 5 cm of 100 cm. Are these canes within the tolerance allowed?

4 The monthly council tax bills payable by the inhabitants of a village is given in the table.

Amount (£)	140–	160–	180–	200–	220–	240–	260–
Frequency	42	37	24	19	7	12	0

Estimate (**a**) the median, and (**b**) the mean council tax bill.

5 A group of students were asked to work out the answer to a calculation. The number of seconds taken is shown in the table.

Time (t, s)	$20 \leqslant t < 40$	$40 \leqslant t < 60$	$60 \leqslant t < 80$	$80 \leqslant t < 100$
No. of students	4	18	25	13

Estimate the mean time taken to do the calculation.

2.2 Measures of spread

Just as with average values in Section 2.1, we will look at three measures of spread which you may have met at GCSE; the range, the interquartile range, and the standard deviation.

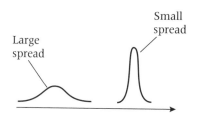

The interquartile range tells you more about the data than the range – it tells you about how much of the data is clustered around the mean.

Range

Even though two sets of data have the same mean value, the data can be more 'spread out' in one of these sets, compared to the other. For example, if A = {4, 5, 5, 6, 7, 9} and B = {1, 3, 3, 5, 6, 8, 10, 12}, then the mean value of each set is 6. Set A values range from 4 to 9 – a **range** of **5** – but set B has a wider **range** of **11** (from 1 to 12).

> The **range** of a set of data is the **difference** between the **highest** value and the **lowest** value of the data. It is very easy to calculate; all you need are two values – the highest and the lowest.

Interquartile range

When a set of data is written in order, you know that the median is $\frac{(n + 1)}{2}$th item of data. The **quartiles** are found in a similar way, the **lower quartile** is the median of the **lower half** of the data, and the **upper quartile** is the median of the **upper half** of the data.

> The range between the quartiles is called the interquartile range (Q_3–Q_1), and covers the middle 50% of the observations.

The upper quartile of a population is the value which is exceeded by the largest quarter of the observations. Similarly the lower quartile is the value which is exceeded by the largest three-quarters of the observations. This definition can lead to difficulties since if, for example, the population has six members it cannot be split exactly into quarters. Most populations have a large number of members and this problem is of no importance. There are minor disagreements among statisticians about how to find the quartiles of small populations. The method given opposite is one acceptable method.

Worked example 5

Find the interquartile range of the following set of data:

24, 24, 25, 26, 26, 26, 27, 27, 30, 33, 33, 35, 35, 36, 43

Solution

The 15 numbers are already given in numerical order. The median value is 8th one $\left\{\frac{(15+1)}{2}\text{th}\right\}$, which is 27, the **lower quartile** is the 4th value, which is **26** and the **upper quartile** is the 12th value, which is **35**.

24, 24, 25, 26, 26, 26, 27, 27, 30, 33, 33, 35,   5, 36, 43

        Q_1 median Q_3

The **interquartile range** is therefore $35 - 26 = \mathbf{9}$.

If only a grouped frequency table is given, then you will have to estimate the quartiles, just as for the median above.

There are seven observations less than the median and the **lower quartile** is the median of these. Similarly the **upper quartile** is the median of the seven observations which are greater than the median.

The lower quartile is often denoted by Q_1 and the upper quartile by Q_3.

If there had been 16 observations the median, *m*, would have divided the sample into two sets of eight. The **lower quartile** would have been the median of the eight observations less than *m* and the **upper quartile** would have been the median of the eight observations greater than *m*.

Worked example 6

When laying pipes, engineers test the soil for 'resistivity'. The table shows the results of 159 tests.

Resistivity (ohms/cm)	Frequency
400–900	5
900–1500	9
1500–3500	40
3500–8000	45
8000–20000	60

Estimate **(a)** the median **(b)** the interquartile range of resistivity.

Solution

The median is the 80th reading, which is the 26th reading in the 3500–8000 group.

$$\textbf{median} = 3500 + \left(\frac{26}{45}\right)(4500) = \mathbf{6100} \text{ ohms/cm}$$

The lower quartile is the 40th reading, which is the 26th reading in the 1500–3000 group.

$$\textbf{lower quartile} = 1500 + \left(\frac{26}{40}\right)(2000) = \mathbf{2800}$$

The upper quartile is the 120th reading, which is the 21st reading in the 8000–20 000 group.

$$\textbf{upper quartile} = 8000 + \left(\frac{21}{60}\right)(12\,000) = \mathbf{12\,000}$$

Hence the **interquartile range** is $12\,200 - 2800 = \mathbf{9400}$ ohms/cm

When dealing with grouped data with a total frequency of *n* the lower quartile is usually taken to be the $\frac{n+1}{4}$ th observation and the upper quartile as the $\frac{3(n+1)}{4}$ th observation. This is consistent with the median being the $\frac{n+1}{2}$ th observation. If *n* is large it is equally acceptable to use the $\frac{n}{4}$ th and $\frac{3n}{4}$ th observations for the quartiles.

There are $5 + 9 + 40 = 54$ readings up to 3500, and so the 80th reading is the $80 - 54 = 26$th reading in the 3500–8000 group.

Worked example 7

Find the interquartile range of the following data:

43, 45, 45, 46, 47, 47, 47, 49, 53, 55, 55, 58

Solution

The lower half of the data are 43, 45, 45, 46, 47, 47. The lower quartile is the median of these six numbers is $\frac{1}{2}(45 + 46) = 45.5$. Similarly, the upper quartile is the median of 47, 49, 53, 55, 55, 58, which is $\frac{1}{2}(53 + 55) = 54$.

The **interquartile range** is therefore $54 - 45.5 =$ **8.5**.

EXERCISE 2C

1 During the last week, I noted down the number of telephone calls that I made each day. The figures were: 12, 28, 9, 17, 15, 6 and 11. What are the lower and upper quartiles.

2 Find the interquartile range for the data below:

12.5 14.7 15.2 18.7 21.1 25.0 39.7 42.4 48.7 50.5 58.2

3 The number of registered players for 13 of the teams in a cricket league are:

15, 15, 16, 16, 18, 19, 19, 19, 20, 20, 22, 22, 24

Evaluate the median, and the lower and upper quartile number of players.

4 Find the lower and upper quartiles, and the median, of these test scores:

4, 13, 10, 5, 8, 17, 15, 15, 9, 12, 15, 18, 20, 11, 16

5 Another two students sat the test in question 4. Their scores were 9 and 14. What are the new median, and the new quartile values?

6 The lengths of the 98 telephone calls that I made in question 1 are given in the table.

Call length (t, min)	$0 \leqslant t < 2$	$2 \leqslant t < 4$	$4 \leqslant t < 6$	$6 \leqslant t < 8$	$8 \leqslant t < 10$
Frequency	21	35	22	14	6

Estimate **(a)** the median, **(b)** the lower and upper quartiles, and **(c)** the interquartile range.

7 The table shows the weekly pay of employees in a company.

Pay (£)	0–	100–	200–	300–	400–	500
Frequency	4	29	21	38	18	7

Estimate **(a)** the median pay, and **(b)** the interquartile range of pay.

8 At a summer fayre, 100 people guessed the amount of money in a large jar. Their guesses are given in the table.

Amount (£x)	$4 \leqslant x < 5$	$5 \leqslant x < 6$	$6 \leqslant x < 7$	$7 \leqslant x < 8$	$8 \leqslant x < 9$	$9 \leqslant x < 10$
Frequency	16	29	35	14	6	0

(a) What is the modal class?

(b) Estimate the median guess.

(c) What is the interquartile range of guesses?

9 What is the mode, median and interquartile range of the number of letters in each day of the week?

10 How many sets of seven non-negative integers can you find that have an interquartile range of 0, a median of 1 and a mean of 2?

Standard deviation

If you work out how much each value differs from the mean (i.e. $x - \mu$), and add up all of these differences, the answer will be zero – the sum of the positive differences will be equal to the sum of the negative differences.

If, however, you **square** each of these deviations from the mean, and find the **mean** value of theses **squared deviations**, and then take the **square root**, you will obtain the **standard deviation** from the mean.

Although the interquartile range considers the clustering around the mean, it does not take into account every data value. The standard deviation is a more comprehensive measure of spread, as it does take into account every value.
If we did not find the square of the deviations, and just used the actual deviations, the result would be zero, because there is as much above the mean as there is below it!

Worked example 8

Find the standard deviation of the following set of data:

4, 4, 5, 6, 6, 6, 7, 7, 10, 13, 13, 15, 15, 16, 23

Solution

Firstly, the mean value is $\frac{150}{15} = 10$.

Subtracting this from each value will give:

$-6, \ -6, \ -5, \ -4, \ -4, \ -4, \ -3, \ -3, \ 0, \ 3, \ 3, \ 5, \ 5, \ 6, \ 13$

Squaring each of these deviations from the mean:

$36, \ 36, \ 25, \ 16, \ 16, \ 16, \ 9, \ 9, \ 0, \ 9, \ 9, \ 25, \ 25, \ 36, \ 169$

The mean of these squared deviations is

$$\frac{(36 + 36 + \ldots + 169)}{15} = \frac{436}{15} = 29.0666 \ldots$$

Taking the square root, the **standard deviation = 5.39**.

> Once we have squared each value, we need to take the square root, in order to get back to the same units (cm, kg, etc.) as the data.

Calculating the standard deviation

In this example the mean value was 10, so the calculation was quite straightforward, albeit long. In most practical situations the mean value is not an integer; this makes the calculation rather tedious. We can, however, do some algebraic manipulation of the formula to make it easier to calculate the standard deviation.

> Standard deviation is denoted by σ.
>
> $$\sigma^2 = \frac{\Sigma(x - \mu)^2}{n}$$

As $(x - \mu)^2 = x^2 - 2x\mu + \mu^2$,

$$\sigma^2 = \frac{\Sigma x^2}{n} - \frac{2\mu \, \Sigma x}{n} + \frac{\Sigma \mu^2}{n}$$

But $\frac{\Sigma x}{n} = \mu$, and $\frac{\Sigma \mu^2}{n} = \frac{n\mu^2}{n} = \mu^2$

Hence $\sigma^2 = \frac{\Sigma x^2}{n} - \mu^2$

In other words, the standard deviation is the **square root** of the **mean of the squared values minus the square of the mean value**.

Worked example 9

Find the mean and standard deviation of these numbers:

$16, \quad 19, \quad 20, \quad 20, \quad 21, \quad 24, \quad 24, \quad 25, \quad 25.$

Solution

The mean value is

$$\frac{(16 + 19 + 20 + \ldots + 25)}{9} = \frac{194}{9} = 21.\dot{5}\ldots$$

The mean of the squared values is

$$\frac{(16^2 + 19^2 + \ldots + 25^2)}{9} = \frac{4260}{9} = 473.\dot{3}\ldots$$

The (standard deviation)$^2 = 473.\dot{3} - 21.\dot{5}^2 = 8.691$

Hence the standard deviation $= \sqrt{8.691} = 2.948$

Summarising, the **mean** is **21.56** and the **standard deviation** is **2.95** (correct to two decimal places).

Sample standard deviation

In the examples above, we have taken the data to be the whole population that we are dealing with.

Usually your data will be a sample from a population. You will not be able to calculate, μ, the population mean. You will only be able to calculate, $\bar{x}$, the sample mean. For reasons which are beyond this section the population standard deviation, σ, is 'best' estimated by s, where

$$s^2 = \frac{\Sigma(x - \bar{x})^2}{n - 1},$$

and $\bar{x}$ is the sample mean, $\dfrac{\Sigma x}{n}$

In the following exercise, assume that the data are *samples*, use the '$n - 1$' formula for standard deviation.

> Calculators with statistics functions give both s and σ. However, they may be labelled in different ways.
> Often σ_{n-1} is used for s and σ_n for σ.
> You will need to check your particular calculator, so that you can distinguish which to use for a sample and which to use for a population.

> $\sigma =$ **population** standard deviation.
> s is an estimate of σ, calculated from a sample.

> Practice obtaining the mean and standard deviation directly from your calculator. This will save you a lot of time.

EXERCISE 2D

1 Calculate the standard deviation of the following data:

$$6 \quad 8 \quad 8 \quad 9 \quad 14 \quad 15.$$

2 Compare the means and standard deviations of the following two sets of data:

$$A = \{3, 4, 5, 6, 7\} \text{ and } B = \{1, 3, 5, 7, 9\}$$

3 The number of shots taken by a golfer in the last 12 rounds played is given below.

$$75, \quad 81, \quad 82, \quad 76, \quad 79, \quad 86, \quad 90, \quad 74, \quad 78, \quad 82, \quad 80, \quad 77.$$

Calculate the mean score, and the standard deviation.

2

4 Calculate the standard deviation of the following data:

16 18 18 19 24 25.

Compare your answer with question 1, and explain it.

5 The weight of each member of a rowing crew was measured, to the nearest 0.1 kg.

107.3, 87.7, 90.2, 93.0, 109.6, 98.8, 86.4, 95.2.

Calculate the standard deviation of their weights.

6 A class of 15 students scored these marks in a module test:

83, 38, 65, 93, 73, 45, 60, 53, 28, 83, 72, 50, 48, 42, 70

Calculate the mean mark, and the standard deviation.

7 In an experiment, 20 students estimated what they thought was a time interval of 1 minute. Their estimates, in seconds, are shown below.

68, 54, 57, 42, 48, 46, 52, 53, 50, 50,

64, 56, 60, 49, 52, 62, 40, 73, 55, 61.

Calculate the mean estimate, and the standard deviation.

Grouped data

Just as in example 2, when we calculated the mean value from a frequency table, a convenient way of calculating the standard deviation of grouped data is to use a table.

> However, it is quicker to obtain this directly from your calculator.

Worked example 10

Find the standard deviation of the number of children per class member, from the following data (from example 2)

Number of children	0	1	2	3	4	5	6
Number of members	9	4	6	5	2	0	1

> This includes all class members so can be regarded as a population.

Solution

Writing the information in columns:

No. of children (x)	No. of class members (f)	x × f	x² × f
0	9	0	0
1	4	4	4
2	6	12	24
3	5	15	45
4	2	8	32
5	0	0	0
6	1	6	36
	27	45	141

The mean value is $\dfrac{45}{27} = 1.66\dot{6}$

$$(\text{standard deviation})^2 = \left\{ \frac{\Sigma(x^2 \times f)}{\Sigma f} \right\} - \mu^2$$

$$= \frac{141}{27} - (1.66\dot{6})^2$$

$$= 2.44\dot{4}$$

Hence the standard deviation $\sigma = \sqrt{2.44\dot{4}} = 1.56$

If the class members are regarded as a sample from a larger population the appropriate calculation would be

$$s^2 = \left[\left\{ \frac{\Sigma(x^2 \times f)}{\Sigma f} \right\} - \bar{x}^2 \right] \times \left[\frac{(\Sigma f)}{(\Sigma f - 1)} \right]$$

In this case $\left[\dfrac{141}{27} - (1.66\dot{6})^2 \right] \times \dfrac{27}{26} = 2.5385$

$s = \sqrt{2.5385} = 1.59$

> There is little difference between this value and the population value of 1.56 calculated above. There is only a large difference if the sample is very small.

EXERCISE 2E

In this exercise assume the data are samples.

1 A die was thrown 100 times. The scores are summarised in the table.

Score	1	2	3	4	5	6
Frequency	19	14	13	21	17	16

Calculate the mean and standard deviation of the scores.

2 Find the mean and standard deviation of the number of children per family, for the 23 families shown in the table.

Number of children	0	1	2	3	4	5	6
Number of families	7	3	8	3	0	1	1

3 Applicants for a sales job sit a test consisting of five questions. The number of correct answers, x, scored by 50 candidates is shown in the table.

x	0	1	2	3	4	5
Frequency	30	2	4	5	4	5

Find the mean and the standard deviation of x.

4 The blood pressures, in millimetres of mercury, of a group of 20 athletes is shown in the table.

Blood pressure	65–	70–	75–	80–	85–	90–
Frequency	4	3	5	2	6	0

Calculate the mean and standard deviation of these blood pressures.

5 The breaking strength of 200 cables is given in the table.

Breaking strength (kg × 100)	0–	5–	10–	15–	20–	25–
Number of cables	4	58	66	48	24	0

Estimate the mean breaking strength, and the standard deviation.

Variance

> The variance is the standard deviation squared and for a population is usually denoted σ^2.

Variance plays an important role in mathematical statistics and will appear later in this book and in later statistics units. However it is of little practical use as a measure of spread because it is in inappropriate units.

2.3 Change of scale

The weekly wages paid to the employees of a small engineering firm have a mean of £290 and a standard deviation of £42. The union negotiates a rise of £15 per week for each employee.

Since each wage is increased by £15 the mean wage will be increased by £15 to £305. However, the standard deviation measures variability and this is unchanged if all wages are increased by the same amount. Thus the standard deviation of the new wages remains £42.

If instead of a flat-rate rise the union had negotiated an increase of 10% for each employee the variability would increase because the higher-paid employees would receive a larger rise than would the lower-paid employees. In this case both the mean and the standard deviation would increase by 10%. The mean to £319 and the standard deviation to £46.20.

The mode and the median are also each increased by £15. The range and the interquartile range are unchanged.

The mode, median, range and interquartile range all increase by 10%.

Worked example 11

A sprinkler, designed to extinguish house fires, is activated at high temperatures. A batch of sprinklers is tested and found to be activated at a mean temperature of 72°C with a standard deviation of 3°C.

Find the mean and standard deviation of the temperatures in degrees Fahrenheit.

Solution

To convert Centigrade to Fahrenheit you must first multiply the temperature by 1.8 and then add 32.

For the mean you should do exactly the same.

Hence the mean in degrees Fahrenheit will be
$72 \times 1.8 + 32 = 161.6$.

For the standard deviation you only carry out the multiplication since the addition of 32 will have no effect on the variability.

Hence the standard deviation in degrees Fahrenheit is
$3 \times 1.8 = 5.4$.

EXERCISE 2F

1 Seedlings in a tray have a mean height of 2.3 cm with a standard deviation of 0.4 cm. Find the mean and standard deviation in millimetres (1 cm = 10 mm).

2 If all the seedlings in question 1 increased in height by 1 cm find the new mean and standard deviation.

3 The mean price of a pair of shoes in a particular shop is £63 with a standard deviation of £18. Find the mean and standard deviation of the prices if, in a sale, all pairs of shoes are reduced in price by:

(i) £12,

(ii) 50%.

After two days of the sale the remaining unsold pairs of shoes have a mean price of £70 with a standard deviation of £24. It is decided to reduce the price of each pair by £10 and then label them 'half price'. Thus an unsold pair previously priced at £110 would be sold for £50.

Find the mean and standard deviation of the new selling prices.

4 The apples in a crate have a median weight of 235 g with an interquartile range of 63 g. Find the median and interquartile range in kilograms (1 kg = 1000 g).

5 It is discovered that the scales used to weigh the apples in question 4 recorded the weights inaccurately. Find the correct median and interquartile range if the weight recorded for each apple was:

(i) 5 g greater than its actual weight

(ii) 5% greater than its actual weight.

6 The members of a workers cooperative had mean earnings of £11 500 with a standard deviation of £1000 last year. Find the mean and standard deviation of their total earnings for the year if at the end of the year an additional bonus of:

(i) £900 was paid to each worker

(ii) 9% of earnings was paid to each worker.

7 The members of an amateur rugby league team attend training sessions during the week. The number of sessions attended by members of the squad in a particular week has a mode of 3 with a range of 4. Each member of the squad agrees to increase their training sessions by one during the next week. If this is achieved, find the mode and range of the number of training sessions that will be attended during the next week.

2.4 Comparing distributions

The main purpose of calculating numerical measures is to provide a numerical summary of a set of data. This is particularly useful when comparing more than one set of data. For example the following data represents the value, in £, of the weekly orders taken by Kamran, a sales representative working for a pharmaceutical company.

1260	1190	1480	1790	990	2080	1860	1750
1320	1100	1960	2080	2290	930	1800	1780
1350	1220	2200	1570				

The weekly orders taken by Debbie, another sales representative working for the same company, over the same period are:

1510	1880	1430	1200	1650	1780	1470	1200
1830	1840	1590	1640	1580	1720	1310	1480
1520	1430	1210	1330				

It is difficult to come to any conclusion by just looking at these blocks of data. You should summarise the data by calculating that Kamran has mean orders of £1600 with a standard deviation of £416 and Debbie has mean orders of £1530 with a standard deviation of £215. It is now easy to see that on average Kamran's orders were slightly higher than Debbie's but Debbie's orders were much less variable from week to week.

> These observations will be a sample of Kamran's sales figures.

> Use s, not σ, when calculating the standard deviation.

> Kamran's mean is higher than Debbie's.
> Kamran's standard deviation is much higher than Debbie's.

EXERCISE 2G

1 The working lives of torch batteries from manufacturer A have mean 630 hours with a standard deviation of 36 hours. Torch batteries from manufacturer B have mean 412 hours with a standard deviation of 98 hours. Compare the manufacturers.

2 A manufacturing firm has two production lines which have to be stopped for repair and/or adjustment from time to time. The number of minutes between recent stoppages is shown below.

Production line 1	257	354	298	122	98	176	234
	342	401	176	86	138	290	120

Production line 2	198	202	164	257	210	213	189
	172	219	234	214	208	188	216

(a) Calculate the mean and standard deviation of stoppage times for each production line.

(b) Compare the two production lines.

3 Calculate the median and interquartile range of each of the production lines in question 2. Compare the two production lines. Have you reached the same conclusion as in question 2?

4 The breaking strength, in kilograms, of a sample of climbing ropes from each of three suppliers was measured. The following table summarises the results.

Supplier	Mean	Standard deviation
A	856	390
B	820	42
C	496	28

(a) Compare the breaking strength of the ropes from the different suppliers.

(b) Which supplier would you recommend to a friend setting out on a climbing holiday?

5 The following data are the most recent weekly sales, in £, of three representatives working for a confectionery company.

Moira	5120	4970	2230	890	3270	2160	660
	5980	4320	2220				

Everton	4440	3980	4370	3990	3000	3420	2990
	3450	2680	2900				

Syra	2340	2220	2500	2280	3010	2690	2400
	2760	2800	2920				

(a) Calculate the mean and standard deviation of the sales of each representative.

(b) Compare the sales of the three representatives.

6 Calculate the median and the interquartile range of the sales of each of the representatives in question 5. Compare the sales of the three representatives. Have you reached the same conclusions as in question 5?

Key point summary

1 The three most common measures of 'average' are the **mean, median** and **mode**.   *p12*

2 The most commonly used is the **mean**. A **sample mean** is denoted $\bar{x}$ and a **population mean** is denoted μ.   *p14*

3 The mean is calculated using the formula $\dfrac{\Sigma x}{n}$.   *p16*

4 The most three common measures of spread are the **range**, **interquartile range** and **standard deviation**.   *p19*

5 The most commonly used is the standard deviation. A **population standard deviation** is denoted σ.   *pp19, 22*
$$\sigma = \sqrt{\frac{\Sigma(x-\mu)^2}{n}}$$

6 The data you deal with will usually be a sample. If this is so it is not possible to calculate σ. You should estimate σ by s *p24*
$$s^2 = \sqrt{\frac{\Sigma(x-\bar{x})^2}{(n-1)}}$$

7 You should practise obtaining the mean and standard deviation directly from your calculator. This saves a lot of time and is acceptable in the examination.   *p24*

8 The standard deviation squared is called the **variance**.   *p27*

9 If a variable is increased by a constant amount its **average** will be **increased** by this amount but its **spread** will be **unchanged**. This applies whichever measures of average and spread are used.   *p27*

10 If a variable is multiplied by a constant amount both its average and spread will be multiplied by this amount. This is true whichever measures of average and spread are used.   *p27*

Test yourself	What to review
1 The following data is the girth, in metres, of a sample of trees in a wood: 2.1 1.8 3.5 0.8 1.9 0.6 4.6 0.7 1.7 Find the median and the interquartile range.	*Sections 2.1 and 2.2*
2 A year later the girth of each tree, in question 1, had increased by 5%. Find the new median and interquartile range.	*Section 2.3*
3 Find the mean and standard deviation of the girth of the trees in question 1.	*Sections 2.1 and 2.2*
4 What symbols would you use to denote the mean and standard deviation you have calculated in question 3. Explain your answer.	*Sections 2.1 and 2.2*
5 Explain why the mode would not be a suitable measure of average for the data in question 1.	*Section 2.1*
6 The following table summarises the times taken by 70 army recruits to complete and obstacle course.	*Section 2.1*

Time in minutes	10–	12–	14–	16–	18–	20–22
Number of recruits	3	14	30	16	5	2

State the modal class.

7 Calculate the estimates of the median and the interquartile range for the times in question 6.	*Sections 2.1 and 2.2*
8 Calculate estimates of the mean and standard deviation of the times in question 6.	*Sections 2.1 and 2.2*

Test yourself ANSWERS

8 Mean 15.3, s.d. 2.13.

7 Median 15.2, interquartile range 2.73.

6 Modal class is 14–.

5 The data is too sparse, all observations have a frequency of 1.

4 $\bar{x}$ and s because the girths are a sample.

3 Mean 1.97, s.d. 1.33.

2 Median 1.89, interquartile range 2.15.

1 Median 1.8, interquartile range 2.05.

CHAPTER 3
Pictorial representation of data

Learning objectives

After studying this chapter you should be able to:
- select a suitable diagram to illustrate qualitative, discrete quantitative and continuous quantitative data
- construct pie charts, bar charts, line diagrams, histograms, box and whisker plots, cumulative frequency curves and scatter diagrams
- interpret statistical diagrams.

3.1 Introduction

The first step in analysing data is usually to illustrate it pictorially. In some cases this will be sufficient and mathematical analysis will not be necessary. In other cases it will reveal unusual features of the data which may make mathematical analysis inappropriate. It is always best to look at the data before undertaking calculations.

Many of the diagrams described in this chapter will already be familiar to you from GCSE. However, as well as constructing diagrams you will be expected to be able to select a diagram appropriate to a particular set of data and to interpret it.

There are many ways of illustrating data and this chapter does not describe them all. However, the diagrams described here will be sufficient for most common statistical data.

3.2 Qualitative data

> To illustrate qualitative data you should normally use a pie chart or a bar chart.

The pie chart opposite illustrates the proportion of votes cast for each party at the 1983 general election.

It is easy to see that the Conservatives received a little less than half the votes, Labour received more than a quarter and the Alliance just under a quarter. Other parties received only a small proportion of the votes.

Votes

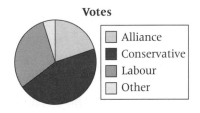

Sometimes the number, or percentage, of votes for each party is written on the corresponding sector.

The diagram below places the seats won by the parties alongside the votes cast. It is easy to see that both Labour and Conservative won a bigger proportion of seats than they received votes, while the Alliance won a much smaller proportion of seats than votes.

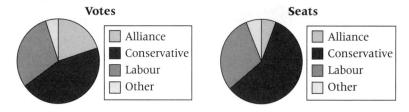

Votes   **Seats**

Alliance
Conservative
Labour
Other

Drawing a pie chart

Roadside checks on the tyres on 300 cars in a suburban area produced the following data:

	Frequency	Proportion (freq/total)	Degrees (prop × 360)
Satisfactory	210	0.7	252
Slightly defective	55	0.1833	66
Seriously defective	35	0.1167	42
Total	**300**		

The angles subtended at the centre of the pie should be proportional to these frequencies. The proportion satisfactory is $\frac{210}{300} = 0.7$. Hence the satisfactory section should subtend an angle of $0.7 \times 360 = 252$ degrees at the centre.

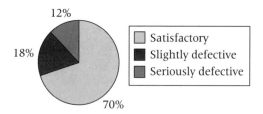

12%
18%
70%

Satisfactory
Slightly defective
Seriously defective

A second set of roadside checks in a rural area produced the following results:

Satisfactory   110
Slightly defective   14
Seriously defective   23

You can compare the distributions by drawing two pie charts. The area of each chart should be made proportional to the total number of observations it represents. In this case there are 300 checks in the suburban area and 147 checks in the rural area.

Therefore the ratio of the areas should be $\frac{147}{300} = 0.49$.

If you choose to represent the suburban area by a circle of radius 2 cm, the area of the pie chart will be $\pi \times 2^2 = 4\pi$. If the circle representing the rural area has radius r its area will be πr^2.

$$\frac{\pi r^2}{4\pi} = 0.49, \quad r^2 = 4 \times 0.49 = 1.96, \quad r = 1.4\,\text{cm}$$

The area of a circle is proportional to the square of the radius. Whatever radius you choose for the circle representing the suburban area, the ratio of the radii of the two pie charts should be $\sqrt{0.49} = 0.7$.

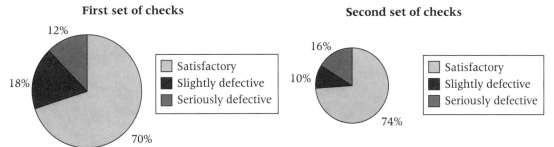

Bar charts

Four parties contested a parliamentary by-election.

The votes cast were as follows:

Labour	19 102
Conservative	18 329
Liberal Democrat	8196
Monster Raving Loony	672

If you drew a pie chart of this data it would not be easy to tell the difference between the Labour and Conservative section. As the most important thing about a by-election result is who got the most votes this information is best illustrated by a bar chart. The length of the bar is proportional to the number of votes received and it is clear to see that Labour got more votes than Conservative.

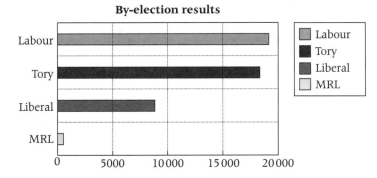

It is equally acceptable to draw the bars vertically instead of horizontally.

The party getting the most votes has been put at the top of the diagram followed by the other parties in order of votes obtained. This is not a compulsory feature of bar charts but is generally helpful in communicating the chart's message.

Worked example 3.1 _____

An advertising campaign to promote electric showers consists of a mailshot which includes a pre-paid postcard requesting further details. Prospective customers who return the postcard are then contacted by one of five sales staff: Gideon, Magnus, Jemma, Pandora or Muruvet. The pie charts below represent the number of potential customers contacted and the number of sales completed during a 1 month period.

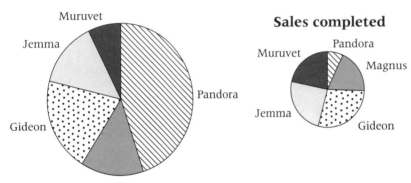

(a) The total number of potential customers contacted is 1100. Find, approximately, the total number of sales completed.

(b) Describe the main features of the data revealed by the pie charts.

(c) The manager wishes to compare the sales staff according to the number of sales completed. What type of diagram would you recommend, in place of a pie chart, so that this comparison could be made easily?   [A]

Solution

(a) The radius of the **Potential customers** pie chart is approximately 2 cm while that of the **Sales completed** pie chart is approximately 1 cm.

$$\text{Total number of sales completed} = \frac{1100 \times 1^2}{2^2} = 275$$

(b) Pandora has contacted the most customers but completed the least sales. Muruvet has contacted the fewest customers but has made a similar number of sales to Jemma, Gideon and Magnus.

(c) Bar chart.

> You only need to comment on obvious differences. For example if you look carefully you can see that Gideon has made slightly more sales than Jemma. The difference is so small it does not require a comment.

EXERCISE 3A

1 The information below relates to people taking out mortgages. Draw an appropriate bar chart.

By type of dwelling (%)	
Type	**All buyers**
Bungalow	10
Detached house	19
Semi-detached house	31
Terraced house	31
Purpose built flat	7
Converted flat	3

2 The drinks purchased by customers at a cafe between 11.00 am and midday were as follows:

coffee, coffee, tea, tea, tea, orange, tea, coffee, orange, orange, coffee, coffee, coffee, tea, tea, orange, coffee, coffee, orange, tea, tea, tea, tea.

Illustrate the data by means of a pie chart.

Between midday and 1.00 pm the cafe sold 24 coffees, 38 teas and nine oranges. Illustrate this data by means of a pie chart making the area of each pie chart proportional to the total frequency.

3 The following data is the usual mode of travel to work for a 1% sample of people in employment from the 1991 census:

Works at home	10 980
Train/tube/metro	13 456
Bus/coach	22 910
Car – driver	124 293
Car – passenger	18 106
Pedal cycle	6924
On foot	27 056
Other	9129

Illustrate the data:

(a) with a bar chart

(b) with a pie chart.

Which features of the data are best illustrated by which diagram?

3.3 **Discrete quantitative data**

The number of times that a machine producing carpet tiles had
to be adjusted on 11 successive night shifts is summarised below:

Number of adjustments	0	1	2	3
Frequency	3	2	5	1

Discrete quantitative data can be best illustrated by a line
diagram. As with a bar chart the length of the line is
proportional to the frequency.

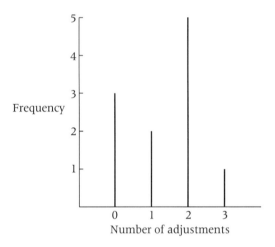

3.4 **Continuous quantitative data**

Continuous quantitative data can be best illustrated by
histograms.

When yarn is delivered to a weaving mill its density is
measured. The following data are the densities of 96 deliveries
of yarn from the same supplier.

6300	6200	6150	6090	5720	5860	6220	6100
5910	5830	5950	6020	6120	6230	6090	6030
5910	5940	5930	5830	5890	5820	6560	5760
5900	5900	5820	6280	5740	6110	6200	6610
5960	6000	6070	5670	6400	6110	6290	6170
6440	6120	6120	6430	6220	6220	6370	6260
5560	6310	5950	5930	6780	6230	6340·	6540
6320	5600	6170	6300	6260	5980	6740	5770
6310	6000	6430	6070	6150	6610	6310	6150
5630	6420	6020	6780	6200	6820	6470	6030
6110	6570	6150	6390	6650	6680	6620	6410
6370	6280	6480	5730	6280	5890	6230	6130

The units are denier which is the
weight in grams of 9000 m of
yarn. The reasons why this
strange unit is used need not
concern us.

Density is a continuous variable but the data recorded has been rounded to the nearest 10. Thus 6150 means that the actual density was between 6145 and 6155. The data may be formed into the frequency distribution below.

Class	Frequency
5495–5595	1
5595–5695	3
5695–5795	5
5795–5895	7
5895–5995	11
5995–6095	10
6095–6195	14
6195–6295	15
6295–6395	10
6395–6495	8
6495–6595	3
6595–6695	5
6695–6795	3
6795–6895	1

These classes would not be satisfactory for some data. For example if the observation 5595 occurred you would not know whether to place it in the first or the second class. However, in this case the data was rounded to the nearest 10 and so an observation such as 5595 cannot occur. The classes are satisfactory for this data.

3

Histograms

This frequency distribution could be illustrated by a histogram. The area under the bar represents the frequency and the vertical axis represents frequency density. In this case the classes are all of equal width and so the height of the bars is proportional to the frequency.

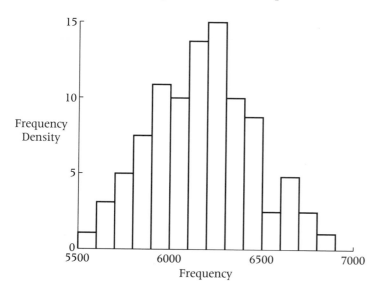

Density of yarn from factory A

Histograms with classes of unequal width

If a frequency distribution has classes of unequal width the height of the bars in the histogram should **not** be proportional to the frequency. They should be proportional to the **frequency density**. The **frequency density** is the frequency divided by the class width.

Worked example 3.2

The table summarises the times between 90 consecutive admissions to an intensive care unit.

Time in hours	Frequency
0–	16
10–	22
30–	17
60–	15
100–200	19

This is an alternative way of showing classes. The first class contains all times between 0 and 10 hours.

Illustrate the data by means of a histogram. [A]

Solution

Time in hours	Class width	Frequency	Frequency density
0–	10	16	1.6
10–	20	22	1.1
30–	30	17	0.567
60–	40	15	0.375
100–200	100	19	0.19

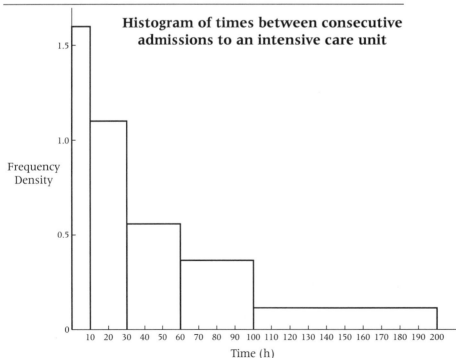

Histogram of times between consecutive admissions to an intensive care unit

Worked example 3.3

A travel agent carried out a survey among people who travel between Manchester and London at least 10 times per year.

Question 1 of the survey asked whether they made their last journey by car, coach, train or plane.

(a) State the type of diagram that would be most appropriate for illustrating the proportion of people using each method of transport.

Question 2 of the survey asked how many of the last four journeys were made by car. A summary of the results is shown below.

Number of journeys by car	Number of people
0	43
1	11
2	6
3	15
4	62

Table 1

(b) Illustrate the data by a line diagram. Comment briefly on the shape of the distribution.

Question 3 of the survey asked how long the last journey had taken from door to door. The following table summarises the journey times, in minutes, of those who had travelled by plane.

Time (minutes)	Frequency
180–	9
210–	11
240–	9
250–	11
260–	10
290–430	13

Table 2

(c) Explain why a histogram is a suitable diagram for illustrating the data in **Table 2** but is not a suitable diagram for illustrating the data in **Table 1**.

Solution

(a) Pie chart.

(b)

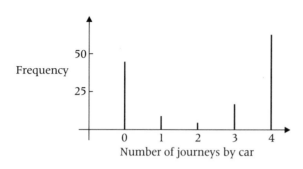

The distribution is U-shaped which is unusual.

(c) A histogram is suitable for the data in Table 2 as it is continuous. It is unsuitable for the data in Table 1 which is discrete quantitative.

EXERCISE 3B

1 The weight of a sample of expired blood donations were as follows:

Weight in g	Frequency
70–79	8
80–89	24
90–99	26
100–109	12
110–119	5

Illustrate the data with a histogram.

2 The breaking strengths of 200 cables, manufactured by a company, are shown in the table below.

Breaking strength (in 100 s of kg)	Frequency
0–	4
5–	48
10–	60
15–	48
20–	24
25–30	16

Draw a histogram of the data.

3

Time in minutes	Frequency
1–2	3
2–3	12
3–4	17
4–6	11
6–10	7

The distribution above refers to the time taken to complete a jigsaw puzzle by 50 people. Draw a histogram of the distribution.

4 The following table is extracted from a census report. It shows the age distribution of the population present on census night in Copeland, an area of Cumbria.

Population aged					
0–4	5–15	16–24	25–44	45–74	75 and over
4462	12 214	10 898	19 309	22 820	3364

Illustrate the data by means of a histogram. Make a suitable assumption about the upper bound of the class '75 and over'.

5 In an investigation children were asked a number of questions about their journeys to school. The data collected are to be illustrated using pie charts, line diagrams or histograms. (In answering this question you should only consider these three types of diagram.)

Question 1 asked the children whether they had travelled to school by bicycle, bus, train, car or on foot.

(a) Which type of diagram would best illustrate the proportion of children using each method of transport?

Question 2 asked the children on how many of the past 5 days they had travelled to school by car. A summary of the results is shown below.

Number of days by car	Number of people
0	112
1	32
2	18
3	7
4	29
5	64

(b) Illustrate these data using a suitable diagram. Comment briefly on the shape of the distribution.

Question 3 asked the children how long their journeys to school had taken on a particular day. A summary of the results is shown below.

Time (minutes)	Number of children
0.5–15.5	129
15.5–25.5	52
25.5–35.5	34
35.5–55.5	26
55.5–90.5	21

(c) Illustrate these data using an appropriate diagram.

Box-and-whisker plots

You will often wish to use a diagram to compare different sets of data. For example the weaving mill mentioned above received yarn from three suppliers. The densities illustrated above were measured on yarn from supplier A. Densities were also measured on samples of yarn from suppliers B and C. The results are shown below.

Densities of yarn from supplier B

(B) 4240	4160	4120	4072	3776	3888	4176	4080
3928	3864	3960	4016	4096	4184	4072	4024
3928	3952	3944	3864	3912	3856	4448	3808
3920	3920	3856	4224	3792	4088	4160	4488
3968	4000	4056	3736	4320	4088	4232	5120
3100	3010	4096	4344	4176	4176	4296	4208
3648	4248	3960	3944	4624	4184	4272	4432
4256	3680	4136	4792	4208	3984	4592	3816
4248	4000	4344	4056	4120	4488	4248	4120
3704	4336	4016	4624	4160	4656	4376	4024
4088	4456	4120	4312	4520	4544	4496	4328
4296	4224	4384	3784	4224	3912	4184	4104

Densities of yarn from supplier C

(C) 6166	5984	5893	5784	5110	5365	6020	5802
5456	5311	5529	5656	5838	6039	5784	5675
5456	5511	5493	5311	5420	5292	6639	5183
5438	5438	5292	6130	5147	5820	5984	6730
5547	5620	5747	5019	6348	5820	6148	5929
6421	5838	5838	6403	6020	6020	6293	6093
4819	6184	5529	5493	7040	6039	6239	6603
6202	4892	5929	7422	6093	5584	6967	5201
6184	5620	6403	5747	5893	6730	6184	5893
4947	6384	5656	7040	5984	7112	6475	7748
5820	6657	5893	6330	6803	6858	6748	6366
6239	6130	6494	5129	6130	5420	6039	5857

It is difficult to compare these distributions from the raw data. You could draw a histogram of each set of data. If the histograms were drawn on the same scale and placed one beneath the other a comparison could be made. An alternative method is to draw a box-and-whisker plot.

This is particularly difficult to do if you are using a computer. Most common statistical packages are very poor at drawing histograms.

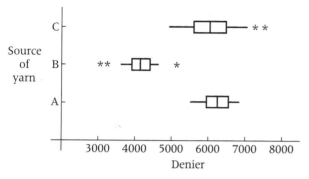

3

For each supplier the vertical line in the 'box' represents the median. The 'box' contains the middle 50% of the observations. The * represent **outliers** – that is observations which are untypical of the rest of the distribution. The 'whiskers' extending from the box join the box to the largest and smallest observations which are not outliers.

From the diagram it is easy to see that Supplier A had a slightly higher average density than Supplier C and that Supplier C was much more variable. Supplier B has a much lower average density than either of the others. The variability of Supplier B is similar to A apart from the three outliers.

This is confirmed by numerical measures.

	Mean	Standard deviation
A	6167	284
B	4125	300
C	5958	568

Constructing a box-and-whisker plot

The following data is the weight, in grams, of 16 pebbles sampled from a beach:

25.6   37.4   27.0   34.3   50.6   42.1   37.4   66.6

33.5   42.9   44.8   49.0   20.9   37.4   44.0   43.2

First you need to identify the median and the upper and lower quartiles. Arranging the data in order of magnitude:

20.9   25.6   27.0   33.5   34.3   37.4   37.4   37.4

42.1   42.9   43.2   44.0   44.8   49.0   50.6   66.5

There are 16 observations, so the median is halfway between the 8th and 9th, i.e. $\frac{(37.4 + 42.1)}{2} = 39.75$.

The lower quartile Q_1 is halfway between the 4th and 5th, i.e.

$Q_1 = \frac{(33.5 + 34.3)}{2} = 33.9$.

Similarly the upper quartile $Q_3 = \frac{(44.0 + 44.8)}{2} = 44.4$.

The generally accepted (but arbitrary) definition of an outlier is any observation:

> greater than $Q_3 + 1.5(Q_3 - Q_1)$
>
> or less than $Q_1 - 1.5(Q_3 - Q_1)$

In this example an outlier is an observation:

> greater than $44.4 + 1.5(44.4 - 33.9) = 60.15$
>
> or less than $33.91.5(44.4 - 33.9) = 18.15$

For this example the only outlier is 66.5.

Box-and-whisker plot of weights of pebbles

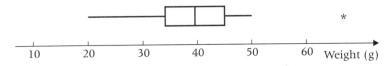

The left-hand whisker is longer than the right-hand whisker and the median is towards the upper end of the box. That is the smaller observations tend to be more spread out than the larger ones. If we ignore the outlier we would say that the distribution is **negative skew**.

Worked example 3.4

A factory manager obtains raw materials from three different suppliers. The time from placing the order to receiving the raw materials is called the **lead time**. For the factory to run smoothly, it is desirable that the distribution of this lead time should have a low average and low variability.

The diagram shows box-and-whisker plots of the lead times of recent deliveries of raw materials from suppliers A, B and C.

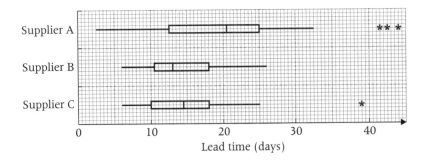

The lead times, in days, for the 12 most recent deliveries from Supplier C, as illustrated in the above diagram, were as follows:

> 7   9   6   12   11   15   17   14   15   25   19   39

(The lead times are in order, i.e. the most recent delivery had lead time 39 days, the second most recent 19 days, etc.)

(a) Explain with the aid of suitable calculations why, in the box-and-whisker plot for Supplier C, the lead time of 39 has been shown as an outlier, but the lead time of 25 has been included in the whisker.

(b) Compare, from the point of view of the factory manager, the lead times of the three suppliers as revealed by the box-and-whisker plots.

(c) What feature of the given data for Supplier C is not revealed by the box-and-whisker plot?

3

Solution

(a) For Supplier C, $Q_1 = 10$, $Q_3 = 18$ (from graph)
an observation $> 18 + 1.5(18 - 10) = 30$ is an outlier

Hence 39 is an outlier.

A value of 25 is not greater than 30 but is greater than 18 the upper quartile. Hence it is included in the upper whisker.

(b) Supplier A's lead times are more variable and have a higher median than B or C. There are also three outliers representing very long lead times. Hence A is unsuitable. There is little to choose between B and C but B has a slightly lower median and C has an undesirable outlier. Hence B would be preferred by the factory manager.

> Comment on the most obvious features. There is no need to go into great detail on, for example, the small differences in the length of the whiskers for Suppliers B and C.

(c) The box-and-whisker plot does not reveal that the lead times for C are tending to increase as time goes on.

In part (b) you could also comment on the skewness. Ignoring outliers Supplier A is negative skew. This is a bad thing in this context as it means that there are more observations towards the upper end of the distribution (long lead times) than towards the lower end (short lead times). Supplier B is positive skew which is a good thing in this context. Supplier C has a longer right-hand whisker but the median is towards the upper end of the box. For this supplier there is no useful comment to make on skewness.

EXERCISE 3C

1 Applicants for an assembly job are required to take a test of manual dexterity. The times, in seconds, taken to complete the task by 19 applicants were as follows:

63,	229,	165,	77,	49,	74,	67,	59,
66,	102,	81,	72,	59,	74,	61,	82,
48,	70,	86.					

For these data find

(a) the median

(b) the upper and lower quartiles.

(c) Identify any outliers in the data.

(d) Illustrate the data by a box-and-whisker plot. Outliers, if any, should each be denoted by a ' * ' and should not be included in the whiskers.

2 The potencies of samples of two different brands of aspirin were as follows:

Brand A	58.7	58.4	59.3	60.4	59.8	59.4	57.7	60.3	61.0
	58.2	58.1	58.8	59.4	60.1	58.9			
Brand B	65.8	56.4	60.3	61.0	59.2	58.7	59.3	61.8	64.1
	61.9	62.8	60.7	55.2	59.9	63.6	60.4	59.9	61.5
	59.3	65.2	57.6	64.9	57.7	61.4	61.8	66.3	65.3

(a) Compare the potencies of the two brands by drawing box-and-whisker plots. You may use the following information about the sample of **Brand B**.

smallest value 55.2; lower quartile 59.3; median 61.0; upper quartile 63.6; largest value 66.3.

(Assume there are no outliers in either sample.)

(b) Comment, briefly, on the features of the data revealed by the diagrams.

3 A school cleaner is approaching pensionable age. She lives halfway between two post offices, A and B, and has to decide from which of the two she will arrange to collect her pension. For a few months she has deliberately used the two post offices alternately when she has required postal services. On each of these visits she has recorded the time taken between entering the post office and being served.

The box-plots below show these waiting times for the two post offices. The symbol * represents an outlier.

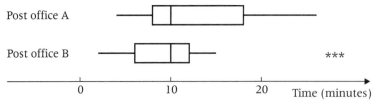

(a) Compare, in words, the distributions of the waiting times in the two post offices.

(b) Advise the cleaner which post office to use if the outliers were due to:

(i) a cable-laying company having severed the electricity supply to the post office;

(ii) the post office being short-staffed.

4 A group of athletes frequently run round a cross-country course in training. The box-and-whisker plots below represent the times taken by athletes A, B, C and D to complete the course.

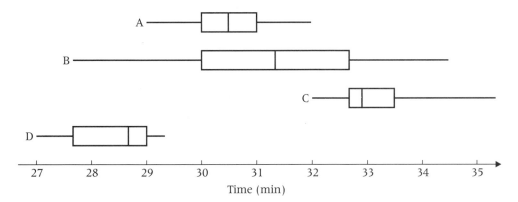

(a) Compare the times taken by athletes C and D.

Assume that the distributions shown above are representative of the times the athletes would take in a race over the same course.

(b) Which of the athletes A or B would you choose if you were asked to select one of them to win a race against:

(i) C

(ii) D?

Give a reason for **each** answer.

(c) Which athlete would be most likely to win a race between A and B?

3.5 Cumulative frequency curves

Cumulative frequency curves provide a useful method of estimating the median and quartiles of grouped data. They are not a particularly good diagram for illustrating or comparing distributions. The cumulative frequency is the number of observations not greater than a given value.

The following table shows the weights of a sample of expired blood donations.

Weight, g	Frequency	Cumulative frequency
70–79	8	8
80–89	24	32
90–99	26	58
100–109	12	70
110–119	6	76

These classes are suitable for data measured to the nearest g. The class 70–79 will contain all blood donations weighing between 69.5 g and 79.5 g.

The cumulative frequency is plotted against the upper class bound. This is because we know there were eight samples weighing not more than 79.5 g, 8 + 24 = 32 samples weighing not more than 89.5 g, 32 + 26 = 58 samples weighing not more than 99.5 g, etc.

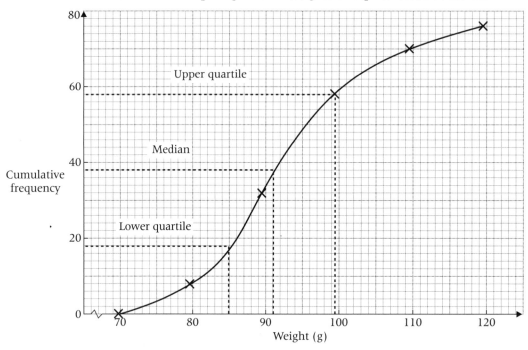

Cumulative frequency curve of weights of expired blood donations

We may estimate the median of the sample by reading off on the horizontal axis the value corresponding to a cumulative frequency of $\frac{(n+1)}{2}$ where n is the sample size. The lower and upper quartiles are estimated by reading off the value corresponding to $\frac{(n+1)}{4}$ and $\frac{3(n+1)}{4}$, respectively.

> Unless n is small it makes little difference if you use $\frac{n}{4}, \frac{n}{2}$ and $\frac{3n}{4}$.

In this example $n = 76$ so we read off at $\frac{(76+1)}{2} = 38.5$ for the median and at $\frac{(76+1)}{4} = 19.25$ and $\frac{3(76+1)}{4} = 57.75$ for the quartiles. This gives an estimate of 91 for the median, 85 for the lower quartile and 99 for the upper quartile.

> As we are estimating these values from grouped data, two significant figures is sufficient. To give more than two significant figures suggests greater accuracy than is possible in this case.

EXERCISE 3D

1 The lengths of 32 fish caught in a competition were measured correct to the nearest mm.

Length	20–22	23–25	26–28	29–31	32–34
Frequency	3	6	12	9	2

  (a) Draw a cumulative frequency curve.

  (b) Estimate the median and quartiles of the lengths of the fish.

2 When laying pipes, engineers test the soil for 'resistivity'. If the reading is low then there is an increasing risk of pipes corroding. In a survey of 159 samples the following results were found:

Resistivity (ohms/cm)	Frequency
400–900	5
901–1500	9
1501–3500	40
3501–8000	45
8001–20000	60

Draw a cumulative frequency curve and estimate the median and quartiles.

3 The gross registered tonnages of 500 ships entering a small port are given in the following table.

Gross registered tonnage (tonnes)	No. of ships
0–	25
400–	31
800–	44
1200–	57
1600–	74
2000–	158
3000–	55
4000–	26
5000–	i8
6000–8000	12

Plot the cumulative frequency curve.

Hence estimate:

(a) the median tonnage

(b) the interquartile range

(c) the percentage of ships with a gross registered tonnage exceeding 2500 tonnes.

Worked example 3.5

The diagram compares the size of comprehensive schools with that of other public sector secondary schools in the United Kingdom.

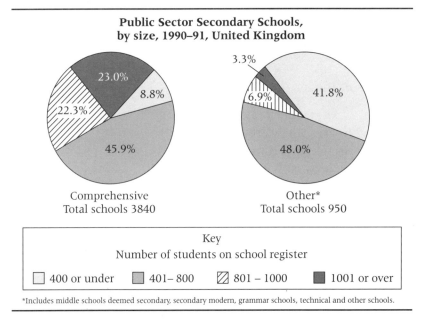

Public Sector Secondary Schools, by size, 1990–91, United Kingdom

Comprehensive
Total schools 3840

Other*
Total schools 950

Key
Number of students on school register

☐ 400 or under   ▦ 401– 800   ▨ 801 – 1000   ■ 1001 or over

*Includes middle schools deemed secondary, secondary modern, grammar schools, technical and other schools.

> Although this diagram is taken from official government statistics it is inappropriate to illustrate quantitative data with a pie chart.
> In this question we extract the data from the pie chart and replace the pie chart with a more suitable diagram.

(a) How could the diagram be modified so that the number of schools in each category could also be compared?

You are not required to redraw the diagram.

(b) Using the percentages and total given in the diagram, or otherwise, construct a grouped frequency table for the size of **comprehensive schools**. (Size is measured by the number of students on the school register.)

For **comprehensive schools** the number of students on the school register is 210 in the smallest school and 1600 in the largest.

(c) (i) Draw a cumulative frequency diagram for the size of **comprehensive schools** and use it to estimate the upper and lower quartiles and the median.

(ii) Draw a box-and-whisker plot for the size of **comprehensive schools**.

(iii) Draw on the same axes a box-and-whisker plot for the size of the **other schools** given the following data.

Smallest	Lower quartile	Median	Upper quartile	Largest
88	290	468	694	1095

(d) Compare briefly, the distributions of size of comprehensive schools and other schools. Which type of diagram is more helpful in making this comparison?

Solution

(a) The area of the pie chart could be made proportional to the number of schools. The ratio of the radii would be

$$\sqrt{\frac{950}{3840}} = 0.497,$$

i.e. radius of other schools' pie chart about half that of comprehensive schools.

(b)

Size of school	Frequency
400 or under	$0.088 \times 3840 = 338$
401–800	$0.459 \times 3840 = 1763$
801–1000	$0.223 \times 3840 = 856$
1001 and over	$0.230 \times 3840 = 883$

(c) (i)

Size of school	Cumulative frequency
400 or under	338
401–800	2101
801–1000	2957
1001 and over	3840

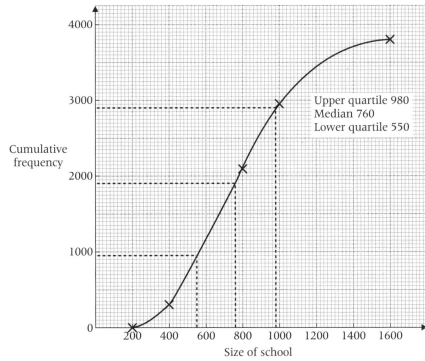

Upper quartile 980
Median 760
Lower quartile 550

You also need to use the additional information that the smallest school has 210 students and the largest 1600.

In this case $n = 3840$.

It makes no difference whether you use $\frac{n}{2}$ or $\frac{n+1}{2}$ for the median.

Read off at $\frac{3}{4} \times 3840 = 2880$ for the upper quartile.

$\frac{3840}{2} = 1920$ for the median.

$\frac{3840}{4} = 960$ for the lower quartile.

(ii)

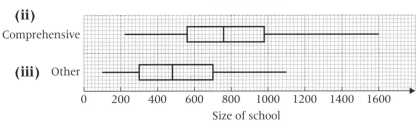

Comprehensive

There are no outliers.

(iii) Other

(d) Comprehensive schools are larger, on average and more variable than other schools.

This is clear from the box-and-whisker plot, but much more difficult to see from the pie chart.

3.6 Scatter diagrams

> Scatter diagrams are used where we are examining possible relationships between two variables.

Scatter diagrams are included here for completeness but this topic will be examined in much more detail in Chapters 8 and 9.

An athlete, recovering from injury, had her pulse rate measured after performing a predetermined number of step-ups in a gymnasium. The measurements were made at weekly intervals. The table below shows the number of step-ups, x, the pulse rate, y beats per minute, and the week in which the measurement was made.

Week	1	2	3	4	5	6	7	8
x	15	50	35	25	20	30	10	45
y	114	155	132	112	96	105	78	113

To construct a scatter diagram you simply plot points with coordinates (x, y) for each of the 8 weeks.

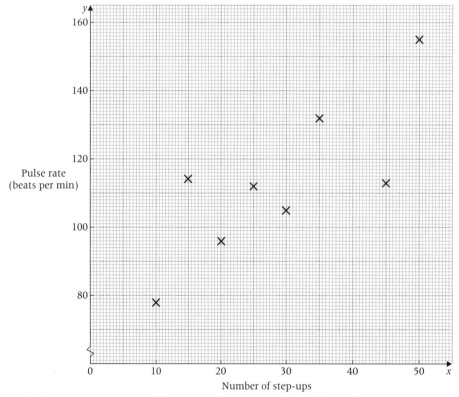

In this case, as you would expect, there appears to be a clear tendency for the pulse rate to increase with the number of step-ups.

EXERCISE 3E

1 A tree surgeon selects jobs suitable for her assistant to carry out without supervision and estimates the time they will take to complete. The table below shows the estimated time, x minutes, and the actual time, y minutes, her assistant took to complete them. Draw a scatter diagram of the data.

job	1	2	3	4	5	6	7	8	9	10	11	12
x	440	260	410	330	210	170	110	310	250	520	170	220
y	585	370	495	365	215	180	90	265	205	435	145	190

2 The following data show the annual income per head, x (in US$), and the infant mortality, y (per thousand live births), for a sample of 11 countries.

Country	A	B	C	D	E	F	G	H	I	J	K
x	130	5950	560	2010	1870	170	390	580	820	6620	3800
y	150	43	121	53	41	169	143	59	75	20	39

Draw a scattergram of the data. Describe any relationships between infant mortality and income per head suggested by the scattergram.

MIXED EXERCISE

1 In a school survey on the number of passengers in cars driving into Norwich in the rush hour the following results were obtained.

No. of passengers	Frequency
0	13
1	25
2	12
3	6
4	1

Illustrate the data with a suitable diagram.

2 According to a report showing the differences in diet between the richest and poorest in the UK the figures opposite were given for the consumption of staple foods (ounces per person per week).

Draw pie charts for this information. What differences in dietary pattern does this information show?

	Poorest 10%	Richest 10%
White bread	26	12.3
Sugar	11.5	8
Potatoes	48.3	33.4
Fruit	13	25.3
Vegetables	21.5	30.7
Brown bread	5.2	8

3 Illustrate the data below using a suitable diagram.

Percentage impurity in samples of raw material	
% Impurity	**Frequency**
0–1	6
1–2	13
2–3	9
3–5	8
5–8	6

4 A frequent rail traveller records the time she has to queue to buy a ticket. The 19 most recent times, in seconds, she recorded were as follows:

136 120   78 132 111 124 109 122 131 162
16 109 117 124   99 127 255 298 113

  (a) Find:

  (i)   the median waiting time

  (ii) the upper and lower quartiles of the waiting times.

  (b) Identify any outliers in the data.

  (c) On graph paper, draw a box-and-whisker plot of the data. Outliers, if any, should each be denoted by a '*' and should not be included in the whiskers.

5 The table below shows the lifetimes of a random sample of 200 mass produced circular abrasive discs.

Lifetime (to nearest hour)	Number of discs
690–709	3
710–719	7
720–729	15
730–739	38
740–744	41
745–749	35
750–754	21
755–759	16
760–769	14
770–789	10

Draw a cumulative frequency curve and estimate the median and quartiles.

6 The following frequency table shows the frequency with which other types of vehicles were involved in cycling accidents in a particular year.

	Number
Motor cycle	96
Motor car	2039
Van	168
Goods vehicle	126
Coach	49
Pedestrian	226
Dog	120
Cyclist	218
None–defective road surface	266
None–weather conditions	129
None–mechanical failure	65
Other	399
Total	3901

(*Source: Cycling Accidents – Cyclists' Touring Club*)

Illustrate the data with a suitable diagram.

7 The weight of luggage belonging to each of the 135 passengers on an aeroplane is summarised in the frequency distribution shown:

Weight (kg)	0–	20–	30–	35–	40–	60–90
Number of passengers	23	28	31	4	33	16

(a) Illustrate these data using a histogram.

(b) Comment on the distribution of luggage weight given the fact that on this flight any passenger taking more than 35 kg of luggage had to pay an excess baggage charge.

(c) Draw a box-and-whisker plot of the data above using the following additional information.

Lightest luggage	Lower quartile	Median	Upper quartile	Heaviest luggage
4 kg	25 kg	32 kg	53 kg	87 kg

There are no outliers

(d) Discuss which of your two diagrams better illustrates the distribution of luggage weight.

8 Each member in a group of 100 children was asked to do a simple jigsaw puzzle. The times, to the nearest five seconds, for the children to complete the jigsaw are as follows:

Time (seconds)	No. of children
60–85	7
90–105	13
110–125	25
130–145	28
150–165	20
170–185	5
190–215	2

(a) Illustrate the data with a cumulative frequency curve.

(b) Estimate the median and the inter-quartile range.

(c) Each member of a similar group of children completed a jigsaw in a median time of 158 seconds with an inter-quartile range of 204 seconds. Comment briefly on the relative difficulty of the two jigsaws.

In addition to the 100 children who completed the first jigsaw, a further 16 children attempted the jigsaw but gave up, having failed to complete it after 220 seconds.

(d) Estimate the median time taken by the whole group of 116 children.

Comment on the use of the median instead of the mean.

9 A company is considering three types of machine *A*, *B*, and *C* for producing tablets containing a certain drug. Samples of about 100 tablets produced by each type of machine were analysed. The box-plot below illustrates the potency of the tablets (the symbol '*' is used to represent outliers).

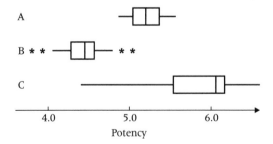

(a) Compare the distributions in words.

(b) Small variability in the potency of the tablets is desirable. The target value for each tablet is 6.0. It is easy to change the mean amount, but not possible to reduce the variability. Recommend, giving reasons, which type of machine should be used.

10 The following table refers to all marriages that ended in divorce in Scotland during 1977. It shows the age of the wife at marriage.

Age of wife (years)	16–20	21–24	25–29	30/over
Frequency	4966	2364	706	524

(a) Draw a cumulative frequency curve for these data.

(b) Estimate the median and the inter-quartile range.

The corresponding data for 1990 revealed a median of 21.2 years and an inter-quartile range of 6.2 years.

(c) Compare these values with those you obtained for 1977. Give a reason for using the median and inter-quartile range, rather than the mean and standard deviation for making this comparison.

The box-and-whisker plots below also refer to Scotland and show the age of the wife at marriage. One is for all marriages in 1990 and the other is for all marriages that ended in divorce in 1990. (The small number of marriages in which the wife was aged over 50 have been ignored.)

Age of wife at marriage, Scotland

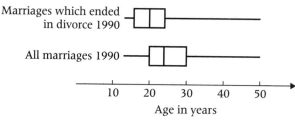

(d) Compare and comment on the two distributions.　[A]

11 Over a period of four years a bank keeps a weekly record of the number of cheques with errors that are presented for payment. The results for the 200 accounting weeks are as follows.

Number of cheques with errors (x)	Number of weeks (f)
0	5
1	22
2	46
3	38
4	31
5	23
6	16
7	11
8	6
9	2

$$(\Sigma fx = 706 \quad \Sigma fx^2 = 3280)$$

Construct a suitable pictorial representation of these data.

State the modal value and calculate the median, mean and standard deviation of the number of cheques with errors in a week.

Some textbooks measure the **skewness** (or asymmetry) of a distribution by

$$\frac{3(\text{mean} - \text{median})}{\text{standard deviation}}$$

and others measure it by

$$\frac{(\text{mean} - \text{mode})}{\text{standard deviation}}$$

Calculate and compare the values of these two measures of skewness for the above data.

State how this skewness is reflected in the shape of your diagram.

12 Cucumbers are stored in brine before being processed into pickles. Data were collected on x, the percentage of sodium chloride in the salt used to make brine, and y, a measure of the firmness of the pickles produced. The data are shown below:

x	6.0	6.5	7.0	7.5	8.0	8.5	9.0	9.5
y	15.3	15.8	16.1	16.7	17.4	17.8	18.2	18.3

Plot a scatter diagram of the data.

13 In addition to its full-time staff, a supermarket employs part-time sales staff on Saturdays. The manager experimented to see if there is a relationship between the takings and the number of part-time staff employed.

He collected the following data on nine successive Saturdays.

Number of part-time staff employed, x	10	13	16	19	22	25	28	31	34
Takings, £'00, y	313	320	319	326	333	342	321	361	355

Plot a scatter diagram of these data.

14 The intervals of time between successive telephone calls received in a school office are summarised in the table below.

Time, s	Frequency
0–60	20
60–120	21
120–240	25
240–360	14
360–480	21
480–720	9

(a) Estimate the median and the upper and lower quartiles.

(b) Given that the shortest interval is 3 seconds and the longest is 665 seconds, draw a box-and-whisker plot of the data. You may assume that there are no outliers.

(c) At a neighbouring school the following information is collected about the intervals between calls to the office.

Smallest	Lower quartile	Median	Upper quartile	Largest
5	34	124	313	526

Using the same axes as in (b), draw a box-and-whisker plot of the interval between calls to this school office. You may assume that there are no outliers.

(d) Compare briefly, the two distributions. [A]

Key point summary

1 Qualitative data may be illustrated by pie charts or bar charts. Pie charts illustrate proportions. Bar charts compare the numbers in each class. *p33*

2 Discrete quantitative data can be illustrated by line diagrams. *p38*

3 Continuous quantitative data should be illustrated by histograms. *p38*

4 Cumulative frequency curves are useful for estimating the median and quartiles of grouped data. *p50*

5 Scatter diagrams illustrate the relationship, if any, between two variables. *p54*

Test yourself	What to review
1 What type of data may be illustrated by a pie chart?	*Section 3.2*
2 A secretary arranges appointments for a company executive. He records the number of appointments on each working day. Why would a histogram be an unsuitable diagram for illustrating this data?	*Section 3.4*
3 Name a suitable type of diagram to illustrate the data in question 2.	*Section 3.3*
4 Which numerical measures may be estimated from a cumulative frequency curve?	*Section 3.5*
5 What, in general terms, is an outlier? In the context of box-and-whisker plots what is the usual definition of an outlier?	*Section 3.4*
6 A pie chart of radius 5 cm illustrates the votes cast for each party at a local by-election. The total number of votes cast was 4000. A second pie chart is to be drawn illustrating the votes cast for each party at a parliamentary by-election. The total number of votes cast at this election was 32 500. Find an appropriate radius for this second pie chart.	*Section 3.2*
7 Name a suitable type of diagram to illustrate a possible relationship between two variables.	*Section 3.6*
8 What does the vertical axis of a histogram represent?	*Section 3.4*
9 A student attempts to draw a histogram using frequency as the vertical scale. Under what circumstances would the resulting diagram be seriously misleading?	*Section 3.4*

Test yourself ANSWERS

9 If the classes were of unequal width.

8 Frequency density.

7 Scatter diagram.

6 14.25 cm.

5 An observation untypical of the distribution as a whole. The usual convention is to define an outlier as any observation less than $Q_1 - 1.5(Q_3 - Q_1)$ or greater than $Q_3 + 1.5 (Q_3 - Q_1)$, where Q_3 is the upper quartile and Q_1 is the lower quartile.

4 Median, quartiles, interquartile range.

3 Line diagram.

2 This data is discrete – a histogram illustrates continuous data.

1 Qualitative.

CHAPTER 4

Probability

Learning objectives

After studying this chapter you should be able to:
- understand the concept of probability and be able to allocate probabilities using equally likely outcomes
- identify mutually exclusive events and independent events
- apply the law $P(A \cup B) = P(A) + P(B)$ to mutually exclusive events
- apply the law $P(A \cap B) = P(A)P(B)$ to independent events or the law $P(A \cap B) = P(A)P(B|A)$ to events which are not independent
- solve simple probability problems using tree diagrams or the laws of probability.

4.1 Probability

The concept of probability is widely understood. For example, Courtney might say that the probability of having to wait more than 5 minutes for a bus on a weekday morning is 0.4. He means that if he carries out a large number of **trials** (that is he waits for a bus on a large number of weekday mornings) he expects to have to wait more than 5 minutes in about 0.4 or 40% of these **trials**.

> Probability is measured on a scale from 0 to 1. Zero represents impossibility and 1 represents certainty.

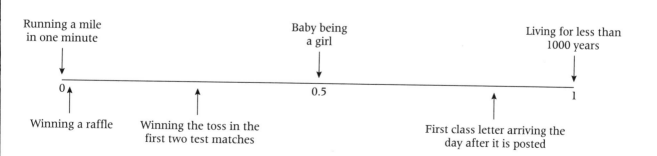

4.2 Equally likely outcomes

Often trials can result in a number of equally likely outcomes. For example, if there are 25 people in a room and a trial consists of choosing one at random there are 25 equally likely outcomes.

> You will understand what is meant by 'equally likely'. Don't try to give it a precise definition – it can't be done.

An **event** consists of one or more of the outcomes. Choosing, a particular person, choosing someone wearing glasses or choosing a male would all be examples of events.

If Janice is one of the people in the room then the probability of the event 'choosing Janice' occurring as a result of the trial is $\frac{1}{25}$.

If there are six people wearing glasses in the room the probability of the event 'choosing someone wearing glasses' occurring as a result of the trial is $\frac{6}{25}$.

> If a trial can result in one of n equally likely outcomes and an event consists of r of these outcomes, then the probability of the event happening as a result of the trial is $\frac{r}{n}$.

> It must be impossible for more than one of the outcomes to occur as a result of the same trial.

Worked example 1

If a fair die is thrown, what is the probability that it lands showing, **(a)** 2, **(b)** an even number, **(c)** more than 4?

Solution

There are six equally likely outcomes. The probability of any one of them occurring is therefore $\frac{1}{6}$.

(a) $P(2) = \frac{1}{6}$

(b) $P(\text{even number}) = P(2, 4 \text{ or } 6) = \frac{3}{6} = \frac{1}{2}$

(c) $P(\text{more than 4}) = P(5 \text{ or } 6) = \frac{1}{3}$.

EXERCISE 4A

1 A box contains 20 counters, numbered 1, 2, 3, … up to 20. A counter is taken out of the box. What is the probability that it **(a)** is the number 7, **(b)** it is a multiple of 4, **(c)** is greater than 14, **(d)** has a 3 on it.

2 The days of the week are written on seven separate cards. One card is chosen. What is the probability that it is: **(a)** Thursday, **(b)** either Monday or Tuesday, **(c)** not Friday, Saturday or Sunday?

3 In a game of Scrabble, Charlie has the letters B, E, E, H, Q, S, and T. One letter accidentally falls on to the floor. What is the probability that it is:

(a) Q, (b) B, E or S, (c) not an E?

4 In a box there are 15 beads. Seven are white, three are yellow, three are blue and two are green. If one bead is selected at random, what is the probability that it is: (a) white, (b) yellow or green, (c) not blue, (d) brown, (e) neither white nor yellow?

5 A cricket team has five batters, a wicket-keeper, three bowlers and two all-rounders. One player is selected at random to pack the cricket bag. What is the probability that the selected player is: (a) the wicket-keeper, (b) a bowler, (c) not an all-rounder, (d) neither a batter nor a bowler?

4.3 Relative frequency

It is not always possible to assign a probability using equally likely outcomes. For example, when Courtney waits for a bus he either has to wait for less than 5 minutes or for 5 or more minutes. However, there is no reason to think that these two outcomes are equally likely. In this case the only way to assign a probability is to carry out the trial a large number of times and to see how often a particular outcome occurs. If Courtney went for a bus on 40 weekday mornings and on 16 of these he had to wait more than 5 minutes he could assign the probability $16/40 = 0.4$ to the event of having to wait more than 5 minutes.

The **relative frequency** of an event is the proportion of times it has been observed to happen.

The **relative frequency** method of assigning probabilities suffers from the problem that if Courtney carried out a large number of further trials it is not possible to prove that the relative frequency would not change completely. However, when this method has been used in practice it has always happened that although the relative frequency may fluctuate over the first few trials, these fluctuations become small after a large number of trials.

In all cases where equally likely outcomes can be used it is also possible to use the relative frequency method. When this has been done it has always been observed that provided a large number of trials are carried out the two methods give very similar although not quite identical results. For example, when a die has been thrown a large number of times the proportion of ones observed is very close to $\frac{1}{6}$.

In examination questions you will either be given the probability of an event or required to find it using equally likely outcomes.

4.4 Mutually exclusive events

When you pick a card from a pack, it must be a club, diamond, heart or a spade. The card cannot be, say, both a club and a heart. The events 'picking a club', 'picking a diamond', 'picking a heart' and 'picking a spade' are said to be '**mutually exclusive**'. The occurrence of one event **excludes** the possibility that any of the other events could occur.

Worked example 2

One card is selected from a pack. Which of these pairs of events are mutually exclusive?

(a) 'The card is a heart' and 'the card is a spade'

(b) 'The card is a club' and 'the card is a Queen'

(c) 'The card is black' and 'the card is a diamond'

(d) 'The card is a King' and 'the card is an Ace'

(e) 'The card is red' and 'the card is a heart'.

Solution

(a), **(c)** and **(d)**. In **(b)** it is possible to have a card which is **both** a club **and** a Queen {the Queen of Clubs}, and in **(e)** a red card could be a heart.

In **(a)**, **(c)** and **(d)** the two events cannot occur simultaneously, hence they are mutually exclusive.

The pack of 52 cards contains 13 clubs, 13 diamonds, 13 hearts and 13 spades. The probability of picking a club is $\frac{13}{52} = 0.25$. The probability of picking a diamond is $\frac{13}{52} = 0.25$. The probability of picking a club or a diamond is $\frac{26}{52} = 0.5$. This is equal to the probability of picking a club plus the probability of picking a diamond. This is an example of the addition law of probability **as it applies to mutually exclusive events**.

If A and B are mutually exclusive events then the probability of A or B occurring as a result of a trial is the sum of the separate probabilities of A and B occurring as a result of the trial. This is usually written:

$$P(A \cup B) = P(A) + P(B)$$

$P(A \cup B)$ denotes the probability of A or B or both occurring. However, here we are dealing with mutually exclusive events so A and B cannot both occur.

If A and B are not mutually exclusive the law is more complicated. You will not need the more complicated form in this module and rarely need it in other modules.

This law can be extended to more than two mutually exclusive events. For example the probability of picking a club, a diamond or a heart is $0.25 + 0.25 + 0.25 = 0.75$.

$P(A \cup B \cup C) = P(A) + P(B) + P(C)$

A person, selected at random from 25 people in a room, must either be wearing glasses or not wearing glasses. These two events are mutually exclusive but one of them must happen. One of these events is called the **complement** of the other. The complement of event A is usually denoted A'.

Another way of saying that one of the events must happen is to say the events are exhaustive.

As one of the events must happen $P(A \cup A') = 1$

As the events are mutually exclusive
$P(A) + P(A') = P(A \cup A') = 1$

or $P(A') = 1 - P(A)$

Sometimes it is much easier to work out $P(A)$ than $P(A')$ or vice versa. You can find whichever is easier and, if necessary, use this rule to find the other.

4

EXERCISE 4B

1 The probability of Brian passing a driving test is 0.6. Write down the probability of him not passing the test.

2 The probability of a TV set requiring repair within 1 year is 0.22. Write down the probability of a TV set not requiring repair within 1 year.

3 When Devona rings her mother the probability that the phone is engaged is 0.1, the probability that the phone is not engaged but no one answers is 0.5 and the probability that the phone is answered is 0.4.

Find the probability that:

(a) the phone is engaged or no one answers, **(b)** the phone is engaged or it is answered, **(c)** the phone is not engaged.

4 Kofi shops exactly once a week. In a particular week the probability that he shops on a Monday is 0.3, on a Tuesday is 0.4 and on a Wednesday is 0.1.

Find the probability that he goes shopping on:

(a) Monday or Tuesday, **(b)** Monday or Wednesday, **(c)** Monday or Tuesday or Wednesday, **(d)** not on Monday, **(e)** Thursday or Friday or Saturday or Sunday.

5 There are 35 customers in a canteen, 12 are aged over 50, 15 are aged between 30 and 50 and 5 are aged between 25 and 29.

Find the probability that the next customer to be served is aged:

(a) 30 or over, **(b)** 25 or over, **(c)** under 25, **(d)** 50 or under.

6 Charlotte is expecting a baby:

A is the event that the baby will have blue eyes

B is the event that the baby will have green eyes

C is the event that the baby will have brown hair.

   (a) Write down two of these events which are:

   (i) mutually exclusive, **(ii)** not mutually exclusive.

   (b) Define the complement of event A.

7 A firm employs 20 bricklayers. The inland revenue selects one for investigation:

A is the event that the bricklayer selected earned less than £20 000 last year

B is the event that the bricklayer selected earned more than £20 000 last year

C is the event that the bricklayer selected earned £20 000 or more last year.

   (a) Which event is the complement of *C*.

   (b) Are the events *A* and *B* mutually exclusive?

   (c) Write down two of the events which are not mutually exclusive.

4.5 Independent events

When the probability of event *A* occurring is unaffected by whether or not event *B* occurs the two events are said to be **independent**.

For example, if event *A* is throwing an even number with a blue die and event *B* is throwing an odd number with a red die then the probability of event *A* is $\frac{3}{6} = 0.5$ regardless of whether or not event *B* occurs. Events *A* and *B* are independent.

If two dice are thrown there are 36 equally likely possible outcomes

1,1	1,2	1,3	1,4	1,5	1,6
2,1	2,2	2,3	2,4	2,5	2,6
3,1	3,2,	3,3	3,4	3,5	3,6
4,1	4,2	4,3	4,4	4,5	4,6
5,1	5,2	5,3	5,4	5,5	5,6
6,1	6,2	6,3	6,4	6,5	6,6

If you wish to find the probability of the total score being 12 you can observe that only one of the outcomes (6,6) gives a total score of 12 and so the probability is $\frac{1}{36}$.

If the question concerned more than two dice there would be a
very large number of equally likely outcomes and this method
would be impractical. An alternative method is to regard
throwing a 6 with the first die as event *A* and throwing a 6 with
the second die as event *B*. Now use the law that the probability
of two independent events both happening is the product of
their separate probabilities. This is usually written:

 If *A* and *B* are independent events P($A \cap B$) = P(A)P(B)

P($A \cap B$) is the probability of
events *A* and *B* both happening.

The law can be extended to
three or more independent
events.

4

The probability of obtaining a total score of 12 (which can only
be achieved by throwing a six with both dice) is
$\frac{1}{6} \times \frac{1}{6} = \frac{1}{36}$ as before.

EXERCISE 4C

1 The probability of Brian passing a driving test is 0.6. The
probability of Syra passing an advanced motoring test is 0.7.
Find the probability of Brian passing a driving test and Syra
passing an advanced motoring test.

2 The probability of a TV set requiring repair within 1 year is
0.22. The probability of a washing machine requiring repair
within a year is 0.10. Find the probability of a TV set and a
washing machine both requiring repair within a year.

3 Two coins are tossed. Find the probability of them both falling
heads.

4 The probability that a vinegar bottle filled by a machine
contains less than the nominal quantity is 0.1. Find the
probability that two bottles, selected at random both contain:

(a) less than the nominal quantity

(b) at least the nominal quantity.

5 Three coins are tossed. Find the probability of them all falling
tails.

If you wish to find the probability of a total score of 4 when two
dice are thrown then you can observe that there are three

outcomes which give a total score of 4 and the probability is $\frac{3}{36}$

1,1	1,2	1,3	1,4	1,5	1,6
2,1	2,2	2,3	2,4	2,5	2,6
3,1	3,2,	3,3	3,4	3,5	3,6
4,1	4,2	4,3	4,4	4,5	4,6
5,1	5,2	5,3	5,4	5,5	5,6
6,1	6,2	6,3	6,4	6,5	6,6

Alternatively you can answer the question using the laws of probability.

There are three outcomes which give a total score of 4:

1,3 with probability $\frac{1}{6} \times \frac{1}{6} = \frac{1}{36}$

2,2 with probability $\frac{1}{6} \times \frac{1}{6} = \frac{1}{36}$

3,1 with probability $\frac{1}{6} \times \frac{1}{6} = \frac{1}{36}$.

Since these three outcomes are mutually exclusive you can apply the addition law of probability and obtain the probability of obtaining a total score of 4 as $\frac{1}{36} + \frac{1}{36} + \frac{1}{36} = \frac{3}{36} = \frac{1}{12}$.

Worked example 3

The probability that telephone calls to a railway timetable enquiry service are answered is 0.7. If three calls are made find the probability that:

(a) all three are answered

(b) exactly two are answered.

Solution

If A is the event of a call being answered $P(A) = 0.7$.

A' is the probability of a call not being answered and $P(A') = 1 - 0.7 = 0.3$.

(a) Using the multiplication law the probability of $AAA = 0.7 \times 0.7 \times 0.7 = 0.343$.

> The law for three independent events is used.

(b) If one call is unanswered it could be the first, second or third call.

$A'AA$ with probability $0.3 \times 0.7 \times 0.7 = 0.147$
$AA'A$ with probability $0.7 \times 0.3 \times 0.7 = 0.147$
AAA' with probability $0.7 \times 0.7 \times 0.3 = 0.147$

> Although A' occurs in different positions the probability of each of the three outcomes is the same.

These three outcomes are mutually exclusive and so you can apply the addition law and find the probability of exactly two calls being answered to be:

$0.147 + 0.147 + 0.147 = 0.441$.

4.6 Tree diagrams

An alternative approach to the problem is to illustrate the outcomes with a tree diagram. Each branch shows the possible outcomes of each call and their probabilities. The outcome of the three calls is found by reading along the branches leading to it and the probability of this outcome is found by multiplying the individual probabilities along these branches.

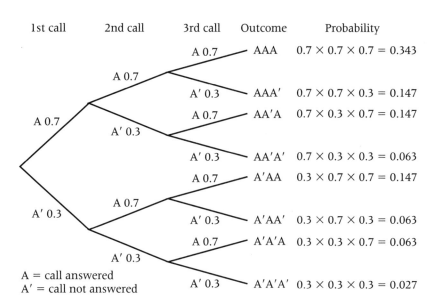

A = call answered
A' = call not answered

The probability of all three calls being answered (*AAA*) can be seen to be 0.343.

The probability of exactly two calls being answered is the sum of the probabilities of the three outcomes *AAA'*, *AA'A* and *A'AA* = 0.147 + 0.147 + 0.147 = 0.441 as before.

Worked example 4

A coin is tossed three times. Find the probability that the number of tails is 0, 1, 2 or 3.

Solution

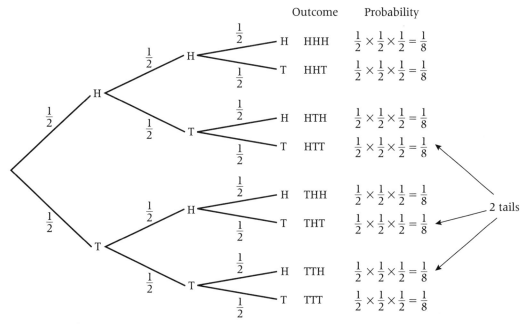

The probability of 0 tails is $\dfrac{1}{8}$

The probability of 1 tail is $\dfrac{1}{8} + \dfrac{1}{8} + \dfrac{1}{8} = \dfrac{3}{8}$

The probability of 2 tails is $\dfrac{1}{8} + \dfrac{1}{8} + \dfrac{1}{8} = \dfrac{3}{8}$

The probability of 3 tails is $\dfrac{1}{8}$.

EXERCISE 4D

Answer the following questions using tree diagrams or the laws of probability.

1 The probability of Michelle passing a mathematics exam is 0.3 and the probability of her passing a biology exam is independently 0.45.

Find the probability that she:

(a) passes mathematics and fails biology

(b) passes exactly one of the two examinations

(c) passes at least one of the two examinations.

2 A civil servant is given the task of calculating pension entitlements. For any given calculation the probability of the result being incorrect is 0.08.

(a) Find the probability that if two pension entitlements are calculated the number incorrect will be:

(i) 0,   **(ii)** 1,   **(iii)** at least 1.

(b) Find the probability that if three pension entitlements are calculated the number incorrect will be:

(i) 0,   **(ii)** 1,   **(iii)** 2 or more.

3 The probability of answering a multiple choice question correctly by guessing is 0.25.

(a) A student guesses the answer to two multiple choice questions. Find the probability that:

(i) both answers are correct,

(ii) exactly one answer is correct.

(b) Another student guesses the answer to three multiple choice questions. Find the probability that:

(i) no answers are correct

(ii) exactly two answers are correct

(iii) at least two answers are correct

(iv) less than two answers are correct.

(c) If the second student guesses the answer to four multiple choice questions find the probability that no answers are correct.

4 An opinion poll is to investigate whether estate agents earnings are thought to be too high, about right or too low. The probabilities of answers from randomly selected adults are as follows:

Too high   0.80
About right   0.15
Too low   0.05.

(a) Find the probability that if two adults are selected at random they will:

(i) both answer 'too high'

(ii) one answer 'too high' and one answer 'about right'

(iii) both give the same answer

(iv) neither answer 'too low'

(v) both give different answers.

(b) Find the probability that if three adults are selected at random they will:

(i) all answer 'too high'

(ii) two answer 'too high' and one answers 'about right'

(iii) none answer 'too high'

(iv) all give the same answer

(v) all give different answers.

4.7 Conditional probability

A room contains 25 people. The table shows the numbers of each sex and whether or not they were wearing glasses.

	Male	**Female**
Glasses	4	5
No glasses	5	11

A person is selected at random.

F is the event that the person selected is female.

G is the event that the person selected is wearing glasses.

There are a total of nine people wearing glasses so $P(G) = \dfrac{9}{25}$. However, only four of the nine males are wearing glasses and so for the males the probability of wearing glasses is $\dfrac{4}{9}$ while for the females the probability is $\dfrac{5}{16}$. That is the probability of event G occurring is affected by whether or not event F has occurred. The two events are **not independent**.

The **conditional probability** that the person selected is wearing glasses given that they are female is denoted **P(G|F)**.

> P(A|B) denotes the probability that event A happens given that event B happens.

> Two events A and B are independent if P(A) = P(A|B).

Worked example 5

Students on the first year of a science course at a university take an optional language module. The number of students of each sex choosing each available language is shown below.

	French	German	Russian	Total
Male	17	9	14	40
Female	12	11	7	30
Total	29	20	21	70

A student is selected at random.

M is the event that the student selected is male

R is the event that the student selected is studying Russian.

Write down the value of:

(a) P(M), **(b)** P(R), **(c)** P(M|R), **(d)** P(M∩R), **(e)** P(M∪R), **(f)** P(R|M), **(g)** P(M'), **(h)** P(R'), **(i)** P(R|M'), **(j)** P(R'|M), **(k)** P(M'∩R), **(l)** P(M∪R').

Solution

(a) There are 40 male students out of a total of 70

$$P(M) = \frac{40}{70} = 0.571.$$

(b) 21 students are studying Russian. $P(R) = \frac{21}{70} = 0.3.$

(c) There are 21 students studying Russian of whom 14 are male. $P(M|R) = \frac{14}{21} = 0.667.$

(d) There are 14 students who are both male and studying Russian. $P(M\cap R) = \frac{14}{70} = 0.2.$

(e) There are $17 + 9 + 14 + 7 = 47$ students who are either male or studying Russian (or both). $P(M\cup R) = \frac{47}{70} = 0.671.$

(f) There are 40 male students of whom 14 are studying Russian. P($R|M$) = 14/40 = 0.35.

(g) There are 30 students who are not male (i.e. are female). P(M') = $\frac{30}{70}$ = 0.429.

(h) There are 17 + 9 + 12 + 11 = 49 students who are not studying Russian. P(R') = $\frac{49}{70}$ = 0.7.

(i) Of the 30 not male (female) students seven are studying Russian. P($R|M'$) = $\frac{7}{30}$ = 0.233.

(j) Of the 40 male students 17 + 9 = 26 are not studying Russian. P($R'|M$) = $\frac{26}{40}$ = 0.65.

(k) There are 7 students who are not male (female) and are studying Russian. P($M'\cap R$) = $\frac{7}{70}$ = 0.1.

(l) There are 17 + 9 + 14 + 12 + 11 = 63 students who are either male or not studying Russian (or both). P($M\cup R'$) = $\frac{63}{70}$ = 0.9.

EXERCISE 4E

1 One hundred and twenty students register for a foundation course. At the end of a year they are recorded as pass or fail. A summary of the results, classified by age, is shown.

	Age (years)	
	Under 20	**20 and over**
Pass	47	33
Fail	28	12

A student is selected at random from the list of those who registered for the course.

Q denotes the event that the selected student is under 20
R denotes the event that the selected student passed
(Q' and R' denote the events 'not Q' and 'not R', respectively).

Determine the value of:

(a) P(Q), **(b)** P(R), **(c)** P(Q'), **(d)** P($Q\cap R$), **(e)** P($Q\cup R$),
(f) P($Q|R$), **(g)** P($R'|Q$), **(h)** P($Q|R'$), **(i)** P($Q'|R$), **(j)** P($Q\cap R'$).

2 Last year the employees of a firm either received no pay rise, a small pay rise or a large pay rise. The following table shows the number in each category, classified by whether they were weekly paid or monthly paid.

	No pay rise	Small pay rise	Large pay rise
Weekly paid	25	85	5
Monthly paid	4	8	23

A tax inspector decides to investigate the tax affairs of an employee selected at random.

D is the event that a weekly paid employee is selected.

E is the event that an employee who received no pay rise is selected.

D' and E' are the events 'not D' and 'not E', respectively.

Find

(a) $P(D)$, **(b)** $P(E')$, **(c)** $P(D|E)$, **(d)** $P(D \cup E)$, **(e)** $P(E \cap D)$,

(f) $P(D \cap E')$, **(g)** $P(E \cup D')$, **(h)** $P(D|E')$, **(i)** $P(E'|D')$.

3 A car hire firm has depots in Falmouth and Tiverton. The cars are classified small, medium and large according to their engine size. The number of cars in each class, based at each depot, is shown in the following table.

	Small	Medium	Large
Falmouth	12	15	13
Tiverton	18	22	10

One of the 90 cars is selected at random for inspection.

A is the event that the selected car is based at Falmouth.

B is the event that the selected car is small.

C is the event that the selected car is large.

A', B' and C' are the events 'not A', 'not B' and 'not C', respectively.

Evaluate

(a) $P(A)$, **(b)** $P(B')$, **(c)** $P(A \cup C)$, **(d)** $P(A \cap B)$, **(e)** $P(A \cup B')$,

(f) $P(A|C)$, **(g)** $P(C|A')$, **(h)** $P(B'|A)$, **(i)** $P(B \cap C)$.

By comparing your answers to (a) and (f) state whether or not the events A and C are independent.

Multiplication law

You have seen that if A and B are independent events $P(A \cap B) = P(A)P(B)$. This is a special case of the more general law that

$$P(A \cap B) = P(A)P(B|A)$$

> *A and B may consist of different outcomes of the same trial or of outcomes of different trials.*

You can verify this using the earlier example

	Male	Female
Glasses	4	5
No glasses	5	11

A person is selected at random.

F is the event that the person selected is female.

G is the event that the person selected is wearing glasses.

> *Here F and G consist of different outcomes of the same trial.*

$P(F \cap G)$, the probability that the person selected is a female wearing glasses is $\dfrac{5}{25}$ or 0.2.

$$P(F) = \frac{16}{25}$$

$P(G|F)$, the probability that the person selected is wearing glasses given that they are female, is $\dfrac{5}{16}$.

$$P(F)P(G|F) = \frac{16}{25} \times \frac{5}{16} = 0.2 = P(F \cap G)$$

Worked example 6

Sheena buys 10 apparently identical oranges. Unknown to her the flesh of two of these oranges is rotten. She selects two of the 10 oranges at random and gives them to her grandson. Find the probability that:

(a) both the oranges are rotten

(b) exactly one of the oranges is rotten.

Solution

(a) P('1st rotten' ∩ '2nd rotten') = P('1st rotten') × P('2nd rotten' | '1st rotten')

$$P(\text{'1st rotten'}) = \frac{2}{10}$$

There are now only nine oranges left to choose from of which one is rotten.

$$P(\text{'2nd rotten'} \mid \text{'1st rotten'}) = \frac{1}{9}$$

The probability that both oranges are rotten is

$$\frac{2}{10} \times \frac{1}{9} = \frac{1}{45} = 0.0222.$$

(b) There are two outcomes which result in one rotten orange.

'1st rotten' '2nd OK' with probability $\dfrac{2}{10} \times \dfrac{8}{9} = \dfrac{16}{90}$

or '1st OK' '2nd rotten' with probability $\dfrac{8}{10} \times \dfrac{2}{9} = \dfrac{16}{90}$.

> Note that although the oranges are selected in a different order the probabilities are the same.

Since these outcomes are **mutually exclusive** we may add their probabilities to obtain the probability of exactly one rotten orange $= \dfrac{16}{90} + \dfrac{16}{90} = \dfrac{32}{90} = 0.356$.

You may prefer to solve examples like this using tree diagrams.

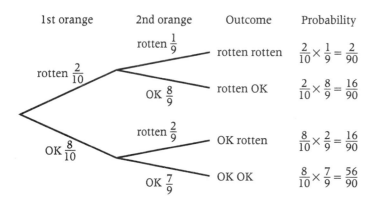

(a) The probability of both oranges being rotten is $\dfrac{2}{90} = 0.222$.

(b) The probability of exactly one orange being rotten is $\dfrac{16}{90} + \dfrac{16}{90} = 0.356$.

Worked example 7

When Bali is on holiday she intends to go for a 5-mile run before breakfast each day. However, sometimes she stays in bed instead. The probability that she will go for a run on the first morning is 0.7. Thereafter, the probability that she will go for a run is 0.7 if she went for a run on the previous morning and 0.6 if she did not.

Find the probability that on the first three days of the holiday she will go for:

(a) three runs

(b) exactly two runs. [A]

Solution

(a) Probability Bali goes for three runs (RRR)

P(R 1st morning) × P(R 2nd morning | R 1st morning) × P(R 3rd morning | R 2nd morning) = 0.7 × 0.7 × 0.7 = 0.343.

(b) Probability that Bali runs the first two mornings and stays in bed (B) on the third morning is

P(R 1st morning) $\times$ P(R 2nd morning$|R$ 1st morning) $\times$ P(B 3rd morning$|R$ 2nd morning) $= 0.7 \times 0.7 \times 0.3 = 0.147$.

There are two other possibilities

RBR with probability $0.7 \times 0.3 \times 0.6 = 0.126$

and

BRR with probability $0.3 \times 0.6 \times 0.7 = 0.126$

These outcomes are mutually exclusive and so the probability of Bali going for exactly two runs is:

$0.147 + 0.126 + 0.126 = 0.399$.

EXERCISE 4F

1 A car hire firm owns 90 cars, 40 of which are based at Falmouth and the other 50 at Tiverton. If two of the 90 cars are selected at random (without replacement) find the probability that:

(a) both are based at Falmouth

(b) one is based at Falmouth and the other at Tiverton.

2 Eight students share a house. Five of them own bicycles and three do not. If two of the students are chosen at random, to complete a survey on public transport, find the probability that:

(i) both own bicycles

(ii) one owns a bicycle and the other does not.

3 A small firm employs two sales representatives, six administrative staff and four others.

(a) If two of the 12 staff are selected at random find the probability that they are:

(i) both sales representatives

(ii) one administrator and one sales representative

(iii) neither administrative staff.

(b) If three of the 12 staff are selected at random without replacement find the probability that they are

(i) all administrative staff

(ii) include two administrative staff and one sales representative

(iii) include exactly one sales representative

(iv) include one sales representative, one administrator and one other.

4 At a Cornish seaside resort, the local council displays warning flags if conditions are considered to be dangerous for bathing in the sea. The probability that flags are displayed on a particular day is 0.4 if flags were displayed on the previous day, and 0.15 if they were not displayed on the previous day.

A family arrives for a 3-day holiday. Assume the probability that flags are displayed on their first day is 0.3.

Determine the probability that flags are displayed on

(a) all three days

(b) none of the three days

(c) exactly one of the three days.   [A]

5 The probability of rain interrupting play at a county cricket ground is estimated to be 0.7 if rain has interrupted play on the previous day and 0.2 if rain has not interrupted play on the previous day.

A 3-day match is scheduled to start on Wednesday. The weather forecast suggests that the probability of rain interrupting play on the first day is 0.4.

Find the probability that rain will interrupt play on:

(i) Wednesday, Thursday and Friday

(ii) Wednesday and Friday but not Thursday

(iii) Thursday and Friday only

(iv) Friday only

(v) exactly one of the first two days (regardless of what happens on Friday)

(vi) exactly one of the three days

(vii) exactly two of the three days.

6 During an epidemic a doctor is consulted by 40 people who claim to be suffering from flu. Of the 40, 15 are female of whom 10 have flu and five do not. Fifteen of the males have flu and the rest do not. If three of the people are selected at random, without replacement, find the probability:

(i) that all three are female

(ii) all three have flu

(iii) all three are females with flu

(iv) all three are of the same sex

(v) one is a female with flu and the other two are females without flu

(vi) one is male and two are female

(vii) one is a male with flu, one is a male without flu and one is a female with flu.

MIXED EXERCISE

1 A group of three pregnant women attend ante-natal classes together. Assuming that each woman is equally likely to give birth on each of the seven days in a week, find the probability that all three give birth:

   (a) on a Monday

   (b) on the same day of the week

   (c) on different days of the week

   (d) at a weekend (either a Saturday or Sunday).

   (e) How large would the group need to be to make the probability of all the women in the group giving birth on different days of the week less than 0.05?   [A]

2 Conveyor-belting for use in a chemical works is tested for strength.

   Of the pieces of belting tested at a testing station, 60% come from supplier A and 40% come from supplier B. Past experience shows that the probability of passing the strength test is 0.96 for belting from supplier A and 0.89 for belting from supplier B.

   (a) Find the probability that a randomly selected piece of belting:

   (i) comes from supplier A and passes the strength test
   (ii) passes the strength test.

   The belting is also tested for safety (this test is based on the amount of heat generated if the belt snaps).

   The probability of a piece of belting from supplier A passing the safety test is 0.95 and is independent of the result of the strength test.

   (b) Find the probability that a piece of belting from supplier A will pass both the strength and safety tests.   [A]

3 Vehicles approaching a crossroads must go in one of three directions – left, right or straight on. Observations by traffic engineers showed that of vehicles approaching from the north, 45% turn left, 20% turn right and 35% go straight on. Assuming that the driver of each vehicle chooses direction independently, what is the probability that of the next three vehicles approaching from the north:

   (i) all go straight on

   (ii) all go in the same direction

   (iii) two turn left and one turns right

   (iv) all go in different directions

   (v) exactly two turn left?   [A]

4 A bicycle shop stocks racing, touring and mountain bicycles. The following table shows the number of bicycles of each type in stock, together with their price range.

	Price range		
	< £250	£250–£500	> £500
Racing	10	18	22
Touring	36	22	12
Mountain	28	32	20

A bicycle is selected at random for testing.

R is the event that a racing bicycle is selected

S is the event that a bicycle worth between £250 and £500 is selected

T is the event that a touring bicycle is selected.

(R', S', T' are the events not R, not S, not T, respectively.)

(a) Write down the value of

(i) P(S), **(ii)** P($R \cap S$), **(iii)** P($T' \cup S'$) **(iv)** P($S|R$).

(b) Express in terms of the events that have been defined the event that a mountain bicycle is selected. [A]

5 The probability that telephone calls to a railway timetable enquiry service are answered is 0.7.

(a) If three calls are made, find the probability that:

(i) all three are answered

(ii) exactly two are answered.

(b) Ahmed requires some timetable information and decides that if his call is not answered he will call repeatedly until he obtains an answer.

Find the probability that to obtain an answer he has to call:

(i) exactly three times

(ii) at least three times.

(c) If a call is answered, the probability that the information given is correct is 0.8. Thus, there are three possible outcomes for each call:

call not answered

call answered but incorrect information given

call answered and correct information given.

If three calls are made, find the probability that each outcome occurs once. [A]

6 At the beginning of 1992 a motor insurance company classified its customers as low, medium or high risk. The following table shows the number of customers in each category and whether or not they made a claim during 1992.

	Low	Medium	High
No claim in 1992	4200	5100	3900
Claim in 1992	200	500	1100

(a) A customer is selected at random.

A is the event that the customer made a claim in 1992

B is the event that the customer was classified low risk

A' is the event 'not *A*''.

Write down the value of:

(i) P(*A*)

(ii) P(*A*|*B*)

(iii) P(*B*|*A'*)

(iv) P(*A*∩*B*)

(v) P(*B*∪*A'*).

(b) As a result of the data in (a) the company decided not to accept any new high risk customers (but existing customers could continue). In June 1993 its customers were 30% low risk, 65% medium risk and 5% high risk. Use the data in the table above to estimate, for each category of customer, the probability of a claim being made in the next year. Hence estimate the probability that a randomly selected customer will make a claim in the next year. [A]

7 A market researcher wishes to interview residents aged 18 years and over in a small village. The adult population of the village is made up as follows:

Age group	Male	Female
18–29	16	24
30–59	29	21
60 and over	15	25

(a) When one person is selected at random for interview

A is the event of the person selected being male

B is the event of the person selected being in the age group 30–59

C is the event of the person selected being aged 60 or over.

(*A'*, *B'*, *C'* are the events not *A*, not *B* and not *C*.)

Write down the value of

(i) P(A)

(ii) P(A∩B)

(iii) P(A∪C′)

(iv) P(B′|A).

(b) When three people are selected for interview, what is the probability that they are all female if:

(i) one is selected at random from each age group

(ii) they are selected at random, without replacement, from the population of 130 people?

Three people are selected at random, without replacement.

(c) What is the probability that there will be one from each of the three age groups? [A]

Key point summary

1	Probability is measured on a scale from 0 to 1.	*p63*
2	If a trial can result in one of n equally likely outcomes and an event consists of r of these, then the probability of the event happening as a result of the trial is $\dfrac{r}{n}$.	*p64*
3	Two events are **mutually exclusive** if they cannot both happen.	*p66*
4	If A and B are **mutually exclusive** events $P(A \cup B) = P(A) + P(B)$.	*p66*
5	The event of A not happening as the result of a trial is called the **complement** of A and is usually denoted A'.	*p67*
6	Two events are **independent** if the probability of one happening is unaffected by whether or not the other happens.	*p68*
7	If A and B are **independent** events $P(A \cap B) = P(A)P(B)$.	*p69*
8	$P(A|B)$ denoted the probability that event A happens given that event B happens.	*p74*
9	If events A and B are **independent** $P(A|B) = P(A)$.	*p74*
10	$P(A \cap B) = P(A)P(B|A) = P(B)P(A|B)$.	*p77*

Test yourself	What to review
1 Twelve components include three that are defective. If two components are chosen at random from the 12 find the probability that **(a)** both are defective, **(b)** exactly one is defective.	*Section 4.7*
2 Under what conditions does $P(R \cap Q) = P(R)P(Q)$?	*Section 4.5*
3 Under what conditions does $P(S \cup T) = P(S) + P(T)$?	*Section 4.4*
4 A student is selected from a class. R is the event that the student is female. Describe the complement of R. How is the complement usually denoted?	*Section 4.4*
5 There are 15 male and 20 female passengers on a tram. Ten of the males and 16 of the females are aged over 25. A ticket inspector selects one of the passengers at random. A is the event that the person selected is female, B is the event that the person selected is over 25. Write down $P(A)$, $P(B)$, $P(A\|B)$, $P(A \cap B)$ and $P(A \cup B)$. Hence verify that $P(A \cap B) = P(B)P(A\|B)$. Why is it not possible to apply the law $P(A \cup B) = P(A) + P(B)$ in this case?	*Section 4.7*
6 It is estimated that the probability of a league cricket match ending in a home win is 0.4, an away win is 0.25 and a draw is 0.35. Find the probability that if three games are played, and the results are independent, there will be: **(a)** three home wins **(b)** exactly one home win **(c)** one home win, one away win and one draw.	*Sections 4.5 and 4.6*

4

Test yourself ANSWERS

1 (a) 0.0455, **(b)** 0.409.

2 R and Q independent events.

3 S and T mutually exclusive events.

4 student is male, R'.

5 $\frac{4}{7}, \frac{26}{35}, \frac{8}{13}, \frac{16}{35}, \frac{6}{7}$, $P(B) \times P(A|B) = \frac{26}{35} \times \frac{8}{13} = \frac{16}{35} = P(A \cap B)$

A and B are not mutually exclusive.

6 (a) 0.064, **(b)** 0.432, **(c)** 0.21.

CHAPTER 5

Binomial distribution

Learning objectives

After studying this chapter, you should be able to:
- recognise when to use the binomial distribution
- state any assumptions necessary in order to use the binomial distribution
- apply the binomial distribution to a variety of problems.

5.1 Introduction to the binomial distribution

Bicycle, **Bi**ennial, **Bi**nary and **Bi**nomial all start with 'Bi' which generally implies that 'two' of something is involved. In the binomial distribution, the random variable concerned has two possible outcomes.

You have already met the binomial situation in Chapter 4, Section 4.6, where the results from a fair coin being thrown three times are considered.

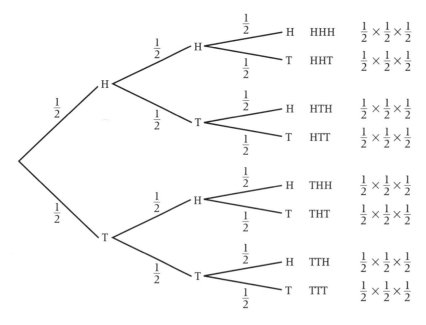

In this situation, the two outcomes are H, a head is showing, or T, a tail is showing.

There are three throws or trials involved and the results which are possible can be written in the following way:

All 3 heads (and 0 tails)	2 heads (and 1 tail)	1 head (and 2 tails)	0 heads (and 3 tails)
HHH	HHT	HTT	TTT
	HTH	THT	
	THH	TTH	
1 way of obtaining all 3 heads	3 ways of obtaining exactly 2 heads	3 ways of obtaining just 1 head	1 way of obtaining no heads

These results are normally written in the following way:

$$P(X = 0) = \left(\frac{1}{2}\right)^3 = \frac{1}{8} \qquad P(X = 1) = 3 \times \left(\frac{1}{2}\right)^3 = \frac{3}{8}$$

$$P(X = 2) = 3 \times \left(\frac{1}{2}\right)^3 = \frac{3}{8} \qquad P(X = 3) = \left(\frac{1}{2}\right)^3 = \frac{1}{8}$$

If the coin was not a fair coin but was a coin which had been squashed with a probability of a head showing being $\frac{1}{4}$, rather than $\frac{1}{2}$, then the tree diagram would look like this:

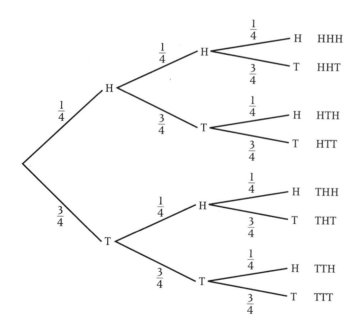

$$P(X = 3) = \left(\frac{1}{4}\right)^3 \qquad P(X = 2) = 3 \times \left(\frac{1}{4}\right)^2 \times \left(\frac{3}{4}\right)$$

$$P(X = 1) = 3 \times \left(\frac{1}{4}\right) \times \left(\frac{3}{4}\right)^2 \qquad P(X = 0) = \left(\frac{3}{4}\right)^3$$

A tree diagram can be used to find binomial probabilities but only in simple situations.

5.2 The essential elements of the binomial distribution

Certain conditions are necessary for a situation to be modelled by the binomial distribution.

- A fixed number of trials, **n**.
- Just two possible outcomes resulting from each trial.
- The probability of each outcome is the same for each trial.
- The trials are independent of each other.

The letters **n** and **p** are the binomial parameters.

These are often referred to as 'success' and 'failure'.

The probability of a 'success' is called **p**.

Either outcome can be called the 'success' but by convention, you usually refer to the **less** likely outcome as the 'success'.

EXERCISE 5A

1 If the probability of a baby being male is 0.5, draw a tree diagram to find the probability that a family of three children has exactly two boys.

2 Four fair coins are thrown. Draw a tree diagram to find the probability that:

(a) only one Head is obtained

(b) exactly two Heads are obtained.

3 At a birthday party, it is time to light the candles on the cake, but there are only three matches left in the box. If the probability that a match lights is only 0.6, find the probability that none of the matches will light.

4 A regular die has six faces. Two have circles on them and four have squares. This die is rolled three times and the shape on the top of the die is noted.

Draw a tree diagram to illustrate the possible outcomes and find the probability that:

(a) none of the rolls resulted in a square shape on the top face

(b) at least two throws resulted in a square shape on the top face.

5.3 Investigating further – Pascal's triangle

For larger values of n, a tree diagram is too difficult to construct and a rule is needed to help find the binomial probabilities.

Remember, in the binomial situation:

n represents the number of trials

p represents the probability of the event concerned.

We can then identify that a random variable X follows a binomial distribution by writing

$X \sim \mathbf{B}(n, p)$

In section 5.1

Example 1, $X \sim B\left(3, \frac{1}{2}\right)$

Example 2, $X \sim B\left(3, \frac{1}{4}\right)$

Worked example 1

Ashoke, Theo, Sadie and Paul will each visit the local leisure centre for a swim one afternoon next week. They have not made any particular arrangement between themselves about which afternoon they will go swimming and they are each equally likely to chose any afternoon of the week. The random variable involved, X, is the number of the four friends who go swimming on the Wednesday afternoon of the following week.

Find the probability that exactly two of the friends go swimming on Wednesday afternoon.

Solution

In this situation, $X \sim B\left(4, \frac{1}{7}\right)$

There are four trials as we are considering the number going out of the four friends. This tells us $n = 4$.

They can choose any afternoon therefore $p = \frac{1}{7}$.

The tree diagram on the next page shows the probabilities for how many of the friends go on Wednesday. It is very tedious to construct as there are 16 branches.

As the friends are equally likely to choose any afternoon out of the seven available, the probability that one of them chooses Wednesday is $\frac{1}{7}$.

$P(X = 0) = \left(\frac{6}{7}\right)^4$ 　　$P(X = 1) = 4 \times \left(\frac{6}{7}\right)^3 \times \left(\frac{1}{7}\right)$

$= \frac{1296}{2401}$ 　　　　　　$= \frac{864}{2401}$

$P(X = 2) = 6 \times \left(\frac{6}{7}\right)^2 \times \left(\frac{1}{7}\right)^2$ 　$P(X = 3) = 4 \times \left(\frac{6}{7}\right) \times \left(\frac{1}{7}\right)^3$

$= \frac{216}{2401}$ 　　　　　　$= \frac{24}{2401}$

$P(X = 4) = \left(\frac{1}{7}\right)^4 = \frac{1}{2401}$

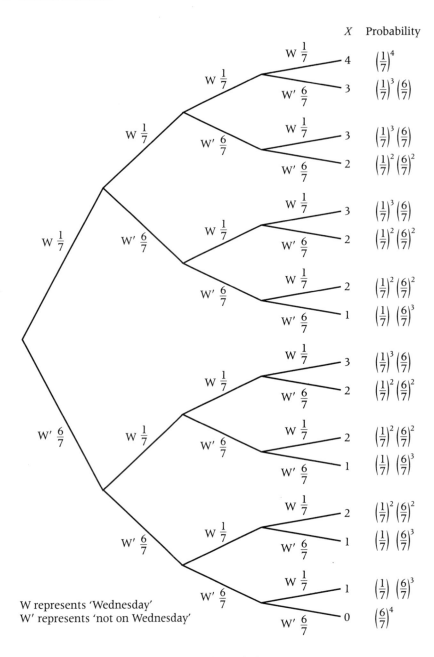

W represents 'Wednesday'
W' represents 'not on Wednesday'

Considering $\mathbf{P(X = 2)} = 6 \times \left(\frac{6}{7}\right)^2 \times \left(\frac{1}{7}\right)^2$.

The fractions involved are easily explained.

As we are interested in having *two* of the group of four going to the leisure centre on Wednesday and, as the probability for each is $\frac{1}{7}$, the $\left(\frac{1}{7}\right)^2$ is explained. Also, *two* out of the four will not be going on Wednesday which gives the $\left(\frac{6}{7}\right)^2$. The 6 is explained by the fact that there are six branches of the tree diagram which give two $\left(\frac{1}{7}\right)$s and two $\left(\frac{6}{7}\right)$s.

The six ways can be seen by examining the tree diagram but we would not want to draw a tree diagram every time (imagine if there were 10 friends involved!) and so another method needs to be developed to find binomial probabilities.

If we can produce the fractions in the expression for a binomial probability fairly easily, then all that is needed is a way to find the right numbers or coefficients to go with them for all the different ways of combining these probabilities.

In examples 1 and 2, the coefficients for the binomial model where $n = 3$ were found to be 1, 3, 3, 1.

In example 3, where $n = 4$, the coefficients were found to be 1, 4, 6, 4, 1.

You might recognise these numbers from Pascal's triangle shown below.

5

Pascal's triangle

```
                1     1
             1     2     1
          1     3     3     1          ←—— n = 3
       1     4     6     4     1       ←—— n = 4
    1     5    10    10     5     1
  1     6    15    20    15     6     1
 1    7    21    35    35    21    7    1
1   8   28   56   70   56   28   8   1
1  9  36  84  126 126  84  36  9   1
1 10 45 120 210 252 210 120 45 10  1  ←—— n = 10
```

You may well have met Pascal's triangle during GCSE investigations.

Worked example 2

Let's imagine now that there are 10 friends, each of whom will visit the leisure centre for a swim one afternoon next week. What is the probability that exactly three of them go for a swim on Wednesday?

Now, $X \sim B\left(10, \frac{1}{7}\right)$

Solution

It is clearly not possible to use a tree diagram this time but we can start to find the probability by finding the fractions needed.

For three to go on Wednesday, we need $\left(\frac{1}{7}\right)^3$. Also, seven must not go on Wednesday which gives $\left(\frac{6}{7}\right)^7$.

There would be 1024 branches for this situation.

We can write down these fractions but how many different ways are there of combining them? According to Pascal's triangle, for the relevant row relating to $n = 10$, there are 120 ways of combining three out of the 10 going on Wednesday and seven not going on Wednesday.

So $P(X = 3) = 120 \times \left(\dfrac{1}{7}\right)^3 \times \left(\dfrac{6}{7}\right)^7 = \dfrac{33\,592\,320}{282\,475\,249}$

$= 0.119$ (three significant figures)

> **The row is labelled $n = 10$**
>
> | 1 | 10 | 45 | 120 |
> |---|----|----|-----|
> | $X = 0$ | $X = 1$ | $X = 2$ | $X = 3$ |

> **Note:**
> The expressions $\dbinom{n}{r}$ or $^nC_r = \dfrac{n!}{r! \times (n-r)!}$
>
> The expressions $\dbinom{10}{3}$ or $^{10}C_3 = \dfrac{10!}{3! \times 7!}$
>
> $= \dfrac{10 \times 9 \times 8 \times 7 \times 6 \times 5 \times 4 \times 3 \times 2 \times 1}{(3 \times 2 \times 1) \times (7 \times 6 \times 5 \times 4 \times 3 \times 2 \times 1)} = \dfrac{10 \times 9 \times 8}{(3 \times 2 \times 1)} = 120.$

This is much easier to write down and calculate, rather than drawing 1024 branches!

The number of ways of choosing 3 from 10 is normally written $\dbinom{10}{3}$ or $^{10}C_3$ so the required probability can written as

$P(X = 3) = \dbinom{10}{3} \times \left(\dfrac{1}{7}\right)^3 \times \left(\dfrac{6}{7}\right)^7.$

Worked example 3

Continuing with the same problem.

Find the probability that exactly half of the friends go to the leisure centre on Wednesday for a swim.

> Half means five do go on Wednesday and five do not go.

Solution

The relevant number this time is 252.

The fractions are $\left(\dfrac{1}{7}\right)^5$ and $\left(\dfrac{6}{7}\right)^5$

Hence $P(X = 5) = 252 \times \left(\dfrac{1}{7}\right)^5 \times \left(\dfrac{6}{7}\right)^5$

$= \dfrac{1\,959\,552}{282\,475\,249} = 0.00694$ (three significant figures).

> Again looking at the row labelled $n = 10$
>
> | 1 | 10 | 45 | 120 | 210 | 252 |
> |---|----|----|-----|-----|-----|
> | $X = 0$ | $X = 1$ | $X = 2$ | $X = 3$ | $X = 4$ | $X = 5$ |
>
> $\dbinom{10}{5}$ or $^{10}C_5 = 252$

Worked example 4

Let's extend the problem further to 20 friends, each of whom will visit the leisure centre for a swim one day next week.

What is the probability that exactly five of them will go for a swim on Wednesday?

Solution

This time, both a tree diagram and Pascal's triangle are too difficult to use, but we can easily find the fractions:

Five out of 20 do swim on Wednesday means $\left(\dfrac{1}{7}\right)^5$ and 15 out of 20 do not which gives $\left(\dfrac{6}{7}\right)^5$.

The number of ways of doing this is $\binom{20}{5}$ which is 15 504.

So $P(X = 5) = 15\,504 \times \left(\dfrac{1}{7}\right)^5 \times \left(\dfrac{6}{7}\right)^{15} = 0.0914$ (three significant figures).

> You may find that you need to find $\binom{20}{5}$ or $^{20}C_5$ using the ^nC_r button on your calculator.

5

5.4 Finding a formula

When the probability of a 'success' is p and an experiment is repeated n times, then the probability that there are x successes is given by:

> So $X \sim B(n, p)$

> n is the number of trials.

$$P(X = x) = \binom{n}{x} p^x (1 - p)^{(n-x)}$$

EXERCISE 5B

1 Ropes produced in a factory are tested to a certain breaking strain. From past experience it is found that one-quarter of ropes break at this strain.

From a batch of four such ropes, find the probability that exactly two break.

2 A distorted coin, where the probability of a head is $\dfrac{3}{5}$, is thrown five times.

Find the probability that a head shows on exactly four of these throws.

3 A group of 10 friends plan to each buy a present for their friend who has a birthday. The probability that they will choose to buy chocolates is 0.4 and the friends all choose their present independently.

Find the probability that only three of the 10 friends decide to buy chocolates.

4 A bank cash dispenser has a probability of 0.2 of being out of order on any one day chosen at random.

Find the probability that, out of the 10 of these machines which this bank owns, exactly three are out of order on any one given day.

5 The probability that Miss Brown will make an error in entering any one set of daily sales data into a database is 0.3.

Find the probability that, during a fortnight (10 working days) she makes an error exactly four times.

6 A restaurant takes bookings for 20 tables on Saturday night. The probability that a party does not turn up for their booking is 0.15.

Find the probability that only two of the parties who have made bookings do not turn up.

7 A school pupil attempts a multiple-choice exam paper but he has not made any effort to learn any of the information necessary. Therefore he guesses the answers to all the questions.

There are five possible answers to each question and there are 30 questions on the paper. Find the probability that the pupil gets eight questions correct out of the 30 on the paper.

8 A batch of 25 lightbulbs is sent to a small retailer. The probability that a bulb is faulty is 0.1.

Find the probability that only two of the bulbs are faulty.

5.5 Using cumulative binomial tables

| Refer to Section 5.4 |

We now have a formula to use for evaluating binomial probabilities for precise numbers of successes. We may, however, need to evaluate more than just one individual probability, often a whole series of such probabilities, and this can become very tedious. Fortunately, cumulative binomial probability tables have been constructed to help out in such cases, for certain values of p and n.

| Tables can be found in the *AQA Formulae Book*, Table 1, and in the back of this book. |

Worked example 5

| In this case $X \sim B(8, 0.5)$ |

If an unbiased coin is thrown eight times, what is the probability of obtaining fewer than four heads.

Solution

For $P(X < 4)$, we will need

$$P(X = 0) + P(X = 1) + P(X = 2) + P(X = 3)$$
$$= P(X \leqslant 3)$$

> 0, 1, 2, 3, |4, 5, ...
> X **less** than 4

This means evaluating and summing four binomial probabilities

$$\left(\frac{1}{2}\right)^8 + \left(\frac{8}{1}\right)\left(\frac{1}{2}\right)^7\left(\frac{1}{2}\right) + \left(\frac{8}{2}\right)\left(\frac{1}{2}\right)^6\left(\frac{1}{2}\right)^2 + \left(\frac{8}{3}\right)\left(\frac{1}{2}\right)^5\left(\frac{1}{2}\right)^3$$

$$= 0.3633 \text{ (four decimal places)}$$

> This may be found directly on some calculators. This is allowed in exams.

but, using the tables, where $n = 8$ and $p = 0.5$, we require $P(X \leqslant 3)$ which is given as a cumulative probability in the tables along the row labelled $x = 3$.

The required probability is found directly as 0.3633!

> Tables should always be the first choice for finding any binomial probabilities – they are so much easier. However, not all values of n and p are included so you may need to calculate probabilities.

5

r \\ p	0.01	0.02	0.03	0.04	0.05	0.06	0.07	0.08	0.09	0.10	0.15	0.20	0.25	0.30	0.35	0.40	0.45	0.50
$n=8$ 0	0.9227	0.8508	0.7837	0.7214	0.6634	0.6096	0.5596	0.5132	0.4703	0.4305	0.2725	0.1678	0.1001	0.0576	0.0319	0.0168	0.0084	0.0039
1	0.9973	0.9897	0.9777	0.9619	0.9428	0.9208	0.8965	0.8702	0.8423	0.8131	0.6572	0.5033	0.3671	0.2553	0.1691	0.1064	0.0632	0.0352
2	0.9999	0.9996	0.9987	0.9969	0.9942	0.9904	0.9853	0.9789	0.9711	0.9619	0.8948	0.7969	0.6785	0.5518	0.4278	0.3154	0.2201	0.1445
3	1.000	1.000	0.9999	0.9998	0.9996	0.9993	0.9987	0.9978	0.9966	0.9950	0.9786	0.9437	0.8862	0.8059	0.7064	0.5941	0.4770	0.3633
4			1.000	1.000	1.000	1.000	0.9999	0.9999	0.9997	0.9996	0.9971	0.9896	0.9727	0.9420	0.8939	0.8263	0.7396	0.6367
5							1.000	1.000	1.000	1.000	0.9998	0.9988	0.9958	0.9887	0.9747	0.9502	0.9115	0.8555
6											1.000	0.9999	0.9996	0.9987	0.9964	0.9915	0.9819	0.9648
7												1.000	1.000	0.9999	0.9998	0.9993	0.9983	0.9961
8														1.000	1.000	1.000	1.000	1.000

> The probability of a 'success' should be chosen so that $p \leqslant 0.5$ as found in these tables.

Worked example 6

The probability that a candidate will guess the correct answer to a multiple-choice question is 0.2. In a multiple-choice test there are 50 questions. A candidate decides to guess the answers to all the questions and he chooses the answers at random, each answer being independent of any other answer.

Find the probability that the candidate:

(a) gets five or fewer answers correct

(b) gets more than 14 answers correct

(c) gets exactly nine answers correct

(d) gets between seven and 12 (inclusive) answers correct.

Solution

In this case, the number of trials, *n* = **50**.

The probability of 'success' (obtaining a correct answer) *p* = **0.2**.

(a) P($X \leq 5$) can be found directly from the tables. As the tables are cumulative, all six probabilities are summed for you

$$P(X = 0) + P(X = 1) + P(X = 2) + P(X = 3) + P(X = 4)$$
$$+ P(X = 5) = 0.0480.$$

(b) P($X > 14$) cannot be found directly from the tables but can be easily worked out from a probability that is given there.

The opposite event to getting more than 14 correct is getting 14 or fewer correct so we need

$$1 - P(X \leq 14) = 1 - 0.9393$$
$$= 0.0607$$

(c) P($X = 9$) is not given in the tables but again, it can be found from probabilities that are there by finding

$$P(X \leq 9) - P(X \leq 8)$$
$$= 0.4437 - 0.3073$$
$$= 0.1364$$

Alternatively, the formula can be used

$$P(X = 9) = \binom{50}{9} \times (0.2)^9 \times (0.8)^{41}$$
$$= 0.1364 \text{ (four decimal places)}.$$

(d) P($7 \leq X \leq 12$) involves summing six individual probabilities which is possible but tedious.

The tables can be used to obtain the answer much more easily by finding

$$P(X \leq 12) - P(X \leq 6)$$
$$= 0.8139 - 0.1034$$
$$= 0.7105$$

> $X \sim B(50, 0.2)$

> **Five or fewer means**
> 0, 1, 2, 3, 4, 5, 6, 7, ...

> **more than 14 means**
> 0, 1, 2, ... , 13, 14, 15, 16, ... , 50
> $X \leq 14$ $X > 14$

> Clearly
> 0, 1, ... , 7, 8, 9, 10, ...
> $X \leq 8$
> $X \leq 9$

> Look back at Section 5.4.

> It is up to you to choose which method you find easier.

> Consider this
> 0, ... , 5, 6, 7, 8, 9, 10, 11, 12, 13, ... , 50
> $X \leq 6$
> $X \leq 12$

Worked example 7

A golfer practises on a driving range. His aim is to drive a ball to within 20 m of a flag.

The probability that he will achieve this with each particular drive is 0.3.

If he drives 20 balls, what is the probability that he achieves:

(a) five or fewer successes

(b) seven or more successes

(c) exactly six successes

(d) between four and eight (inclusive) successes.

Solution

Clearly, in this situation **n = 20** and **p = 0.3**.

	$X \sim B(20, 0.3)$

(a) We require $P(X \leq 5) = 0.4164$

$\overline{0, 1, 2, 3, 4, 5,}6, \ldots, 20$

(b) This time the tables do not supply the answer directly, but it can be found by evaluating

$$1 - P(X \leq 6) = 1 - 0.6080$$
$$= 0.3920$$

For 7 or more successes
$0, 1, \ldots, 5, 6, \overline{7, 8, \ldots, 20}$

$X \leq 6$ 7 or more

(c) $P(X = 6)$ can either be found from the tables by evaluating

$$P(X \leq 6) - P(X \leq 5)$$
$$= 0.6080 - 0.4164$$
$$= 0.1916$$

Clearly
$\overline{0, 1, 2, 3, 4, 5, 6,} 7, \ldots$
$X \leq 5$
$X \leq 6$

or from the formula where

$$P(X = 6) = \binom{20}{6} \times (0.3)^6 \times (0.7)^{14}$$
$$= 0.1916$$

(d) $P(4 \leq X \leq 8)$ again can be found from the tables by evaluating

$$P(X \leq 8) - P(X \leq 3)$$
$$= 0.8867 - 0.1071$$
$$= 0.7796$$

Consider this
$\overline{0, 1, 2, 3,} 4, 5, 6, 7, 8, 9, 10, \ldots, 20$
$X \leq 3$
$X \leq 8$

5

5.6 The mean and variance of the binomial distribution

If you played 10 games of table tennis against an opponent who, from past experience, you know has a chance of only $\frac{1}{5}$ of winning a game against you, how many games do you expect your opponent to win?

In this example, $X \sim B(10, \frac{1}{5})$

Most people would instinctively reply 'two games' and would argue that, an opponent who wins, on average $\frac{1}{5}$ of the games, can expect to be successful in $\frac{1}{5}$ of the ten games played. Hence $\frac{1}{5} \times 10 = 2$.

Mean $= \mu = \frac{1}{5} \times 10 = 2$

In general, if $X \sim B(n, p)$ then the mean of X is given by

The proof for the results for the mean and the variance are not required but you should be able to quote the results.

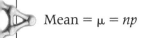
Mean $= \mu = np$

The variance of X is given by

$$\text{Variance} = \sigma^2 = np(1-p)$$

> The standard deviation is obtained by taking the square root of the variance.

In this example, the variance is $10 \times \dfrac{1}{5} \times \dfrac{4}{5} = 1.6$.

> In this case, $\sigma = \sqrt{1.6} = 1.265$.

Worked example 8

A biased die is thrown 300 times and the number of sixes obtained is 80. If this die is then thrown a further 12 times, find:

(a) the probability that a six will occur exactly twice

(b) the mean number of sixes

(c) the variance of the number of sixes.

Solution

(a) The probability that a six is obtained is $\dfrac{80}{300} = \dfrac{4}{15}$

> Since the die is biased p has to be estimated from the data

The binomial model in this case is $X \sim \text{B}\left(12, \dfrac{4}{15}\right)$

So $\text{P}(X=2) = \dbinom{12}{2}\left(\dfrac{4}{15}\right)^2\left(\dfrac{11}{15}\right)^{10} = 0.211$

(b) Mean $= np = 12 \times \dfrac{4}{15} = 3.2$

(c) Variance $= np(1-p) = 12 \times \dfrac{4}{15} \times \dfrac{11}{15} = 2.347$

Worked example 9

A group of 50 pensioners are all given a flu vaccination at their doctor's surgery. The probability that any one of this group will actually catch flu after this vaccination is known to be 0.1.

Find the distribution of X, the number of pensioners catching flu, and find the mean number and the variance of the number who catch flu.

Solution

The distribution is clearly binomial with $n = 50$ and $p = 0.1$.

So $X \sim \text{B}(50, 0.1)$

The mean number from the vaccinated group who will catch flu $= n \times p = 50 \times 0.1 = 5$.

The variance of the number catching flu $= n \times p \times (1-p)$
$$= 50 \times 0.1 \times 0.9 = 4.5.$$

EXERCISE 5C

1 Components produced in a factory are tested in batches of 20. The proportion of components which are faulty is 0.2. Find the probability that a randomly chosen batch has:

   (a) three or fewer faulty components

   (b) less than three faulty components

   (c) more than one faulty component.

2 A biased die, where the probability of a six showing is $\frac{2}{5}$, is thrown eight times. Find the probability that

   (a) a six shows fewer than three times

   (b) a six shows at least twice

   (c) no sixes show.

3 A group of 25 school pupils are asked to write an essay for a GCSE project. They each independently choose a subject for their essay from a selection of five. One of the choices available is to write a horror story. Find the probability that, out of this group,

   (a) more than five write a horror story

   (b) at least six write a horror story

   (c) less than four write a horror story.

4 A cashier at a cinema has to calculate and balance the takings each evening. The probability that the cashier will make a mistake is 0.3. The manager of the cinema wishes to monitor the accuracy of the calculations over a 25-day working month. Find the probability that the cashier makes:

   (a) fewer than five mistakes

   (b) no more than eight mistakes

   (c) more than three mistakes.

5 A manufacturer of wine glasses sells them in presentation boxes of 20. Random samples show that three in every hundred of these glasses are defective. Find the probability that a randomly chosen box contains:

   (a) no defective glasses

   (b) at least two defective glasses

   (c) fewer than three defective glasses

   (d) exactly one defective glass.

5

6 The probability that a certain type of vacuum tube will shatter during a thermal shock test is 0.15. What is the probability that, if 25 such tubes are tested:

   (a) four or more will shatter

   (b) no more than five will shatter

   (c) between five and ten (inclusive) will shatter?

7 A researcher calls at randomly chosen houses in a large city and asks the householder whether they will agree to answer questions on local services. The probability that a householder will refuse to answer the questions is 0.2. What is the probability that, on a day when 12 households are visited,

   (a) three or fewer will refuse

   (b) exactly three will refuse

   (c) no more than one will refuse

   (d) at least ten **will agree** to answer?

8 The organiser of a school fair has organised raffle tickets to be offered to all adults who attend. The probability that an adult declines to buy a ticket is 0.15. What is the probability that if 40 adults attend and are asked to buy tickets:

   (a) five or fewer will decline

   (b) exactly seven will decline

   (c) between four and 10 (inclusive) decline

   (d) 36 or more **will agree** to buy.

5.7 The binomial model

In Section 5.2, the essential elements of the binomial distribution are outlined.

Whilst it may be clear that a situation has a fixed number of trials and that two outcomes only are involved, often it can be a more difficult decision to make the assumption that the probability of each outcome is fixed and that the trials are independent of each other.

Examining situations to assess the suitability of the binomial model is an important aspect of this topic.

Worked example 10

A monkey in a cage is rewarded with food if it presses a button when a light flashes. Say, giving a reason, whether it is likely that the following variables follow the binomial distribution:

(a) X, the number of times that the light flashes before the monkey is twice successful in obtaining the food.

(b) Y, the number of times that the monkey obtains food by the time the light has flashed 20 times.

Solution

(a) In this case, the number of trials is clearly not fixed as we do not know how many times in total the light will need to flash in order for the monkey to achieve two successes. Therefore, it is immediately clear that a binomial model is not appropriate.

(b) Here, we clearly have a fixed value for n, the total number of trials involved. We have $n = 20$. However, we cannot assume that the probability of the monkey pressing the button to obtain food will remain constant. It would seem very likely that, once the monkey has made the connection between the light flashing, pressing the button and obtaining food, it will learn that a connection exists and the probability that it will press the button in subsequent trials in order to obtain food will increase.

Worked example 11

For each of the experiments described below, state, giving reasons, whether a binomial distribution is appropriate.

Experiment 1

A bag contains black, white and red marbles which are selected at random, one at a time, with replacement. Ten marbles are taken out of the bag and the colour of each marble is noted.

Experiment 2

This experiment is a repeat of Experiment 1 except that the bag contains black and white marbles only.

Experiment 3

This experiment is a repeat of Experiment 2 except that the marbles are not replaced after selection.

Solution

In each experiment, the total number of trials is fixed at $n = 10$.

Experiment 1 cannot be modelled using the binomial distribution because there are **three outcomes**, black, white and red, being considered.

Experiment 2 has only two outcomes involved, black or white, and the probability of obtaining each outcome is fixed because the marbles are replaced after each trial. The trials are independent of each other so a binomial model would be suitable.

Experiment 3 cannot be modelled using the binomial distribution because the probability of each outcome is not constant since the marbles are not being replaced into the bag after each trial.

Worked example 12

A consultant wishes to test a new treatment for a particular skin condition. She asks patients who come to her clinic suffering from this condition if they are willing to take part in a trial in which they will be randomly allocated to the standard treatment or to the new treatment. She observes that the probability of such a patient agreeing to take part in this trial is 0.3.

(Assume throughout this question that the behaviour of any patient is independent of the behaviour of all other patients.)

(a) If she asks 25 patients to take part in the trial, find the probability that

    (i) four or fewer will agree

    (ii) exactly six will agree

    (iii) more than two will agree.

During 1 year, this doctor finds a total of 40 patients who are willing to join the trial.

There are many reasons why patients, who have agreed to take part in the trial, may withdraw before the end of the trial. It is found that the probability of a patient who receives the standard treatment withdrawing before the end of the trial is 0.14.

(b) Out of the 15 patients who are receiving the standard treatment, find the probability that no more than one withdraws before the end of the trial.

The probability that a patient who is receiving the new treatment withdraws before the end of the trial is 0.22.

(c) For each of the following cases, state, giving a reason, whether or not the binomial distribution is likely to provide an adequate model for the random variable R.

    (i) R is the total number of patients (out of 40) withdrawing before the end of the trial.

    (ii) R is the total number of patients asked in order to obtain the 40 to take part in the trial.

Solution

(a) In this case $X \sim B(25, 0.3)$ and cumulative binomial tables can be used

    (i) $P(X \leq 4)$ is required which is obtained directly from the tables $= 0.0905$

    (ii) $P(X = 6)$ can be evaluated directly as

$$\binom{25}{6} \times 0.3^6 \times 0.7^{19} = 0.1472 \text{ (four decimal places)}$$

    or obtained from the tables by finding

$$P(X \leq 6) - P(X \leq 5) = 0.3407 - 0.1935$$
$$= 0.1472$$

    (iii) $P(X > 2) = 1 - P(X \leq 2) \quad = 1 - 0.009 \text{ (from tables)}$
$$= 0.991$$

(b) In this case $X \sim B(15, 0.14)$ and we require $P(X \leq 1)$.

We do not have $n = 15$ and $p = 0.14$ available in the tables and so must evaluate $P(X = 0) + P(X = 1)$

$$= \binom{15}{0} \times 0.14^0 \times 0.86^{15} + \binom{15}{1} \times 0.14^1 \times 0.86^{14}$$
$$= 0.1041 + 0.2542$$
$$= 0.358$$

(c) (i) Binomial will not be a suitable model for R as p is not constant. The probability of a patient withdrawing is 0.14 if they received the standard treatment and 0.22 if they are on the new treatment.

    (ii) Binomial will not be a suitable model for R as n is not fixed. We have no idea how many patients in total may need to be asked.

5

0,1,2,3,4,5,6,7,8,...
$X \leq 5$
$X \leq 6$

0,1,2,3,4,5,...
more than 2
$X \leq 2$

EXERCISE 5D

1 A tour operator organises a trip for cricket enthusiasts to the
   Caribbean in March. The package includes a ticket for a one-
   day International in Jamaica. Places on the tour must be
   booked in advance. From past experience, the tour operator
   knows that the probability of a person who has booked a
   place subsequently withdrawing is 0.08 and is independent of
   other withdrawals.

   (a) Twenty people book places. Find the probability that:
        (i)   none withdraw
        (ii) two or more withdraw
        (iii) exactly two withdraw.

   (b) The tour operator accepts 22 bookings but has only 20
        tickets available for the one day International. What is
        the probability that he will be able to provide tickets for
        everyone who goes on tour?

2 The organiser of a fund raising event for a sports club finds
   that the probability of a person who is asked to buy a raffle
   ticket refusing is 0.15.

   (a) What is the probability that, if 40 people are asked to
        buy raffle tickets:
        (i)   five or fewer will refuse
        (ii) exactly seven will refuse
        (iii) more than four will refuse.

   The club also owns a fruit machine for the use of members.
   Inserting a 20p coin enables a member of the club to attempt
   to win a prize. The probability of winning a prize is a constant
   0.2.

   (b) Find the probability that a member, who has 25 attempts
        at winning on this machine, gains:
        (i)   three or more prizes
        (ii) no more than five prizes.

   Another member of the club asks people to pay £1 to enter a
   game of chance. She continues to ask until 50 people have
   agreed to participate.

   (c) X is the number of people she asks before obtaining the
        50 participants. Say, giving a reason whether it is likely
        that X will follow a binomial distribution.

3 An examination consists of 25 multiple choice questions each with five alternatives only one of which is correct and allocated one mark.

(a) No marks are subtracted for incorrect answers. For a candidate who guesses the answers to all 25 questions, find:

    (i) the probability of obtaining at most eight marks

    (ii) the probability of obtaining more than 12 marks

    (iii) the probability of obtaining exactly 10 marks.

(b) It is decided to subtract one mark for each incorrect answer and to award four marks for each correct answer

    (i) find the mean mark for a candidate who guesses all the answers

    (ii) find the mean mark for a candidate whose chance of correctly answering each question is 0.8.

(c) For another candidate, the probability of correctly answering a question is 0.3. Find how many questions out of the 25 this candidate should answer to be 99.9% confident of answering at least one question correctly.

4 A railway company employs a large number of drivers. During a dispute over safety procedures, the drivers consider taking strike action.

Early in the dispute, a polling organisation asks a random sample of 20 of the drivers employed by the company whether they are in favour of strike action.

(a) If the probability of a driver answering 'yes' is 0.4 and is independent of the answers of the other drivers, find the probability that 10 or more drivers answer 'yes'.

Later in the dispute, the probability of a driver answering 'yes' rises to 0.6.

(b) If the polling organisation asks the same question to a second random sample of 20 drivers, find the probability that 10 or more drivers answer 'yes'.

A union meeting is now called and attended by 20 drivers. At the end of the meeting, those drivers in favour of strike action are asked to raise their hands.

(c) Give **two** reasons why the probability distribution you used in part (b) is unlikely to be suitable for determining the probability that 10 or more of these 20 drivers raise their hands.

Key point summary

1 The binomial distribution can only be used to model   *p88* situations in which certain conditions exist. These conditions are:

- a fixed number of trials
- two possible outcomes only at each trial
- fixed probabilities for each outcome
- trials independent of each other.

2 The parameters involved in describing a binomial   *p88* distribution are **n** and **p**, where **n** represents the number of trials and **p** represents the probability of a success.

This is written $X \sim \mathrm{B}(n, p)$.

3 The formula for evaluating a binomial probability   *p93* of x successes out of n trials when the probability of a success is p is

$$P(X = x) = \binom{n}{x} \times p^x \times (1 - p)^{(n - x)}$$

where $\binom{n}{x}$, which can also be written as ^nC_x is found on most calculators.

It can also be found from Pascal's triangle or from the definition

$$\frac{n!}{x!(n - x)!}.$$

4 Cumulative binomial tables can be used for   *p94* evaluating binomial probabilities of the type $P(X \leq x)$ for certain values of n and p.

Use these tables if you can as it will save a lot of time.

Remember to choose $p \leq 0.5$

5 The mean and variance of the binomial   *pp97, 98* distribution are given by

$$\mathrm{Mean} = np$$

and

$$\mathrm{Variance} = np(1 - p)$$

Test yourself	What to review
1 Teenage girls are known to declare a fear of snakes with probability 0.4.	*Section 5.4*
If a group of four teenage girls are chosen at random from a large school, what is the probability that exactly two of them will be afraid of snakes?	
2 A recent survey suggested that the proportion of 14-year-old boys who never consider their health when deciding what to eat is 0.2. What is the probability that, in a random sample of 20 14-year-old boys, the number who never consider their health is	*Section 5.5*
(a) exactly three	
(b) exactly two?	
3 Among the blood cells of a particular animal species, it is known that the proportion of cells of type α is 0.4.	*Section 5.5*
In a sample of 30 blood cells from this species, find the probability that:	
(a) 10 or fewer are of type α	
(b) at most eight are of type α	
(c) less than 15 are of type α.	
4 A market research company carried out extensive research into whether people believed in astrological predictions. It was found that the probability a person selected at random did believe in such predictions was 0.3.	*Section 5.5*
Out of a group of 15 randomly selected people, what is the probability that:	
(a) more than four believed	
(b) at least six believed	
(c) two or more believed?	
5 A nationwide survey discovered that 3% of the population believed that infants should be fed only on organic produce.	*Section 5.7*
A group of 12 mothers, four of whom were selected from members at a Health club and the remaining eight from customers at a large supermarket, were invited to a meeting and asked to raise their hand if they felt that infants should be fed only on organic produce. Give two reasons, why the number raising their hands should not be modelled using a binomial distribution.	

5

Test yourself (continued)	What to review
6 In a manufacturing process, it is observed that 8% of the rods produced do not conform to the required specifications. A sample of 40 components is taken at random from a large batch. What is the mean number of components not conforming in this sample and also, what is the variance?	*Section 5.6*
7 A car repair firm has eight enquiries for estimates one day. Over many years, the manager has found that the probability that any estimate will be accepted is 0.15. Calculate the probability that, out of the eight estimates given: **(a)** exactly two will be accepted **(b)** more than half will be refused. Write down the mean and standard deviation of the number accepted.	*Sections 5.5 and 5.6*

Test yourself ANSWERS

1 $X \sim B(4, 0.4)$

$P(X = 2) = \binom{4}{2}(0.4)^2(0.6)^2 = 0.346$

2 $X \sim B(20, 0.2)$ use tables

(a) $P(X = 3) = 0.2053$

(b) $P(X = 2) = 0.1369$

3 $X \sim B(30, 0.4)$ use tables

(a) $P(X \leq 10) = 0.2915$

(b) $P(X \leq 8) = 0.0940$

(c) $P(X < 15) = P(X \leq 14) = 0.8246$

4 $A \sim B(15, 0.3)$ use tables

(a) $P(A > 4) = 1 - P(A \leq 4) = 1 - 0.5155 = 0.4845$

(b) $P(A \geq 6) = 1 - P(A \leq 5) = 1 - 0.7216 = 0.2784$

(c) $P(A \geq 2) = 1 - P(A \leq 1) = 1 - 0.0353 = 0.9647$

5 The value of p will probably be high at the health club and lower at the supermarket. A show of hands would mean that the trials are not independent, as people will be influenced by the way other people voted.

6 Mean $= 40 \times 0.08 = 3.2$

Variance $= 40 \times 0.08 \times 0.92 = 2.944$

7 $X \sim B(8, 0.15)$

(a) $P(X = 2) = P(X \leq 2) - P(X \leq 1) = 0.8948 - 0.6572 = 0.2376$

(b) $P(X \geq 3) = 0.9786$

Mean of $X = 8 \times 0.15 = 1.2$

Standard deviation of $X = \sqrt{8 \times 0.15 \times 0.85} = 1.010$

CHAPTER 6

Poisson distribution

Learning objectives

After studying this chapter, you should be able to:
- recognise circumstances where a Poisson distribution will provide a suitable model
- use tables of the Poisson distribution
- calculate Poisson probabilities.

6.1 Introduction

> The Poisson distribution arises when events occur independently, at random at a constant average rate.

For example the number of cars passing a point, per minute, on a quiet stretch of motorway might be modelled by a Poisson distribution. The number of telephone calls arriving at a switchboard over a 5-minute interval might also be modelled by a Poisson distribution. As for the binomial distribution, only discrete, whole number outcomes are possible (0, 1, 2, 3, 4 …). However, unlike the binomial distribution there is no upper limit to the possible number of outcomes.

> A constant average rate does *not* mean that the same number of cars pass the point in each minute.

Other examples where the Poisson distribution might provide a suitable model are:

- the number of faults in a metre of dressmaking material
- the number of accidents per month on a particular stretch of motorway
- the number of daisies in a square metre of lawn.

6.2 The Poisson distribution

The French mathematician Simeon Denis Poisson showed that if events occur, in a given interval, independently at random at a constant average rate λ (that is if they follow a Poisson distribution), the probability that exactly r events will occur in a particular interval is:

> This distribution is sometimes denoted Po(λ).

$$\frac{e^{-\lambda}\lambda^r}{r!}$$

6.3 Tables of the Poisson distribution

It is often unnecessary to use the Poisson formula because tables of the cumulative Poisson distribution are available. As with the binomial tables these tabulate the probability of 'r or fewer' events occurring. An extract is shown below.

Table 1 Poisson Distribution Function

The tabulated value is $P(R \leqslant r)$, where R has a Poisson distribution with mean λ.

r \ λ	0.1	0.2	0.3	0.4	0.5	0.6	0.7	0.8	0.9	0.10	1.2	1.4	1.6	1.8	λ / r
0	0.9048	0.8187	0.7408	0.6703	0.6065	0.5488	0.4966	0.4493	0.4066	0.3679	0.3012	0.2466	0.2019	0.1653	0
1	0.9953	0.9825	0.9631	0.9384	0.9098	0.8781	0.8442	0.8088	0.7725	0.7358	0.6626	0.5918	0.5249	0.4628	1
2	0.9998	0.9989	0.9964	0.9921	0.9856	0.9769	0.9659	0.9526	0.9371	0.9197	0.8795	0.8335	0.7834	0.7306	2
3	1.000	0.9999	0.9997	0.9992	0.9982	0.9966	0.9942	0.9909	0.9865	0.9810	0.9662	0.9463	0.9212	0.8913	3
4		1.000	1.000	0.9999	0.9998	0.9996	0.9992	0.9986	0.9977	0.9963	0.9923	0.9857	0.9763	0.9636	4
5				1.000	1.000	1.000	0.9999	0.9998	0.9997	0.9994	0.9985	0.9968	0.9940	0.9896	5
6							1.000	1.000	1.000	0.9999	0.9997	0.9994	0.9987	0.9974	6
7											1.000	1.000	0.9999	0.9997	0.9994	7
8													1.000	1.000	0.9999	8
9														1.000	9

For example for a Poisson distribution with mean 0.9 the probability of two or fewer events occurring is 0.9371.

Worked example 6.1

On average eight vehicles pass a point on a free-flowing motorway in a 10-second interval. Find the probability that in a particular 10-second interval the number of cars passing this point is:

(a) seven or fewer

(b) 12 or more

(c) fewer than nine

(d) more than eight

(e) exactly nine

(f) between seven and 10, inclusive.

> We can use the Poisson distribution here since we know the vehicles arrive at a constant average rate and that the traffic is free-flowing so that vehicles arrive independently and at random during this time interval.

Solution

(a) $P(R \leqslant 7) = 0.4530$
$\qquad = 0.453$

(b) $P(R \geqslant 12) = 1 - P(R \leqslant 11)$
$\qquad = 1 - 0.8881$
$\qquad = 0.1119$
$\qquad = 0.112$

> Here we use the $\lambda = 8.0$ column of the Poisson distribution tables.

$$11 \mid \overline{12 \ \ 13}$$

(c) $P(R < 9) = P(R \leq 8)$
$\qquad\qquad = 0.5925$

$\boxed{7\ 8}\ 9\ 10$

(d) $P(R > 8) = 1 - P(R \leq 8)$
$\qquad\qquad = 1 - 0.5925$
$\qquad\qquad = 0.4075$

$\overline{7\ 8}\,|9\ 10$

(e) $P(R = 9) = P(R \leq 9) - P(R \leq 8)$
$\qquad\qquad = 0.7166 - 0.5925$
$\qquad\qquad = 0.1241$
$\qquad\qquad = 0.124$

$7\ 8\,\boxed{9}\,10\ 11$

(f) $P(7 \leq R \leq 10) = P(R \leq 10) - P(R \leq 6)$
$\qquad\qquad\qquad\quad = 0.8159 - 0.3134$
$\qquad\qquad\qquad\quad = 0.5025$

$5\ 6\,\boxed{7\ 8\ 9\ 10}\,11\ 12$

EXERCISE 6A

1 The number of telephone calls arriving at a switchboard follow a Poisson distribution with mean 6 per 10-minute interval. Find the probability that the number of calls arriving in a particular 10-minute interval is:

  (a) eight or fewer

  (b) more than three

  (c) fewer than six

  (d) between four and seven inclusive

  (e) exactly seven.

2 The number of customers arriving at a supermarket checkout in a 10-minute interval may be modelled by a Poisson distribution with mean 4. Find the probability that the number of customers arriving in a specific 10-minute interval is:

  (a) two or fewer

  (b) fewer than seven

  (c) exactly three

  (d) between three and seven inclusive

  (e) five or more.

3 People arrive at a ticket office independently, at random, at an average rate of 12 per half-hour. Find the probability that the number of people arriving in a particular half-hour interval is:

  (a) exactly 10

  (b) fewer than eight

  (c) more than 16

  (d) between nine and 15 inclusive

  (e) 14 or fewer.

6

4 The number of births announced in the personal column of a local weekly newspaper may be modelled by a Poisson distribution with mean 9.5. Find the probability that the number of births announced in a particular week will be:

(a) fewer than five

(b) between six and 12 inclusive

(c) eight or more

(d) exactly 11

(e) more than 11.

Worked example 6.2

As part of a feasibility study into introducing tolls on a motorway it is estimated that the number of cars arriving at a toll-booth site could be modelled by a Poisson distribution with mean 3.4 per 10-second interval. It is recommended that k toll-booths be installed where the number of cars arriving is $\leq k$ in at least 85% of 10-second intervals. Find k.

Solution

This question is answered by reading down the column $\lambda = 3.4$ until we find the first probability greater than 0.85. In this case we find that the probability of five or fewer cars arriving in a 10-second interval is 0.8705. Hence the required value of k is 5.

EXERCISE 6B

1 The number of customers arriving at an office selling tickets for a festival, may be modelled by a Poisson distribution with mean 1.2 per 2-minute interval. Find the number of arrivals which will not be exceeded in at least 90% of 2-minute intervals.

2 A garage offering a quick change service for exhausts finds that the demand for exhausts to fit a Metro may be modelled by a Poisson distribution with mean 8 per day. Find the demand which will not be exceeded on at least

(a) 95% of days

(b) 99% of days

(c) 99.8% of days.

3 A small newsagent finds that weekday demand for the *Independent* follows a Poisson distribution with mean 12. How many *Independents* should the newsagent stock if the demand is to be satisfied on at least:

(a) 90% of days

(b) 99% of days.

4 Demand for an item in a warehouse may be modelled by a Poisson distribution with mean 14 per day. The warehouse can only be stocked at the beginning of each day. How many items should the stock be made up to in order to ensure that demand can be met on:

(a) 95% of days

(b) 99% of days

(c) 99.5% of days.

6.4 Calculating Poisson probabilities

Tables of the Poisson distribution, although quick to use, may not always be sufficiently detailed to enable us to obtain the probabilities required. In this case we will need to use the fact that if the random variable, R, follows a Poisson distribution with mean λ then:

$$P(R = r) = e^{-\lambda}\frac{\lambda^r}{r!} \text{ for } r = 0, 1, 2, 3\ldots$$

Remember $0! = 1$.

Worked example 6.3

The number of calls arriving at a switchboard may be modelled by a Poisson distribution with mean 4.3 per 10-minute interval.

Find the probability that in a 10-minute interval:

(a) no calls arrive

(b) exactly one call arrives

(c) exactly two calls arrive

(d) exactly three calls arrive

(e) between one and three calls, inclusive, arrive

(f) more than two calls arrive.

Solution

(a) $P(R = 0) = \dfrac{e^{-4.3}4.3^0}{0!} = 0.0135686 = 0.0136$

(b) $P(R = 1) = \dfrac{e^{-4.3}4.3^1}{1!} = 0.0583448 = 0.0583$

These probabilities can be obtained directly from some calculators. This is acceptable in the examinations.

(c) $P(R = 2) = \dfrac{e^{-4.3}4.3^2}{2!} = 0.1254413 = 0.125$

(d) $P(R = 3) = \dfrac{e^{-4.3}4.3^3}{3!} = 0.1797992 = 0.180$

(e) $P(1 \leq R \leq 3) = P(R = 1) + P(R = 2) + P(R = 3)$
$$= 0.058345 + 0.12544 + 0.17980$$
$$= 0.364$$

> $0\boxed{1\ 2\ 3}4$
> Using the answers above correct to five significant figures in order to give the final answer correct to three significant figures.

(f) $P(R > 2) = 1 - P(R \leq 2)$
$$= 1 - [P(R = 0) + P(R = 1) + P(R = 2)]$$
$$= 1 - [0.013569 + 0.058345 + 0.12544]$$
$$= 1 - 0.19735$$
$$= 0.803$$

> $0\ 1\ 2\boxed{3\ 4\ 5}$
> Using the above results correct to five significant figures in order to give the final answer correct to three significant figures.

EXERCISE 6C

1 In a Poisson distribution the mean rate of occurrence of an event is 5.3 per hour. Find the probability that in a given hour:

   (a) none of these events happen

   (b) exactly one of these events happens

   (c) exactly two of these events happen

   (d) exactly three of these events happen

   (e) more than three of these events happen

   (f) between one and three, inclusive, of these events happen.

2 In a Poisson distribution the mean rate of occurrence of an event is 2.95 per 10 minutes. Find the probability that in a given 10 minutes:

   (a) none of these events happen

   (b) exactly one of these events happens

   (c) exactly two of these events happen

   (d) exactly three of these events happen

   (e) more than one of these events happen

   (f) between one and three, inclusive, of these events happen.

3 In a Poisson distribution the mean rate of occurrence of an event is 0.84 per minute. Find the probability that in a given minute:

   (a) none of these events happen

   (b) exactly one of these events happens

(c) exactly two of these events happen

(d) exactly three of these events happen

(e) more than two of these events happen

(f) between one and three, inclusive, of these events happen.

6.5 The sum of independent Poisson distributions

If cars, going north, pass a point on a motorway independently at random and cars, going south, on the same motorway pass the point independently at random then all cars on the motorway will pass the point independently at random. If the cars going north follow a Poisson distribution with mean 5 per minute and cars going south follow a Poisson distribution with mean 6 per minute then the total number of cars passing the point will follow a Poisson distribution with mean $5 + 6 = 11$ per minute. This is a particular example of the general result that:

> If X_1, X_2, X_3... follow independent Poisson distributions with means $\lambda_1, \lambda_2, \lambda_3$, respectively, then $X = X_1 + X_2 + X_3...$ follows a Poisson distribution with mean
> $\lambda = \lambda_1 + \lambda_2 + \lambda_3... .$

In the example, above, of cars passing a point on a motorway, X_1 and X_2 are from different Poisson distributions. However, the result also applies if they are from the same distribution. For example X_1 could be the number of cars, going north, passing the point in a one minute interval and X_2 the number of cars, going north, passing the point in the next one minute interval. Both would be from a Poisson distribution with mean 5. $X_1 + X_2$ would be the number of cars, going north, passing the point in a 2-minute interval and would follow a Poisson distribution with mean $5 + 5 = 10$.

Worked example 6.4

The sales of a particular make of video recorder at two shops which are members of the same chain follow independent Poisson distributions with means 3 per day at the first shop and 4.5 per day at the second shop. Find the probability that on a given day:

(a) the first shop sells more than five

(b) the second shop sells more than five

(c) the total sales by the two shops is:

    (i) five or fewer

    (ii) more than 10

    (iii) between five and nine inclusive.

Solution

(a)
$$P(X_1 > 5) = 1 - P(X_1 \leqslant 5)$$
$$= 1 - 0.9161$$
$$= 0.0839$$

(b)
$$P(X_2 > 5) = 1 - P(X_2 \leqslant 5)$$
$$= 1' - 0.7029$$
$$= 0.297$$

(c) Total sales of the two shops is Poisson with mean $3 + 4.5 = 7.5$

    (i)
$$P(X \leqslant 5) = 0.2414$$
$$= 0.241$$

    (ii)
$$P(X > 10) = 1 - P(X \leqslant 10)$$
$$= 1 - 0.8622$$
$$= 0.1378$$
$$= 0.138$$

    (iii)
$$P(5 \leqslant X \leqslant 9) = P(X \leqslant 9) - P(X \leqslant 4)$$
$$= 0.7764 - 0.1321$$
$$= 0.6443$$
$$= 0.644$$

Worked example 6.5

A 1-day course on statistics for teachers of A-level geography is first advertised 8 weeks before it is due to take place.

Throughout these 8 weeks, the number of places booked follows a Poisson distribution with mean 2 per week.

(a) Find the probability that, during the first week, two or fewer places are booked.

The organisers are hoping for at least 20 participants. They decide that, if at the end of the first 5 weeks less than 10 places have been booked, then they will cancel the guest speaker.

(b) Find the probability that the guest speaker will be cancelled.

(c) Find the probability of exactly nine places being booked during the first 5 weeks.

(d) Exactly nine places were booked during the first 5 weeks. Find the probability that sufficient places are booked in the remaining 3 weeks to give a total of 20 or more bookings during the 8 week period. [A]

Solution

(a) $P(X \leqslant 2) = 0.6767$
$$= 0.677$$

(b) The number of bookings in 5 weeks will follow a Poisson distribution with mean $2 + 2 + 2 + 2 + 2 = 10$
$$P(X \leqslant 9) = 0.4579$$
$$= 0.458 \rightarrow \text{course cancelled}$$

(c) $P(X = 9) = 0.4579 - 0.3328$
$$= 0.1251$$
$$= 0.125$$

(d) 20 or more in 8 weeks $\rightarrow$ 11 or more in last 3 weeks. Number of bookings in 3 weeks will follow a Poisson distribution with mean $3 \times 2 = 6$.
$$P(X \geqslant 11) = 1 - P(X \leqslant 10)$$
$$= 1 - 0.9574$$
$$= 0.0426$$

EXERCISE 6D

1 The sales of cricket bats in a sports shop may be modelled by a Poisson distribution with mean 1.2 per day. Find the probability that:

(a) two or more bats are sold on a particular day

(b) eight or more bats are sold in a 5-day period

(c) exactly seven bats are sold in a 5-day period

(d) between four and seven bats are sold in a 5-day period.

2 Calls arrive at a switchboard independently at random at an average rate of 1.4 per minute. Find the probability that:

(a) more than two calls will arrive in a particular minute

(b) more than 10 calls will arrive in a 5-minute interval

(c) between five and nine calls, inclusive, will arrive in a 5-minute interval

(d) more than 20 calls will arrive in a 10-minute interval

(e) 10 or fewer calls will arrive in a 10-minute interval.

3 The flaws in cloth produced on a loom may be modelled by a Poisson distribution with mean 0.4 per metre. Find the probability that there will be:

(a) two or fewer flaws in a metre of this cloth

(b) more than three flaws in a 5-metre length of this cloth

(c) between three and six flaws, inclusive, in a 10-metre length of this cloth

(d) fewer than 10 flaws in a 30-metre roll of this cloth.

4 Two types of parasite were found on fish in a pond. They were distributed independently, at random with a mean of 0.8 per fish for the first type and 2.0 per fish for the second type. Find the probability that a fish will have:

(a) three or fewer parasites of the first type

(b) more than one parasite of the second type

(c) a total of three or fewer parasites

(d) a total of exactly three parasites

(e) a total of more than five parasites

5 A garage has two branches. The sales of batteries may be modelled by a Poisson distribution with mean 2.4 per day at the first branch and by a Poisson distribution with mean 1.6 per day at the second branch. Find the probability that there will be:

(a) exactly three batteries sold at the first branch on a particular day

(b) exactly three batteries sold at the second branch on a particular day

(c) a total of five or more batteries sold at the two branches on a particular day

(d) a total of between one and five, inclusive, batteries sold at the two branches on a particular day

(e) 15 or fewer batteries sold at the first branch in a 5-day period

(f) more than eight batteries sold at the second branch in a 5-day period.

6.6 Using the Poisson distribution as a model

The Poisson distribution occurs when events occur independently, at random, at a constant average rate. A common example is cars passing a point on a motorway. However, if the motorway was busy, cars would obstruct each other and so would not pass at random. Hence the Poisson distribution would not be a suitable model. Also if we observed over a 24-hour period the mean number of cars per minute would not be constant. In the middle of the night the mean would be less than in the middle of the day. Again the Poisson distribution would not provide a suitable model. It probably would provide a suitable model if we counted the number of cars per minute on a free-flowing motorway over a relatively short period of time.

Telephone calls arriving at a switchboard are also often modelled by a Poisson distribution. However, if there were a queueing system or the switchboard was frequently engaged the calls would not be arriving independently at random. Also over a 24-hour period the mean would change and so the Poisson distribution would not be a suitable model. The Poisson distribution will often provide an adequate model for people joining queues in a supermarket or at a train station. However, if a family of four are shopping together they will probably all join the queue at the same time and so events will not be independent. Again if the queue is long people may be deterred from entering the supermarket and so once again the events would not be independent.

Despite all these qualifications the Poisson distribution provides a useful model in many practical situations. As with any probability distribution, we can never prove that events follow a Poisson distribution exactly, but we can recognise circumstances where it is likely to provide an adequate model.

EXERCISE 6E

State whether or not the Poisson distribution is likely to provide a suitable model for the random variable, X, in the following examples. Give a reason where you believe the Poisson distribution would not provide a suitable model.

The random variable, X, represents number of:

(a) lorries per minute passing a point on a quiet motorway over a short period of time

(b) lorries per minute passing a point on a very busy motorway

(c) cars per minute passing a point close to traffic lights on a city centre road

(d) components which do not meet specification in a sample of 20 from a production line

(e) dandelions in a square metre of lawn in a small garden

(f) boxes of expensive chocolates sold per day at a small shop

(g) passengers per minute arriving at a bus stop, over a short period of time

(h) passengers per minute arriving at a bus stop over a 24-hour period

(i) breakdowns of a power supply per year

(j) accidents per year in a large factory

(k) people injured per year in accidents at a large factory.

Worked example 6.6

Travellers arrive at a railway station, to catch a train, either alone or in family groups. On an August Saturday afternoon, the number, X, of travellers who arrive alone during a one-minute interval may be modelled by a Poisson distribution with mean 7.5.

(a) Find the probability of six or fewer passengers arriving alone during a particular minute.

The number, Y, of family groups who arrive during a one-minute interval may be modelled by a Poisson distribution with mean 2.0.

(b) Find the probability that three or more family groups arrive during a particular minute.

It is usual for one person to buy all the tickets for a family group. Thus the number of people, Z, wishing to buy tickets during a one-minute interval may be modelled by $X + Y$.

(c) Find the probability that more than 18 people wish to buy tickets during a particular minute.

If four booking clerks are available, they can usually sell tickets to up to 18 people during a minute.

(d) State, giving a reason in **each** case, whether:

  (i) more than four booking clerks should be available on an August Saturday afternoon.

  (ii) the Poisson distribution is likely to provide an adequate model for the total number of travellers (whether or not in family groups) arriving at the station during a 1-minute interval.

  (iii) the Poisson distribution is likely to provide an adequate model for the number of passengers, travelling alone, leaving the station, having got off a train, during a 1-minute interval.

(e) Give **one** reason why the model $Z = X + Y$, used in part **(c)**, may not be exact.

Solution

(a) $P(X \leqslant 6) = 0.3782$
$$= 0.378$$

(b) $P(X \geqslant 3) = 1 - P(\leqslant 2)$
$$= 1 - 0.6767 = 0.3233$$
$$= 0.323$$

(c) $X + Y \rightarrow$ Poisson mean $7.5 + 2 = 9.5$
$$P(X > 18) = 1 - P(X \leqslant 18)$$
$$= 1 - 0.9957 = 0.0043$$

> *Examiner's tip:*
> Only two significant figures in the answer can be obtained from the tables. In these circumstances a two significant figure answer will be accepted in an examination.

(d) (i) No, the probability of more than 18 people wishing to buy tickets in a minute has been shown in part **(c)** to be very small. Hence four booking clerks should be adequate.

  (ii) No, the people arriving in family groups will not be arriving independently. Hence Poisson unlikely to be an adequate model.

  (iii) No, the average rate will not be constant. Immediately after a train arrives there will be a high average rate, between train arrivals there will be a low average rate.

(e) Some people or groups may have bought tickets in advance/some family groups may buy tickets individually.

6.7 Variance of a Poisson distribution

The Poisson distribution has the interesting property that the variance is equal to the mean. That is, a Poisson distribution, with mean 9, will have a variance of 9. You will probably be more interested in the standard deviation which will be $\sqrt{9} = 3$.

> You will remember from Chapter 2 that the variance is used by theoretical statisticians but is a poor measure of spread.

A Poisson distribution with mean λ has a variance of λ (and a standard deviation of $\sqrt{\lambda}$).

The number of items of post delivered to a particular address, daily, follows a Poisson distribution with mean 9. On 10 days the number of items delivered was

$$10 \quad 8 \quad 13 \quad 9 \quad 4 \quad 9 \quad 12 \quad 15 \quad 11 \quad 8$$

> mean $\bar{x} = 9.9$
> standard deviation $s = 3.07$
> variance $s^2 = 9.43$

This is a sample from a Poisson distribution with mean 9 and so the mean of the sample will almost certainly not be exactly 9 nor will the variance be exactly 9. However for a large sample we would expect the mean and the variance both to be very close to 9.

This result will be used in later modules but for now its only application is to provide you with an extra piece of information when deciding whether or not the Poisson distribution may provide an adequate model. If you expected the number of items of post delivered per day to follow a Poisson distribution, then the fact that the mean (9.9) and variance (9.43) of the sample were close together would support this. Suppose the number of letters delivered on a sample of ten days had been:

$$12 \quad 6 \quad 15 \quad 7 \quad 2 \quad 7 \quad 14 \quad 17 \quad 13 \quad 6$$

with a mean of 9.9 and a variance of 24.1. You would have to say that it was very unlikely that the Poisson distribution would provide an adequate model as the mean and variance are so far apart.

MIXED EXERCISE

1 A small shop stocks expensive boxes of chocolates whose sales may be modelled by a Poisson distribution with mean 1.8 per day. Find the probability that on a particular day the shop will sell

(a) No boxes.

(b) Three or more boxes of these chocolates. [A]

2 The number of births announced in the personal column of a local weekly newspaper may be modelled by a Poisson distribution with mean 2.4.

Find the probability that, in a particular week:

(a) three or fewer births will be announced

(b) exactly four births will be announced. [A]

3 The number of customers entering a certain branch of a bank on a Monday lunchtime may be modelled by a Poisson distribution with mean 2.4 per minute.

Find the probability that, during a particular minute, four or more customers enter the branch. [A]

4 A shop sells a particular make of video recorder.

(a) Assuming that the weekly demand for the video recorder is a Poisson variable with mean 3, find the probability that the shop sells

(i) at least three in a week

(ii) at most seven in a week

(iii) more than 20 in a month (4 weeks).

Stocks are replenished only at the beginning of each month.

(b) Find the minimum number that should be in stock at the beginning of a month so that the shop can be at least 95% sure of being able to meet the demand during the month.

5 Incoming telephone calls to a school arrive at random times. The average rate will vary according to the day of the week. On Monday mornings in term time there is a constant average rate of four per hour. What is the probability of receiving:

(a) six or more calls in a particular hour

(b) three or fewer calls in a particular period of two hours?

During term time on Friday afternoons the average rate is also constant and it is observed that the probability of no calls being received during a particular hour is 0.202. What is the average rate of calls on Friday afternoons? [A]

6 State giving a reason whether or not the Poisson distribution is likely to provide an adequate model for the following distributions.

(a) A transport cafe is open 24 hours a day. The number of customers arriving in each 5-minute period of a particular day is counted.

(b) Following a cup semi-final victory, a football club ticket office receives a large number of telephone enquiries about tickets for the final, resulting in the switchboard frequently being engaged. The number of calls received during each 5-minute period of the first morning after the victory is recorded.

(c) A machine produces a very large number of components of which a small proportion are defective. At regular intervals samples of 150 components are taken and the number of defectives counted.

7 A car-hire firm finds that the daily demand for its cars follows a Poisson distribution with mean 3.6.

   (a) What is the probability that on a particular day the demand will be:

   (i) two or fewer

   (ii) between three and seven (inclusive)

   (iii) zero?

   (b) What is the probability that 10 consecutive days will include two or more on which the demand is zero?

   (c) Suggest reasons why daily demand for car hire may not follow a Poisson distribution.   [A]

8 The number of letters received by a household on a weekday follows a Poisson distribution with mean 2.8.

   (a) What is the probability that on a particular weekday the household receives three or more letters.

   (b) Explain briefly why a Poisson distribution is unlikely to provide an adequate model for the number of letters received on a weekday throughout the year.   [A]

9 The number of telephone calls to a university admissions office is monitored.

   (a) During working hours in January the number of calls received follows a Poisson distribution with mean 1.8 per 15-minute interval. During a particular 15-minute interval:

   (i) what is the probability that two or fewer calls are received

   (ii) what number of calls is exceeded with probability just greater than 0.01?

   (b) On any particular working day the number of attempts to telephone the office is distributed at random at a constant average rate. Usually an adequate number of staff are available to answer the telephone. However, for a short period in August, immediately after the publication of A level results, the number of calls increases and the telephones are frequently engaged.

   State, giving a reason, whether the Poisson distribution is likely to provide an adequate model for each of the following distributions:

   (i) the number of calls received in each minute during working hours of a day in June

   (ii) the number of calls received in each minute during working hours of a day immediately after the publication of A-level results

   (iii) the number of calls received on each working day throughout the year.   [A]

Key point summary

1 The Poisson distribution is the distribution of events which occur independently, at random, at a constant average rate. *p109*

2 For a constant average rate λ, the probability of r events occurring, $P(R = r) = e^{-\lambda}\dfrac{\lambda^r}{r!}$ *p113*

3 Dependent on the value of λ, Poisson probabilities may be found from tables. *p113*

4 If $X_1, X_2, X_3 \dots$ follow independent Poisson distributions with means $\lambda_1, \lambda_2, \lambda_3 \dots$, respectively, then $X = X_1 + X_2 + X_3 \dots$ follows a Poisson distribution with mean $\lambda = \lambda_1 + \lambda_2 + \lambda_3 \dots$. *p115*

5 A Poisson distribution with mean λ has a variance of λ. *p122*

6

Test yourself

What to review

1 A Poisson distribution has a mean of 1.2 events per minute. Find, from tables, the probability that in a particular minute *Section 6.3*

(a) three or fewer events occur

(b) exactly three events occur

(c) less than three events occur

(d) more than three events occur.

2 What is the largest number of events which could occur in a given minute for the Poisson distribution in question 1? *Section 6.1*

3 A Poisson distribution has mean 1.12 events per minute. Calculate the probability that in a particular minute *Section 6.4*

(a) exactly one event will occur

(b) less than two events will occur

(c) more than two events will occur.

4 The number of calls received at a switchboard may be modelled by a Poisson distribution with mean 12 per hour. Find the probability that more than one call will be received in a particular 5-minute interval. *Section 6.3*

5 State two conditions which must be fulfilled if the number of bicycles crossing a bridge per minute is to follow a Poisson distribution. *Sections 6.1 and 6.6*

Test yourself (continued)	**What to review**
6 Explain why the Poisson distribution is unlikely to form an adequate model for the number of bicycles crossing a bridge	*Sections 6.1 and 6.6*

    (a) over a 24-hour period

    (b) in the rush hour when a large number of bicycles are attempting to cross.

7 The number of newspapers sold by a newsagent in eight successive hours on a weekday was	*Sections 6.6 and 6.7*

    84   92   22   12   13   9   8   104.

    (a) Calculate the mean and variance of the data.

    (b) Give a reason based on your calculations why it is unlikely that the Poisson distribution will provide an adequate model for the data.

    (c) Give a reason, not based on your calculations, why it is unlikely that a Poisson distribution will provide an adequate model for the hourly sales of newspapers throughout a day.

Test yourself ANSWERS

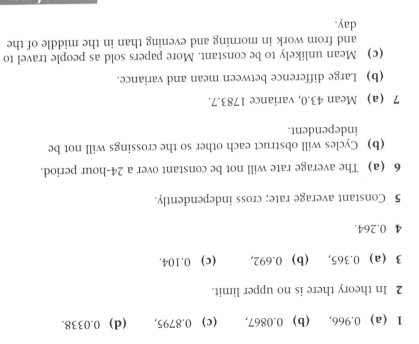

1 (a) 0.966,   **(b)** 0.0867,   **(c)** 0.8795,   **(d)** 0.0338.

2 In theory there is no upper limit.

3 (a) 0.365,   **(b)** 0.692,   **(c)** 0.104.

4 0.264.

5 Constant average rate; cross independently.

6 (a) The average rate will not be constant over a 24-hour period.

    (b) Cycles will obstruct each other so the crossings will not be independent.

7 (a) Mean 43.0, variance 1783.7.

    (b) Large difference between mean and variance.

    (c) Mean unlikely to be constant. More papers sold as people travel to and from work in morning and evening than in the middle of the day.

CHAPTER 7

The normal distribution

Learning objectives

After studying this chapter, you should be able to:
- use tables to find probabilities from any normal distribution
- use tables of percentage points of the normal distribution
- understand what is meant by the distribution of the sample mean
- find probabilities involving sample means.

7.1 Continuous distributions

In previous chapters you have studied discrete probability distributions where the possible outcomes can be listed and a probability associated with each. For continuous variables such as height, weight or distance it is not possible to list all the possible outcomes. In this case probability is represented by the area under a curve (called the probability density function).

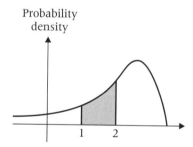

The probability that an observation, selected at random from the distribution lies, between 1 and 2 is represented by the shaded area. Note that the probability that an observation from a continuous distribution is exactly equal to 2 (or any other value) is zero.

There are two conditions for a curve to be used as a probability density function:
- the total area under the curve must be 1
- the curve must not take negative values, i.e. it must not go below the horizontal axis.

7.2 The normal distribution

Many continuous variables, which occur naturally, have a
probability density function like this.

This is called a normal distribution. It has a high probability
density close to the mean and this decreases as you move away
from the mean.

> The main features of normal distribution are that it is:
> - bell shaped
> - symmetrical (about the mean)
> - the total area under the curve is 1 (as with all
>   probability density functions).

Examples of variable which are likely to follow a normal
distribution are the heights of adult females in the United
Kingdom, the lengths of leaves from oak trees, the widths of
car doors coming off a production line and the times taken by
12-year-old boys to run 100 metres.

7.3 The standard normal distribution

Normal distributions may have any mean and any standard
deviation. The normal distribution with mean 0 and
standard deviation 1 is called the **standard normal
distribution**.

> The equation of the probability density function (p.d.f.) is
>
> $$\frac{1}{\sqrt{2\pi}} e^{-\frac{z^2}{2}}$$

Z is, by convention, used to denote a standard normal variable.

Finding areas under this curve would involve some very difficult
integration. Fortunately this has been done for you and the
results tabulated. The tables are in the back of this book and an
extract is shown on the opposite page.

7.4 The normal distribution function

The table gives the probability p that a normally distributed random variable Z, with mean $= 0$ and variance $= 1$, is less than or equal to z.

0.06
row

z	0.00	0.01	0.02	0.03	0.04	0.05	0.06	0.07	0.08	0.09	
1.2	0.88493	0.88688	0.88877	0.89065	0.89251	0.89435	0.89617	0.89796	0.89973	0.90147	1.2
1.3	0.90320	0.90490	0.90658	0.90824	0.90988	0.91149	0.91309	0.91466	0.91621	0.91774	1.3
1.4	0.91924	0.92073	0.92220	0.92364	0.92507	0.92647	0.92785	0.92922	0.93056	0.93189	1.4
1.5	0.93319	0.93448	0.93574	0.93699	0.93822	0.93943	0.94062	0.94179	0.94295	0.94408	1.5
1.6	0.94520	0.94630	0.94738	0.94845	0.94950	0.95053	0.95154	0.95254	0.95352	0.95449	1.6

1.3 row

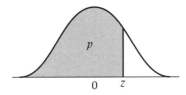

As the diagram above shows, the area to the left of a particular value of z is tabulated. This represents the probability, p, that an observation, selected at random from a standard normal distribution (i.e. mean 0, standard deviation 1), will be less than z.

> The probability of an observation $< z$ is the same as the probability of an observation $\leqslant z$.

7

To use these tables for a positive values of z, say **1.36**, take the digits before and after the decimal point and locate the appropriate row of the table. In this case the row, where z is **1.3** (see diagram in the margin). Then look along this row to find the probability in the column headed **0.06**. This gives 0.91309 meaning that the probability that an observation from a standard normal distribution is less than 1.36 is 0.91309.

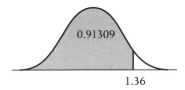

If the z value is given to more than two decimal places, say 0.468 the appropriate value of p will lie between 0.67724 (the value for $z = 0.46$) and 0.68082 (the value for $z = 0.47$). An exact value could be estimated using interpolation. However, it is easier and perfectly acceptable to round the z to 0.47 and then use the tables.

> We will never need a final answer correct to five significant figures but if this is an intermediate stage of a calculation as many figures as possible should be kept

EXERCISE 7A

Find the probability that an observation from a standard normal distribution will be less than:

(a) 1.23, (b) 0.97, (c) 1.85, (d) 0.42, (e) 0.09,

(f) 1.57, (g) 1.94, (h) 0.603, (i) 2.358, (j) 1.05379.

Probability $> z$

If we wish to find the probability of a value greater than 1.36 this is represented by the area to the right of 1.36. We need to use the fact that the total area under the curve is 1.

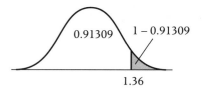

In this case $P(z > 1.36) = 1 - 0.91309 = 0.0869$.

EXERCISE 7B

1 Find the probability that an observation from a standard normal distribution will be greater than

(a) 1.36,   (b) 0.58,   (c) 1.23,   (d) 0.86

(e) 0.32,   (f) 1.94,   (g) 2.37,   (h) 0.652,

(i) 0.087,   (j) 1.3486.

Negative values of z

Negative values of z are not included in the tables. This is because we can use the fact that the normal distribution is symmetrical to derive them from the positive values.

For example $P(z < -1.52) = P(z > 1.52)$

$\qquad P(z < -1.52) = 1 - 0.93574 = 0.06426$

Similarly $P(z > -0.59) = P(z < 0.59) = 0.72240$.

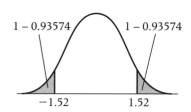

EXERCISE 7C

1 Find the probability that an observation from a standard normal distribution will be

(a) less than -1.39

(b) less than -0.58

(c) more than -1.09

(d) more than -0.47

(e) less than or equal to -0.45

(f) greater than or equal to -0.32

(g) less than -0.64

(h) -0.851 or greater

(i) more than -0.747

(j) less than -0.4398.

7.5 Probability between z-values

To find the probability that z lies between two values we may have to use both symmetry and the fact that the total area under the curve is 1. It is essential to draw a diagram. Remember that the mean of a standard normal distribution is 0 and so positive values are to the right of the mode and negative values to the left. The following three examples cover the different possibilities.

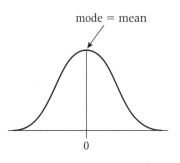

(i) $P(0.6 < z < 1.2)$

We require:

(area to left of 1.2) − (area to left of 0.6)

$= 0.88493 - 0.72575$

$= 0.159$

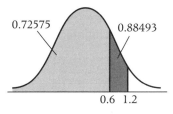

(ii) $P(-2.1 < z < -1.7)$

Here the z values are negative, and so although we could still use areas to the left of z it is easier to use:

(area right of -2.1) − (area right of -1.7)

$= 0.98214 - 0.95543$

$= 0.0267$

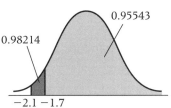

(iii) $P(-0.8 < z < 1.4)$

We require

(area left of 1.4) − (area left of -0.8)

$= 0.91924 - (1 - 0.78814)$

$= 0.707$

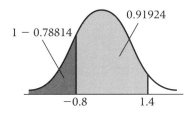

EXERCISE 7D

1 Find the probability that an observation from a standard normal distribution will be between:

(a) 0.2 and 0.8

(b) −1.25 and −0.84

(c) −0.7 and 0.7

(d) −1.2 and 2.4

(e) 0.76 and 1.22

(f) −3 and −2

(g) −1.27 and 2.33

(h) 0.44 and 0.45

(i) −1.2379 and −0.8888

(j) −2.3476 and 1.9987.

7.6 Standardising a normal variable

The wingspans of a population of birds are normally distributed with mean 14.1 cm and standard deviation 1.7 cm. We may be asked to calculate the probability that a randomly selected bird has a wingspan less than 17.0 cm. Tables of the normal distribution with mean 14.1 and standard deviation 1.7 do not exist. However, we can use tables of the standard normal distribution by first standardising the value of interest. That is we express it as standard deviations from the mean.

For example for a normal distribution with mean 50 cm and standard deviation 5 cm a value of 60 cm is:

$$60 - 50 = 10 \text{ cm from the mean.}$$

To express this as standard deviations from the mean we divide by 5 cm.

$$\frac{10}{5} = 2$$

this is the standardised or z score of 60 cm.

> For a value, x, from a normal distribution with mean μ and standard deviation σ
>
> $$z = \frac{x - \mu}{\sigma}$$

For the distribution with mean 50 cm, standard deviation 5 cm the z score of 47 cm is $\dfrac{(47 - 50)}{5} = -0.6$. Note the importance of the sign which tells us whether the value is to the left or the right of the mean.

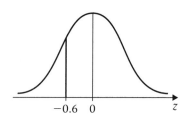

EXERCISE 7E

1 A normal distribution has mean 40 cm and standard deviation 5 cm. Find the standardised values of:

   (a) 47 cm,   **(b)** 43 cm,   **(c)** 36 cm,   **(d)** 32 cm,

   (e) 50.5 cm.

2 A normal distribution has mean 36.3 s and standard deviation 4.6 s. Find the z-scores of:

   (a) 39.3 s,   **(b)** 30.0 s,   **(c)** 42.5 s   **(d)** 28.0 s.

3 The wingspans of a population of birds are approximately normally distributed with mean 18.1 cm and standard deviation 1.8 cm. Find standardised values of:

   (a) 20.2 cm, **(b)** 17.8 cm, **(c)** 19.3 cm, **(d)** 16.0 cm.

7.7 Probabilities from a normal distribution

We said at the beginning of the previous section that you might want to find the probability that a bird randomly selected from a population with mean wingspan 14.1 cm and standard deviation 1.7 cm would have a wingspan less than 17 cm. We can now do this. First calculate the z-score:

$$z = \frac{(17 - 14.1)}{1.7} = 1.71$$

Now enter the tables at 1.71.

We find that the probability of a wingspan less than 17 cm is 0.956.

Some students wonder whether less than 17 cm really means less than 16.5 cm. **Don't.** Just use the value given. Otherwise you would also have to say that the standard deviation is between 1.65 and 1.75 cm and the calculation becomes impossible to carry out.

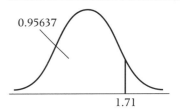

Worked example 1

The chest measurements of adult male customers for T-shirts may be modelled by a normal distribution with mean 101 cm and standard deviation 5 cm. Find the probability that a randomly selected customer will have a chest measurement which is:

(a) less than 103 cm

(b) 98 cm or more

(c) between 95 cm and 100 cm

(d) between 90 cm and 110 cm.

Solution

(a) $z = \frac{(103 - 101)}{5} = 0.4$

probability less than 103 cm is 0.655

(b) $z = \frac{(98 - 101)}{5} = -0.6$

probability 98 cm or more is 0.726

(c) $z_1 = \frac{(95 - 101)}{5} = -1.2$

$z_2 = \frac{(100 - 101)}{5} = -0.2$

probability between 95 cm and 100 cm is
$0.88493 - 0.57926 = 0.306$

(d) $z_1 = \frac{(90 - 101)}{5} = -2.2$

$z_2 = \frac{(110 - 101)}{5} = 1.8$

probability between 90 cm and 101 cm is
$0.96407 - (1 - 0.98610) = 0.950.$

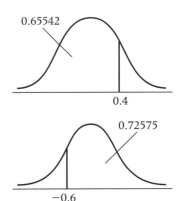

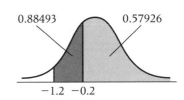

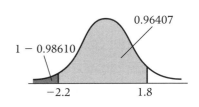

EXERCISE 7F

(In this exercise give the answers correct to three significant figures or to the accuracy found from tables if this is less than three significant figures.)

1 A variable is normally distributed with a mean of 19.6 cm and a standard deviation of 1.9 cm. Find the probability that an item chosen at random from this distribution it will have a measurement

  (a) less than 20.4 cm

  (b) more than 22.0 cm

  (c) 17.5 cm or less

  (d) 22.6 cm or less

  (e) between 19.0 and 21.0 cm

  (f) between 20.5 cm and 22.5 cm.

2 The weights of a certain animal are approximately normally distributed with a mean of 36.4 kg and a standard deviation of 4.7 kg. Find the probability that when one of these animals is chosen at random it will have a weight:

  (a) 40.0 kg or less

  (b) between 32.0 kg and 41.0 kg

  (c) more than 45.0 kg

  (d) less than 28.0 kg

  (e) 30.0 kg or more

  (f) between 30.0 kg and 35.0 kg.

3 The weights of the contents of jars of jam packed by a machine are approximately normally distributed with a mean of 460.0 g and a standard deviation of 14.5 g. A jar of jam is selected at random. Find the probability that its contents will weigh:

  (a) less than 450 g

  (b) 470.0 g or less

  (c) between 440.0 and 480.0 g

  (d) 475 g or more

  (e) more than 454 g

  (f) between 450 g and 475 g.

4 The lengths of leaves from a particular plant are approximately normally distributed with a mean of 28.4 cm and a standard deviation of 2.6 cm. When a leaf is chosen at random what is the probability its length is:

(a) between 25.0 cm and 30.0 cm

(b) more than 32.0 cm

(c) less than 24.0 cm

(d) 27.0 cm or more

(e) 26.0 cm or less

(f) between 24.0 cm and 28.0 cm?

5 The volumes of the discharges made by a drink dispensing machine into cups is approximately normally distributed with a mean of 465.0 cm³ and a standard deviation of 6.8 cm³. When the volume of the contents of a cup chosen at random from this machine is measured what is the probability that it will be:

(a) 470 cm³ or more

(b) less than 458.0 cm³

(c) between 455.0 cm³ and 475.0 cm³.

7

7.8 Percentage points of the normal distribution

This is an alternative way of tabulating the standard normal distribution. The z-score for a given probability, p, is tabulated.

The table gives the values of z satisfying $P(Z \leq z) = p$, where Z is the normally distributed random variable with mean $= 0$ and variance $= 1$.

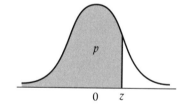

0.00
column

p	0.00	0.01	0.02	0.03	0.04	0.05	0.06	0.07	0.08	0.09	
0.5	0.0000	0.0251	0.0502	0.0753	0.1004	0.1257	0.1510	0.1764	0.2019	0.2275	0.5
0.6	0.2533	0.2793	0.3055	0.3319	0.3585	0.3853	0.4125	0.4399	0.4677	0.4958	0.6
0.7	0.5244	0.5534	0.5828	0.6128	0.6433	0.6745	0.7063	0.7388	0.7722	0.8064	0.7
0.8	0.8416	0.8779	0.9154	0.9542	0.9945	1.0364	1.0803	1.1264	1.1750	1.2265	0.8
0.9	1.2816	1.3408	1.4051	1.4758	1.5548	1.6449	1.7507	1.8808	2.0537	2.3263	0.9

0.9 row →

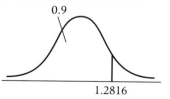

If we require the z-score which exceeds 0.9 or 90% of the normal distribution we would locate the row **0.9** and then take the entry in the column **0.00**. This gives a z-score of 1.2816.

Values of p less than 0.5 are not tabulated. To find the z-score which exceeds 0.05 or 5% of the distribution we need to use symmetry. The z-score will clearly be negative but will be of the same magnitude as the z-score which exceeds $1 - 0.05 = 0.95$ of the distribution. Thus the required value is -1.6449.

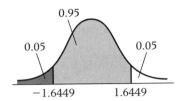

We often require to find the z-scores which are symmetrical about the mean and contain 95% of the distribution. The two tails will contain 5% in total. They will therefore contain $\dfrac{5}{2} = 2.5\%$ each. The upper z-score will exceed $100 - 2.5 = 97.5\%$ of the distribution. Entering the table at 0.975 we find a z-score of 1.96. The lower z-score is, by symmetry, -1.96.

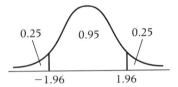

p	0.00	0.01	0.02	0.03	0.04	0.05	0.06	0.07	0.08	0.09	
0.95	1.6449	1.6546	1.6646	1.6747	1.6849	1.6954	1.7060	1.7169	1.7279	1.7392	0.95
0.96	1.7507	1.7624	1.7744	1.7866	1.7991	1.8119	1.8250	1.8384	1.8522	1.8663	0.96
0.97	1.8808	1.8957	1.9110	1.9268	1.9431	1.9600	1.9774	1.9954	2.0141	2.0335	0.97
0.98	2.0537	2.0749	2.0969	2.1201	2.1444	2.1701	2.1973	2.2252	2.2571	2.2094	0.98
0.99	2.3263	2.3656	2.4089	2.4573	2.5121	2.5758	2.6521	2.7478	2.8782	3.0902	0.99

EXERCISE 7G

1 Find the z-score which:

(a) is greater than 97.5% of the population

(b) is less than 90% of the population

(c) exceeds 5% of the population

(d) is exceeded by 7.5% of the population

(e) is greater than 2.5% of the distribution

(f) is less than 15% of the population

(g) exceeds 20% of the distribution

(h) is greater than 90% of the distribution.

(i) is less than 1% of the population.

2 Find the z-scores which are symmetrical about the mean and contain:

(a) 90% of the distribution

(b) 99% of the distribution

(c) 99.8% of the distribution.

Applying results to normal distributions

To apply these results to normal distributions, other than the standard normal we need to recall that z-scores are in units of standard deviations from the mean. Thus if x is normally distributed with mean μ and standard deviation σ

$$x = \mu + z\sigma$$

Note. This is only a rearrangement of the formula $z = (x - \mu)/\sigma$.

Worked example 2

The wingspans of a population of birds are normally distributed with mean 14.1 cm and standard deviation 1.7 cm.

(a) Find the wingspan which will exceed 90% of the population

(b) Find the wingspan which will exceed 20% of the population

(c) The limits of the central 95% of the wingspans.

Solution

(a) The z-score which exceeds 90% of the population is 1.2816. The value required is therefore 1.2816 standard deviations above the mean, i.e.

$$14.1 + 1.2816 \times 1.7 = 16.3 \text{ cm}.$$

(b) The z-score which will exceed 20% of the population will be exceeded by 80% of the population.

$$z = -0.8416$$
$$x = 14.1 - 0.8416 \times 1.7 = 12.7 \text{ cm}.$$

(c) $z = \pm 1.96$

The central 95% of wingspans are $14.1 \pm 1.96 \times 1.7$, i.e.

$$14.1 \pm 3.33 \text{ or } 10.8 \text{ cm to } 17.4 \text{ cm}.$$

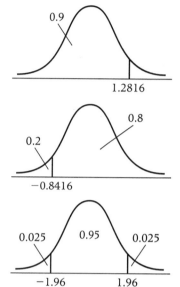

EXERCISE 7H

1 A large shoal of fish have lengths which are normally distributed with mean 74 cm and standard deviation 9 cm.

  (a) What length will be exceeded by 10% of the shoal?

  (b) What length will be exceeded by 25% of the shoal?

  (c) What length will be exceeded by 70% of the shoal?

  (d) What length will exceed 95% of the shoal?

  (e) Find the limits of the central 90% of lengths.

  (f) Find the limits of the central 60% of lengths.

2 Hamburger meat is sold in 1 kg packages. The fat content of the packages is found to be normally distributed with mean 355 g and standard deviation 40 g.

Find the fat content which will be exceeded by:

  (a) 5% of the packages

  (b) 35% of the packages

  (c) 50% of the packages

  (d) 80% of the packages

  (e) 99.9% of the packages.

Find the limits of the central 95% of the contents.

7

3 When Kate telephones for a taxi, the waiting time is normally distributed with mean 18 minutes and standard deviation 5 minutes. At what time should she telephone for a taxi if she wishes to have a probability of:

(a) 0.9 that it will arrive before 3.00 pm

(b) 0.99 that it will arrive before 3.00 pm

(c) 0.999 that it will arrive before 3.00 pm

(d) 0.2 that it will arrive before 3.00 pm

(e) 0.3 that it will arrive after 3.00 pm

(f) 0.8 that it will arrive after 3.00 pm.

Worked example 3

A vending machine discharges soft drinks. A total of 5% of the discharges have a volume of more than 475 cm³, while 1% have a volume less than 460 cm³. The discharges may be assumed to be normally distributed. Find the mean and standard deviation of the discharges.

Solution

5% of z-scores exceed 1.6449.

Hence if the mean is μ and the standard deviation is σ:

$$\mu + 1.6449\sigma = 475 \tag{1}$$

Therefore 1% of z-scores are below -2.3263.

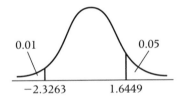

Hence

$$\mu - 2.3263\sigma = 460 \tag{2}$$

Subtracting equation (2) from equation (1) gives

$$3.9712\sigma = 15$$
$$\sigma = 3.7772$$

Substituting in equation (1)

$$\mu + 1.6449 \times 3.7772 = 475$$
$$= 468.787$$

The mean is 468.79 cm³ and the standard deviation is 3.78 cm³.

Worked example 4

Adult male customers for T-shirts have chest measurements which may be modelled by a normal distribution with mean 101 cm and standard deviation 5 cm. T-shirts to fit customers with chest measurements less than 98 cm are classified **small**. Find the median chest measurement of customers requiring **small** T-shirts.

Solution

First find the proportion of customers requiring **small** T-shirts.

$$z = \frac{(98 - 101)}{5} = -0.6$$

Proportion is $1 - 0.72575 = 0.27425$.

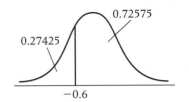

The chest measurement will be less than the median for half of these customers. That is for;

$$\frac{0.27425}{2} = 0.137125 \text{ of all customers.}$$

The proportion of customers with chest measurements exceeding the median of those requiring small T-shirts is $1 - 0.137125 = 0.862875$.

The z-score is -1.08

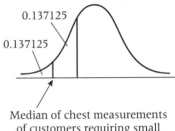

Median of chest measurements of customers requiring small T-shirts

This the median is $101 - 1.08 \times 5 = 95.6$ cm.

7.9 Modelling data using the normal distribution

Textbooks and examination questions often use phrases such as 'the weights of packs of butter in a supermarket may be **modelled** by a normal distribution with mean 227 g and standard deviation 7.5 g'.

The word **modelled** implies that the weights may not follow a normal distribution exactly but that calculations which assume a normal distribution will give answers which are very close to reality. For example if you use the normal distribution to calculate the proportion of packs which weigh less than 224 g the answer you obtain will be very close to the proportion of packs which actually weigh less than 224 g.

There are at least two reasons why the word **modelled** is used in this context:

1 We could never obtain sufficient data to prove that the weights followed a particular distribution exactly without the smallest deviation in any respect.

2 The theoretical normal distribution does not have any limits. That is it would have to be theoretically possible for the packs of butter to have any weight, including negative weights, to fit a normal distribution exactly. However this is not a practical problem since, for a normal distribution with mean μ and standard deviation σ, the central:

    68% of the area lies in the range $\mu \pm \sigma$

    95.5% of the area lies in the range $\mu \pm 2\sigma$

    99.7% of the area lies in the range $\mu \pm 3\sigma$

7

For example for the packs of butter we would expect 99.7% to lie in the range

$$227 \pm 3 \times 7.5, \text{ i.e. } 204.5 \text{ g to } 249.5 \text{ g}$$

It would be theoretically possible to find a pack weighing 260 g which is well outside this range. However, this is so unlikely that, if we did, it would be sensible to conclude that the model was incorrect.

EXERCISE 7I

1 Shoe shop staff routinely measure the length of their customer's feet. Measurements of the length of one foot (without shoes) from each of 180 adult male customers yielded a mean length of 29.2 cm and a standard deviation of 1.47 cm.

Given that the lengths of male feet may be modelled by a normal distribution, and making any other necessary assumptions, calculate an interval within which 90% of the lengths of male feet will lie.

2 Consultants employed by a large library reported that the time spent in the library by a user could be modelled by a normal distribution with mean 65 minutes and standard deviation 20 minutes.

(a) Assuming that this model is adequate, what is the probability that a user spends
  (i) less than 90 minutes in the library,
  (ii) between 60 and 90 minutes in the library?

The library closes at 9.00 pm.

(b) Explain why the model above could not apply to a user who entered the library at 8.00 pm.

(c) Estimate an approximate latest time of entry for which the model above could still be plausible.

3 The bar receipts at a rugby club after a home league game may be modelled by a normal distribution with mean £1250 and standard deviation £210.

The club treasurer has to pay a brewery account of £1300 the day after the match.

(a) What is the probability that she will be able to pay the whole of the account from the bar receipts?

Instead of paying the whole of the account she agrees to pay the brewery £*x*.

(b) What value of *x* would give a probability of 0.99 that the amount could be met from the bar receipts?

(c) What is the probability that the bar receipts after four home league games will all exceed £1300?

(d) Although the normal distribution may provide an adequate model for the bar receipts, give a reason why it cannot provide an exact model. [A]

7.10 Notation

Many textbooks use the notation $X \sim N(\mu, \sigma^2)$ to mean that the variable X is normally distributed with mean μ and standard deviation σ. The symbol σ^2 is the square of the standard deviation and as we have seen earlier is called the variance.

The variance is not a natural measure of spread as it is in different units from the raw data. It does however have many uses in mathematical statistics. We will not use it further in this book but it will appear in later modules.

$X \sim N(27.0, 16.0)$ means that the variable X is distributed with mean 27.0 and standard deviation $\sqrt{16.0} = 4.0$.

7

7.11 The central limit theorem

A bakery makes loaves of bread with a mean weight of 900 g and a standard deviation of 20 g. An inspector selected four loaves at random and weighed them. It is unlikely that the mean weight of the four loaves she chose would be exactly 900 g. In fact the mean weight was 906 g. A second inspector then chose four loaves at random and found their mean weight to be 893 g. There is no limit to how many times a sample of four can be chosen and the mean weight calculated. These means will vary and will have a distribution.

This distribution is known as **the distribution of the sample mean**.

> This is one of the most important statistical ideas in this book. You may not find it easy to grasp at first but you will meet it in many different contexts and this will help you to understand it.

The **central limit theorem** is a remarkable result concerning both the shape and the parameters of this distribution.

If a random sample of size n is taken from any distribution with mean μ and standard deviation σ then $\bar{x}$, the sample mean, will be:

1 distributed with mean μ and standard deviation $\dfrac{\sigma}{\sqrt{n}}$.

2 The distribution will be approximately normal provided n is sufficiently large. The larger the size of n the better the approximation.

> This result is exact. There is no approximation.

The second part of the central limit theorem enables us to make statements about sample means without knowing the shape of the distribution they have come from. As a rule of thumb most textbooks say that the sample size, n, needs to be at least 30 to assume that the mean is normally distributed. For the purpose of examination questions it is best to stick to this figure, however it is undoubtedly on the cautious side. How large the sample needs to be depends on how much the distribution varies from the normal. For a unimodal distribution which is somewhat skew even samples of five or six will give a good approximation.

> If the parent distribution is normal, the distribution of the sample mean is exactly normal.

If a random sample of size 50 is taken from any distribution with mean 75.2 kg and standard deviation 8.5 kg then the mean will be approximately normally distributed with mean 75.2 kg and standard deviation $\dfrac{8.5}{\sqrt{50}} = 1.20$ kg.

If the sample is of size 100 the mean will be approximately normally distributed with mean 75.2 kg and standard deviation $\dfrac{8.5}{\sqrt{100}} = 0.85$ kg.

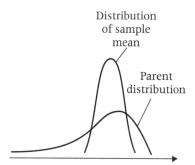

Distribution of sample mean

Parent distribution

Hence we can see that as the sample gets larger the standard deviation of the sample mean (called the **standard error**) gets smaller.

The sample means will be packed tightly around the population mean. The larger the samples become the tighter the means will be packed. This has major implications for topics which arise in later modules, including confidence intervals, hypothesis testing and quality control.

Worked example 5

The weights of pebbles on a beach are distributed with mean 48.6 g and standard deviation 8.5 g.

(a) A random sample of 50 pebbles is chosen. Find the probability that:

  (i) the mean weight will be less than 49.0 g

  (ii) the mean weight will be 47.0 g or less

  (iii) Find limits within which the central 95% of such sample means would lie.

(b) How large a sample would be needed in order that the central 95% of sample means would lie in an interval of width at most 4 g?

Solution

(a) The distribution of the pebble weights is unknown but since the samples are of size 50 it is safe to use the central limit theorem and assume that the sample means are approximately normally distributed. This distribution of sample means will have mean 48.6 g and standard deviation $\frac{8.5}{\sqrt{50}} = 1.2021$ g.

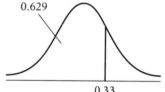

(i) We first standardise 49.0

$$z = \frac{(49.0 - 48.6)}{(8.5/\sqrt{50})} = 0.333$$

Note: we have rounded 0.333 to 0.33. This is adequate but not exact. A more accurate result could be found using interpolation.

Note for the mean of samples of size n

$$z = \frac{(x - \mu)}{\left(\frac{\sigma}{\sqrt{n}}\right)}$$

The probability that the mean is less than 49.0 g is 0.629.

(ii) $z = \dfrac{(47.0 - 48.6)}{\left(\dfrac{8.5}{\sqrt{50}}\right)} = -1.331$

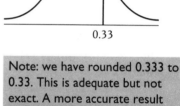

The probability that the mean will be less than 47.0 g is $1 - 0.90824 = 0.0918$.

(iii) The central 95% of sample means will lie in the

interval $\mu \pm \dfrac{1.96\sigma}{\sqrt{n}}$, i.e.

$$48.6 \pm 1.96 \times \frac{8.5}{\sqrt{50}}, \quad 48.6 \pm 2.36$$

or 46.2 g to 51.0 g

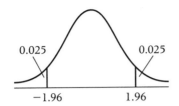

(b) As in (a) (iii) the central 95% of sample means will lie in the interval $\mu \pm 1.96 \frac{\sigma}{\sqrt{n}}$. The width of this interval is

$$\frac{3.92 \times 8.5}{\sqrt{n}}, \text{ i.e. } \frac{33.32}{\sqrt{n}}.$$

If the interval is to be at most 4 then;

$$\frac{33.32}{\sqrt{n}} < 4$$

i.e.

$$\frac{33.32}{4} < \sqrt{n}$$

$$69.4 < n$$

Thus a sample of size at least 70 is needed. (Fortunately the sample size has turned out to be quite large thus justifying our earlier assumption of a normally distributed sample mean.)

EXERCISE 7J

1 A population has a mean of 57.4 kg and a standard deviation of 6.7 kg. Samples of 80 items are chosen at random from this population. Find the probability that a sample mean:

(a) will be 58.4 g or less

(b) will be less than 56.3 kg

(c) will lie between 56.3 kg and 58.4 kg.

2 It is found that the mean of a population is 46.2 cm and its standard deviation is 2.3 cm. Samples of 100 items are chosen at random.

(a) Between what limits would you expect the central 95% of the means from such samples to lie?

(b) What limit would you expect to be exceeded by only 5% of the sample means?

(c) How large should the sample size be in order for the central 95% of such sample means to lie in an interval of width at most 0.8 cm?

3 The times taken by people to complete a task are distributed with a mean of 18.0 s and a standard deviation 8.5 s. Samples of 50 times are chosen at random from this population.

(a) What is the probability that a randomly selected sample mean

   (i) will be at least 19.4 s?

   (ii) will be 17.5 s or more?

   (iii) will lie between 17.4 and 19.0 s?

(b) Between what limits would you expect the central 95% of such sample means to lie?

4 A population has a mean of 124.3 cm and a standard deviation of 14.5 cm. What size samples should be chosen in order to make the central 95% of their means lie in an interval of width as close to 5.0 cm as possible.

Explain why, provided the samples are chosen at random, your answer is valid.

Under what circumstances might an answer to a similar question be invalid?

MIXED EXERCISE

1 A smoker's blood nicotine level, measure in ng/ml, may be modelled by a normal random variable with mean 310 and standard deviation 110.

(a) What proportion of smokers have blood nicotine levels lower than 250?

(b) What blood nicotine level is exceeded by 20% of smokers? [A]

2 The lengths of components from a machine may be modelled by a normal distribution with mean 65 mm and standard deviation 2 mm. Find the probability that the length of a component selected at random will be less than 67 mm [A]

3 A health food co-operative markets free-range eggs. Eggs weighing less than 48 g are graded small, those weighing more than 59 g are graded large and the rest are graded medium.

The weight of an egg from a particular supplier is normally distributed with mean 52 g and standard deviation 4 g.

Find

(a) the proportion of eggs graded small

(b) the proportion of eggs graded medium

(c) the median weight of the eggs graded large. [A]

4 Shamim drives from her home in Sale to college in Manchester every weekday during term. On the way she collects her friend David who waits for her at the end of his road in Chorlton. Shamim leaves home at 8.00 am, and the time it takes her to reach the end of David's road is normally distributed with mean 23 minutes and standard deviation 5 minutes.

  (a) Find the probability that she arrives at the end of David's road before 8.30 am.

  (b) If David arrives at the end of his road at 8.05 am what is the probability that he will have to wait less than 15 minutes for Shamim to arrive?

  (c) What is the latest time, to the nearest minute, that David can arrive at the end of his road to have a probability of at least 0.99 of arriving before Shamim? [A]

5 Free-range eggs supplied by a health food co-operative have a mean weight of 52 g with a standard deviation of 4 g. Assuming the weights are normally distributed find the probability that:

  (a) a randomly selected egg will weigh more than 60 g

  (b) the mean weight of five randomly selected eggs will be between 50 g and 55 g

  (c) the mean weight of 90 randomly selected eggs will be between 52.1 g and 52.2 g.

  Which of your answers would be unchanged if the weights are not normally distributed?

6 Bags of sugar are sold as 1 kg. To ensure bags are not sold underweight the machine is set to put a mean weight of 1004 g in each bag. The manufacturer claims that the process works to a standard deviation of 2.4 g. What proportion of bags are underweight?

7 The lengths of components produced by a machine are normally distributed with a mean of 0.984 cm and a standard deviation of 0.006 cm. The specification requires that a component should measure between 0.975 cm and 0.996 cm in length. Find the probability that a randomly selected component will meet the specification. [A]

8 The weights of bags of fertiliser may be modelled by a normal distribution with mean 12.1 kg and standard deviation 0.4 kg. Find the probability that:

  (a) a randomly selected bag will weigh less than 12.0 kg

  (b) the mean weight of four bags selected at random will weigh more than 12.0 kg

  (c) the mean weight of 100 bags will be between 12.0 and 12.1 kg.

  How would your answer to part **(c)** be affected if the normal distribution was not a good model for the weights of the bags?

9 The masses of plums from a certain orchard have mean 24 g and standard deviation 5 g. The plums are graded small, medium or large. All plums over 28 g in mass are regarded as large and the rest equally divided between small and medium. Assuming a normal distribution find:

  (a) the proportion of plums graded large

  (b) the upper limit of the masses of the plums in the small grade.   [A]

10 A survey showed that the value of the change carried by an adult male shopper may be modelled by a normal distribution with mean £3.10 and standard deviation £0.90. Find the probability that

  (a) an adult male shopper selected at random will be carrying between £3 and £4 in change

  (b) the mean amount of change carried by a random sample of nine adult male shoppers will be between £3.00 and £3.05.

  Give two reasons why, although the normal distribution may provide and adequate model, it cannot in these circumstances provide an exact model.

11 The weights of pieces of home-made fudge are normally distributed with mean 34 g and standard deviation 5 g.

  (a) What is the probability that a piece selected at random weighs more than 40 g?

  (b) For some purposes it is necessary to grade the pieces as small, medium or large. It is decided to grade all pieces weighing over 40 g as large and to grade the heavier half of the remainder as medium. The rest will be graded as small. What is the upper limit of the small grade?   [A]

7

12 Yuk Ping belongs to an athletics club. In javelin throwing competitions her throws are normally distributed with mean 41.0 m and standard deviation 2.0 m.

(a) What is the probability of her throwing between 40 m and 46 m?

(b) What distance will be exceeded by 60% of her throws?

Gwen belongs to the same club. In competitions 85% of her javelin throws exceed 35 m and 70% exceed 37.5 m. Her throws are normally distributed.

(c) Find the mean and standard deviation of Gwen's throws, each correct to two significant figures.

(d) The club has to choose one of these two athletes to enter a major competition. In order to qualify for the final round it is necessary to achieve a throw of at least 48 m in the preliminary rounds. Which athlete should be chosen and why?   [A]

13 A machine is used to fill tubes, of nominal content 100 ml, with toothpaste. The amount of toothpaste delivered by the machine is normally distributed and may be set to any required mean value. Immediately after the machine has been overhauled, the standard deviation of the amount delivered is 2 ml. As time passes, this standard deviation increases until the machine is again overhauled.

The following three conditions are necessary for a batch of tubes of toothpaste to comply with current legislation:

(I)   the average content of the tubes must be at least 100 ml

(II) not more than 2.5% of the tubes may contain less than 95.5 ml

(III) not more than 0.1% of the tubes may contain less than 91 ml.

(a) For a batch of tubes with mean content 98.8 ml and standard deviation 2 ml, find the proportion of tubes which contain

(i) less than 95.5 ml

(ii) less than 91 ml.

Hence state which, if any, of the three conditions above are **not** satisfied.

(b) If the standard deviation is 5 ml, find the mean in **each** of the following cases:

    (i) exactly 2.5% of tubes contain less than 95.5 ml

    (ii) exactly 0.1% of tubes contain less than 91 ml.

Hence state the smallest value of the mean which would enable all three conditions to be met when the standard deviation is 5 ml.

(c) Currently exactly 0.1% of tubes contain less than 91 ml and exactly 2.5% contain less than 95.5 ml.

    (i) Find the current values of the mean and the standard deviation.

    (ii) State, giving a reason, whether you would recommend that the machine is overhauled immediately. [A]

Key point summary

1 The normal distribution is continuous, symmetrical and bell shaped.   *p128*

2 The normal distribution with mean 0 and standard deviation 1 is called the standard normal distribution. Tables of this distribution are at the back of this book.   *p128*

3 An observation, x, from a normal distribution with mean μ and standard deviation σ is standardised using the formula   *p132*

$$z = \frac{x - \mu}{\sigma}$$

This must be done before the tables can be used.

4 If a random sample of size n is taken from any distribution with mean μ and standard deviation σ, then $\bar{x}$, the sample mean, will be: *pp141, 142*

● distributed with mean μ and standard deviation

$$\frac{\sigma}{\sqrt{n}}$$

● the distribution will be approximately normal provided n is reasonably large.

7

Test yourself	**What to review**
1 Why do tables of the standard normal distribution not tabulate negative values of z?	*Sections 7.1 and 7.4*
2 For a standard normal distribution find the value of z which is exceeded with probability: **(a)** 0.06, **(b)** 0.92.	*Section 7.4*
3 A normal distribution has mean 12 and standard deviation 4. Find the probability that an observation from this distribution **(a)** exceeds 10, **(b)** is less than 5, **(c)** is between 14 and 16, **(d)** is between 8 and 15.	*Section 7.7*
4 What is the probability that an observation from the distribution in question **3** is exactly equal to 10?	*Section 7.1*
5 Under what circumstances may tables of the normal distribution be useful when dealing with a variable which is not normally distributed?	*Section 7.11*
6 A random sample of size 25 is taken from a normal distribution with mean 20 and standard deviation 10. **(a)** Find the probability that the sample mean exceeds 21? **(b)** What value will the mean exceed with a probability of 0.6?	*Section 7.11*
7 Give a reason why, although the normal distribution may provide a good model for the weights of new-born mice, it cannot provide an exact model.	*Section 7.9*

Test yourself ANSWERS

7 It is impossible for the mice to have negative weights. A normal distribution would give an infinitesimal but non-zero probability of a baby mouse having a negative weight.

6 (a) 0.309,   **(b)** 19.5.

5 The mean of a large sample will be normally distributed.

4 0.

3 (a) 0.691,   **(b)** 0.0401,   **(c)** 0.150,   **(d)** 0.615.

2 (a) 1.555,   **(ii)** − 1.405.

1 These are unnecessary as the distribution is symmetrical about zero.

CHAPTER 8

Correlation

Learning objectives

In earlier chapters, only single variables have been considered. Now you will be working with pairs of variables.

After studying this chapter you should be able to:

■ investigate the strength of a linear relationship between two variables by using suitable statistical analysis

■ evaluate and interpret the product moment correlation coefficient.

8.1 Interpreting scatter diagrams

Interpreting a scatter diagram is often the easiest way for you to decide whether correlation exists. Correlation means that there is a linear relationship between the two variables. This could mean that the points lie on a straight line but it is much more likely to mean that they are scattered about a straight line.

The four main types of scatter diagram

Positive correlation   Negative correlation   No correlation

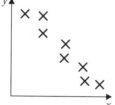
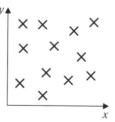

- positive or direct correlation

- negative or inverse correlation

- little or no correlation no linear relationship

- x increases as y increases

- x decreases as y increases

- x and y are not linked

- clear linear relationship exists.

- clear linear relationship exists.

- x and y appear to be independent.

 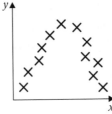

- *x* and *y* are clearly linked by a non-linear relationship.

8.2 Studying results

The table below gives the marks obtained by 10 pupils taking maths and physics tests.

Pupil	A	B	C	D	E	F	G	H	I	J
Maths mark (out of 30) x	20	23	8	29	14	11	11	20	17	17
Physics mark (out of 40) y	30	35	21	33	33	26	22	31	33	36

Is there a connection between the marks obtained by the 10 pupils in the maths and physics tests?

The starting point would be to plot the marks on a scatter diagram.

The areas in the bottom-right and top-left of the graph are almost empty so there is a clear tendency for the points to run from bottom-left to top-right. This indicates that positive correlation exists between *x* and *y*.

Calculating the means:

$$\bar{x} = \frac{170}{10} = 17$$

and

$$\bar{y} = \frac{300}{10} = 30.$$

Using these lines, the graph can be divided into four regions to show this tendency very clearly.

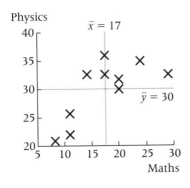

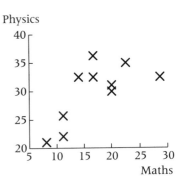

Note: importance of scale:

Consider this change

The appearance of the scatter diagram is now very different. The existence of correlation is much more difficult to identify. Scales should cover the range of the given data.

The table below gives the marks obtained by the 10 pupils taking maths and history tests.

Pupil	A	B	C	D	E	F	G	H	I	J
Maths mark (out of 30) x	20	23	8	29	14	11	11	20	17	17
History mark (out of 60) z	28	21	42	32	44	56	36	24	51	26

Calculating the mean for z:

$$\bar{z} = \frac{360}{10} = 36$$

The scatter diagram for maths and history shows a clear tendency for points to run from top-left to bottom-right. This indicates that negative correlation exists between x and z.

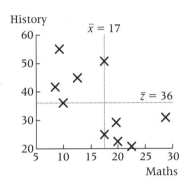

8.3 Product moment correlation coefficient

(This is often known as **Pearson's correlation coefficient** after **Karl Pearson**, an applied mathematician who worked on the application of statistics to genetics and evolution.)

How can the strength of correlation be quantified?

There are two main points to consider:

- how close to a straight line are the points?
- is the correlation positive or negative?

The product moment correlation coefficient gives a standardised measure of correlation which can be used for comparisons between different sets of data.

S_{XX}, S_{YY} and S_{XY} are used to evaluate r where:

$S_{XX} = \sum(x_i - \bar{x})^2$, $S_{YY} = \sum(y_i - \bar{y})^2$ and

$S_{XY} = \sum(x_i - \bar{x})(y_i - \bar{y})$

r is given by $\dfrac{S_{XY}}{\sqrt{S_{XX}S_{YY}}}$

These formulae are given in the AQA formulae book.

Formula

The computational form of this equation which is most commonly used is:

$$r = \frac{\sum xy - \dfrac{\sum x \sum y}{n}}{\sqrt{\left\{\sum x^2 - \dfrac{(\sum x)^2}{n}\right\}\left\{\sum y^2 - \dfrac{(\sum y)^2}{n}\right\}}}$$

r is obtainable directly from all calculators with regression facility. This is permitted in the exam.

Values of *r*

Some worked examples

Returning to the maths and physics marks in Section 8.2

To illustrate the calculation involved in evaluating *r*, the following additional summations are needed:

$$\sum x^2 = 3250, \quad \sum y^2 = 9250, \quad \sum xy = 5313,$$

you can then see that

$$S_{XX} = 3250 - \frac{170^2}{10} = 360$$

and

$$S_{YY} = 9250 - \frac{300^2}{10} = 250$$

Then $S_{XY} = 5313 - \dfrac{170 \times 300}{10} = 213$

So

$$r = \frac{213}{\sqrt{360 \times 250}} = 0.71$$

This, of course, can be found directly from your calculator.

The interpretation of the value of *r* is very important. The value of *r* tells you how close the points are to lying on a straight line.

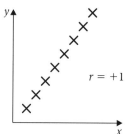

Exact positive correlation

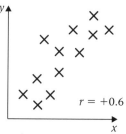

Weak positive correlation

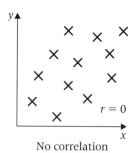

No correlation

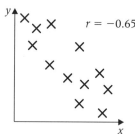

Weak negative correlation

It is always true that

$$-1 \leq r \leq +1$$

$r = +1$ indicates **ALL the points lie on a line** with positive gradient

$r = -1$ indicates **ALL the points lie on a line** with negative gradient

$r = 0$ indicates that there is **no linear connection** at all between the two sets of data.

The value obtained in this example, $r = 0.71$ would indicate a fairly strong positive correlation between the test score in maths and the test score in physics.

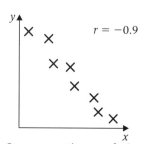

Strong negative correlation

Worked example 1

A group of 12 children participated in a psychological study designed to assess the relationship, if any between age, *x* years and average total sleep time (ATST) *y* minutes. To obtain a measure for ATST, recordings were taken on each child on five consecutive nights and then averaged. The results are below.

Child	Age x (years)	ATST y (minutes)
A	4.4	586
B	6.7	565
C	10.5	515
D	9.6	532
E	12.4	478
F	5.5	560
G	11.1	493
H	8.6	533
I	14.0	575
J	10.1	490
K	7.2	530
L	7.9	515

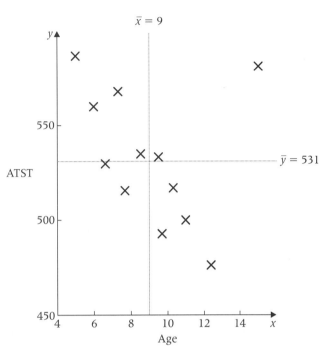

Calculate the product moment correlation coefficient between *x* and *y* and interpret your result.

Solution

$\sum x = 108$ and $\sum y = 6372$

$\sum x^2 = 1060.1$, $\sum y^2 = 3\,396\,942$

$\sum xy = 56\,825.4$

$$S_{XX} = 1060.1 - \frac{108^2}{12} = 88.1$$

$$S_{YY} = 3\,396\,942 - \frac{6372^2}{12} = 13410$$

Then

$$S_{XY} = 56\,825.4 - \frac{108 \times 6372}{12} = -522.6$$

So

$$r = \frac{-522.6}{\sqrt{88.1 \times 13\,410}} = -0.481 \text{ (three significant figures)}$$

Considering the value of *r* and the scatter diagram, there is evidence of weak negative correlation between age and ATST. This would indicate that older children have less ATST than younger children. However, the relationship is fairly weak.

Note: it would be worth investigating child I who seems to have an abnormally high ATST. Perhaps the child was ill during the experiment or perhaps there is some other reason for the excessive amount of sleep.

8

Worked example 2

The following data indicates the level of sales for 10 models of pen sold by a particular company. The sales, together with the selling price of the pen, are given in the table below.

Model	Price, x (£)	Sales, y (00s)
A	2.5	30
B	5	35
C	15	25
D	20	15
E	7.5	25
F	17.5	10
G	12	15
H	6	20
I	25	8
J	30	10

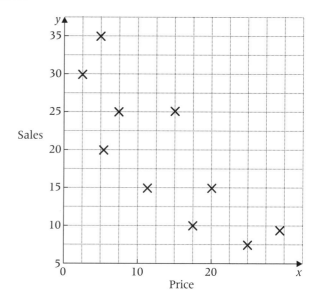

$\sum x = 140.5$ $\sum y = 193$

$\sum x^2 = 2723.75$ $\sum y^2 = 4489$ $\sum xy = 2087.5$

Plot these data on a scatter diagram. Evaluate the product moment correlation coefficient and interpret your answers with reference to the data supplied.

Solution

$$S_{XX} = 2723.75 - \frac{140.5^2}{10} = 749.725$$

$$S_{YY} = 4489 - \frac{193^2}{10} = 764.1$$

Then

$$S_{XY} = 2087.5 - \frac{140.5 \times 193}{10} = -624.15$$

So

$$r = \frac{-624.15}{\sqrt{749.725 \times 764.1}} = -0.825 \text{ (three significant figures)}$$

Considering the value of r and the scatter diagram, there is evidence of quite strong negative correlation between x and y.

This would indicate that there are fewer sales of the more expensive pens and this trend follows a straight line relationship.

Note: care must be taken not to approximate prematurely in calculations or else r may be inaccurate.

Using prematurely rounded figures:

$S_{XX} = 750$ and $S_{YY} = 764$

$S_{XY} = -624$

$$r = \frac{-624}{\sqrt{750 \times 764}}$$

$$= \frac{-624}{757} = -0.824$$

(three significant figures) an error has now occurred.

It is only the **final answer** which should be rounded to three significant figures.

8.4 Limitations of correlation

It is very important to remember a few key points about correlation.

Non-linear relationships

As illustrated in Section 8.1, r measures linear relationships only. It is of no use at all when a non-linear relationship is evident. There may well be a very clear relationship between the variables being considered but if that relationship is not linear then r will not help at all.

Note: clear non-linear relationships identified on scatter diagrams should always be commented upon but the evaluation of r is not appropriate.

The scatter diagram should reveal this.

Cause and effect

A student does some research in a primary school and discovers a very strong direct correlation between length of left foot and score in a mental maths test. Does this mean that stretching a child's foot will make them perform better in maths?

Note: any suggestion that correlation may indicate cause and effect in the relationship between two variables should be considered very carefully!

Clearly this is ridiculous and the probable hidden factor is age: older children have bigger feet and a better ability at maths.

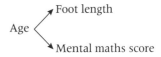

The correlation found between foot length and score in maths is often called *spurious* and should be treated with caution.

Freak results

An unusual result can drastically alter the value of r. Unexpected results should always be commented upon and investigated further as their inclusion or exclusion in any calculations can completely change the final result.

Imagine the effect on r if the point P were to be removed from correlation calculations using the data below.

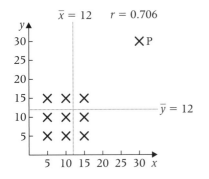

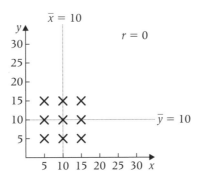

Worked example 3

Plot scatter diagrams on separate axes for the following data sets:

(a)

x	15	10	5	20	25	10	25	10
y	3	2.5	5	5	4	5	5	3

(b)

x	2.5	2.8	3	3.2	4.5	5	6	8
y	20	14	10	8	6	4	3	2

It has been suggested that the product moment correlation coefficient should be evaluated for both sets of data. By careful examination of your scatter diagrams, comment on this suggestion in each case.

Solution

(a) Scatter diagram indicates little or no correlation between the two variables. r could be evaluated but would clearly be close to zero.

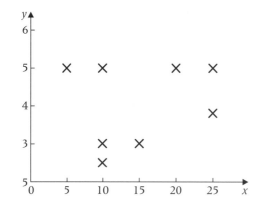

(b) r may well indicate fairly strong negative correlation between the two variables **but** the scatter diagram clearly shows that the relationship is non-linear and hence r is irrelevant.

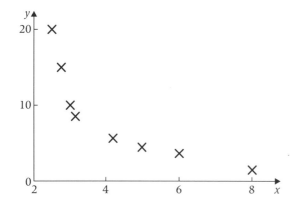

Worked example 4

A tasting panel was asked to assess biscuits baked from a new recipe. Each member was asked to assign a score from 0 to 100 for texture (X), for flavour (Y) and for sweetness (Z).

The scores assigned by the ten tasters were as follows:

Taster	1	2	3	4	5	6	7	8	9	10
X	43	59	76	28	53	55	81	49	38	47
Y	67	82	75	48	91	63	67	51	44	54

(a) Draw a scatter diagram to illustrate the data.

(b) Calculate the value of the product moment correlation coefficient between X and Y.

(c) State, briefly, how you would expect the scatter diagram to alter if the tasters were given training in how to assign scores before the tasting took place.

(d) Given that $\sum Z = 601$ $\sum Z^2 = 38\,637$ and $\sum YZ = 40\,564$ calculate the product moment correlation coefficient between Y and Z.

Solution

(a)

> Scatter diagram clearly shows a positive correlation.

(b) $\sum X = 529$ $\overline{X} = 52.9$ $\sum Y = 642$ $\overline{Y} = 64.2$

$\sum XY = 35\,187$ $\sum X^2 = 30\,339$ $\sum Y^2 = 43\,334$

$$S_{XX} = 30\,339 - \frac{529^2}{10} = 2354.9$$

and $$S_{YY} = 43\,334 - \frac{642^2}{10} = 2117.6$$

and $$S_{XY} = 35\,187 - \frac{529 \times 642}{10} = 1225.2$$

therefore $$r = \frac{1225.2}{\sqrt{2354.9 \times 2117.6}} = 0.549$$

> **Note:** a calculator can be used to obtain r directly.

8

(c) Scores would be less variable.

Scatter diagram would be more compact but the overall shape would be similar.

> Training would lead to a more consistent scale for X and Y. Without training, people's views on texture or flavour would vary widely.

(d) $\overline{Z} = 60.1$, $S_{ZZ} = 38\,637 - \dfrac{601^2}{10} = 2516.9$

and

$$S_{YZ} = 40\,564 - \frac{642 \times 601}{10} = 1979.8$$

therefore

$$r = \frac{1979.8}{\sqrt{2117.6 \times 2516.9}} = 0.858$$

> Calculator cannot be used to obtain *r* directly in this case – formula must be used.

> Be careful not to round prematurely.

Worked example 5

The following data show the annual income per head, x (US$), and the infant mortality, y (per thousand live births) for a sample of 11 countries.

Country	x	y
A	130	150
B	5950	43
C	560	121
D	2010	53
E	1870	41
F	170	169
G	390	143
H	580	59
I	820	75
J	6620	20
K	3800	39

$\sum x = 22\,900$, $\sum x^2 = 102\,724\,200$

$\sum y = 913$, $\sum y^2 = 103\,517$, $\sum xy = 987\,130$.

(a) Draw a scatter diagram of the data. Describe the relationship between income per head and infant mortality suggested by the diagram.

(b) An economist asks you to calculate the product moment correlation coefficient.

(i) Carry out this calculation.

(ii) Explain briefly to the economist why this calculation may not be appropriate.

Solution

(a)

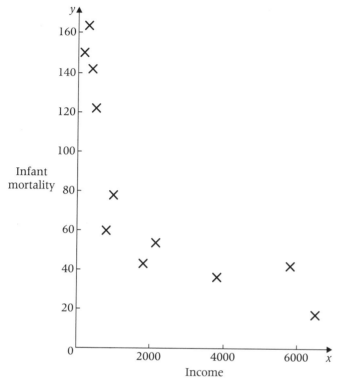

Infant mortality appears to decline as income per head increases.

The decrease is not uniform but is much more marked for the very low incomes than for the higher income countries.

8

(b) (i) $S_{XX} = 102\,724\,200 - \dfrac{22\,900^2}{11} = 55\,050\,563.64$

and $S_{YY} = 103\,517 - \dfrac{913^2}{11} = 27\,738$

and $S_{XY} = 987\,130 - \dfrac{22\,900 \times 913}{11} = 913\,570$

therefore $r = \dfrac{913\,570}{\sqrt{55\,050\,563.64 \times 27\,738}} = -0.739$

Note: this can be found directly from the calculator.

(ii) PMCC measures the strength of a linear relationship. It is not a suitable measure for data which clearly shows a non-linear relationship as in this case.

Look back to Section 8.4. A clear curve is seen.

EXERCISE 8A

1 (a) For each of the following scatter diagrams, state whether or not the product moment correlation coefficient is an appropriate measure to use.

(b) State, giving a reason, whether or not the value underneath each diagram might be a possible value of this correlation coefficient.

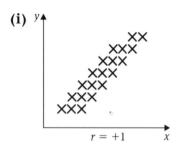

(i) $r = +1$

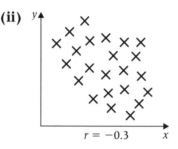

(ii) $r = -0.3$

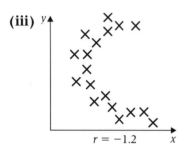

(iii) $r = -1.2$

2 Estimate, **without undertaking any calculations**, the product moment correlation coefficient between the variables in each of the scatter diagrams given:

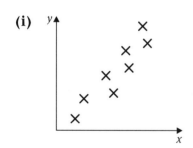

(i)

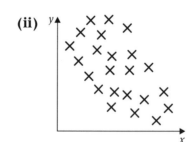

(ii)

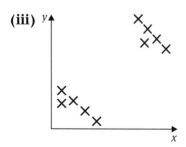

(iii)

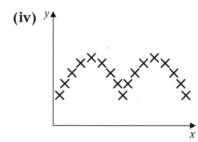

(iv)

3 For each of the following sets of data:

  (a) draw a scatter diagram

  (b) calculate the product moment correlation coefficient between X and Y.

  (i)

X	1	3	6	10	12
Y	5	13	25	41	49

  (ii)

X	1	3	6	10	12
Y	44	34	24	14	4

  (iii)

X	1	1	3	5	5
Y	5	1	3	1	5

  (iv)

X	1	3	6	9	11
Y	12	28	37	28	12

4 The diameters of the longest lichens growing on gravestones were measured.

Age of gravestone (x years)	Diameter of lichen (y mm)
9	2
18	3
20	4
31	20
44	22
52	41
53	35
61	22
63	28
63	32
64	35
64	41
114	51
141	52

Plot a scatter diagram to show the data.

Calculate the values of $\bar{x}$ and $\bar{y}$ and show these as vertical and horizontal lines.

Find the values of S_{XX}, and S_{YY} and r.

8

5 In a biology experiment, a number of cultures were grown in the laboratory. The numbers of bacteria, in millions, and their ages, in days, are given below.

Age (x days)	No. of bacteria (y millions)
1	34
2	106
3	135
4	181
5	192
6	231
7	268
8	300

   (i) Plot these data on a scatter diagram with the x axis having a scale up to 15 days and the y axis up to 410 millions.

   (ii) Find the value of r, the product moment correlation coefficient.

  (iii) Some late readings were taken and are given below.

X	13	14	15
Y	400	403	405

     Add these points to your scatter diagram and describe what they show.

6 A metal rod was gradually heated and its length, L, was measured at various temperatures, T.

Temperature, T (°C)	Length, L (cm)
15	100
20	103.8
25	106.1
30	112
35	116.1
40	119.9

Draw a scatter diagram to show the data, plotting L against T.

Find the value of r, the product moment correlation coefficient.

It is suspected that a major inaccuracy may have occurred in one or more of the recorded values. Discard any readings which you consider may be untrustworthy and find the new value for r.

Comment on your results.

7 In a workshop producing hand-made goods a score is assigned to each finished item on the basis of its quality (the better the quality the higher the score). The number of items produced by each of 15 craftsmen on a particular day and their average quality score are given below.

Craftsman	No. of items produced, x	Average quality score, y
1	14	6.2
2	23	7.3
3	17	4.9
4	32	7.1
5	16	5.2
6	19	5.7
7	17	5.9
8	25	6.4
9	27	7.3
10	31	6.1
11	17	5.4
12	18	5.7
13	26	6.9
14	24	7.2
15	22	4.8

8

(a) Draw a scatter diagram to show the data.

(b) Calculate the product moment correlation coefficient between x and y.

(c) The owner of the firm believes that the quality of the output is suffering because some of the craftsmen are working too fast in order to increase bonus payments. Explain to him the meaning of your results, and state what, if any, evidence they provide for or against his belief.

8 During the summer of 1982 the National Leisure Council, on behalf of the government, conducted a survey into all aspects of the nation's leisure time. The table on the opposite page shows the amount spent per month on sporting pastimes and the total amount per month on all leisure activities for a random sample of 13 young married men.

Man	Amount on sport, x	Total amount, y
A	9.0	50.1
B	4.2	46.6
C	12.9	52.4
D	6.1	45.1
E	14.0	56.3
F	1.5	46.6
G	17.4	52.0
H	10.2	48.7
I	18.1	56.0
J	2.9	48.0
K	11.6	54.1
L	15.2	53.3
M	7.3	51.7

(a) Draw a scatter diagram for this data.

(b) Calculate the product moment correlation coefficient for the data.

(c) Comment, with reasons, upon the usefulness or otherwise of the above correlation analysis.

9 A clothing manufacturer collected the following data on the age, x months, and the maintenance cost, y (£), of his sewing machines.

Machine	Age, x	Cost, y
A	13	24
B	75	144
C	64	110
D	52	63
E	90	240
F	15	20
G	35	40
H	82	180
I	25	42
J	46	50
K	50	92

(a) Plot a scatter diagram of the data.

(b) Calculate the product moment correlation coefficient.

(c) Comment on your result in (b) by making reference to the scatter diagram drawn in (a).

10 The following data relates to a random sample of 15 males, all aged between 40 and 60 years. The measurements given are the level of heart function (out of 100), the percentage of baldness and the average number of hours spent watching television each day.

Male	Heart function	Baldness (%)	Hours of TV
1	42	83	6.2
2	65	66	2.2
3	86	32	1.8
4	32	74	8.3
5	56	69	7.6
6	48	74	6.5
7	92	25	0.8
8	78	30	5.9
9	68	32	2.2
10	52	54	4.4
11	53	58	4.6
12	69	76	2.7
13	57	63	5.8
14	89	38	0.2
15	65	41	4.6

(a) Calculate the value of the product moment correlation coefficient between heart function and % baldness.

(b) Calculate the value of the product moment correlation coefficient between heart function and average number of hours of television watched per day.

(c) Comment on the values of the correlation coefficients found in **(a)** and **(b)** and interpret your results.

(d) Do you consider that males aged between 40 and 60 should be advised to reduce the number of hours that they spend watching television in order to ensure a better heart function? Explain your answer.

8

Key point summary

1 A scatter diagram should be drawn to judge whether *p151* correlation is present.

The product moment correlation coefficient

$$r = \frac{\sum xy - \frac{\sum x \sum y}{n}}{\sqrt{\left\{\sum x^2 - \frac{(\sum x)^2}{n}\right\}\left\{\sum y^2 - \frac{(\sum y)^2}{n}\right\}}} \quad \text{or} \quad \frac{S_{XY}}{\sqrt{S_{XX}S_{YY}}}$$

Remember, this can be found directly from a calculator.

r is a measure of **linear** relationship only and $-1 \le r \le +1$

Do not refer to *r* if a scatter diagram clearly shows a non-linear connection.

2 $r = +1$ or $r = -1$ implies that the points all **exactly** *p154* lie on a **straight line**.

$r = 0$ implies **no** linear relationship is present.

But ... no linear relationship between the variables does not necessarily mean that $r = 0$.

3 Even if *r* is close to $+1$ or -1, **no causal link** should *p157* be assumed between the variables without thinking very carefully about the nature of the data involved.

Remember the feet stretching! Will it really help you to get better at maths?

Test yourself	**What to review**

1 Which of the following could **not** be a value for a product moment correlation coefficient?   *Section 8.3*

(a) $r = 0.98$

(b) $r = -0.666$

(c) $r = 1.2$

(d) $r = 0.003$.

2 Which of the following scatter diagrams has a corresponding product moment correlation coefficient given which is not appropriate?   *Section 8.3*

(a) $r = -0.86$

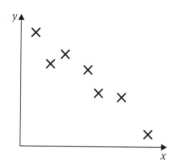

(b) $r = 0.784$

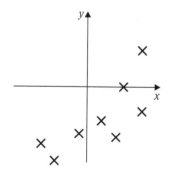

(c) $r = -0.145$

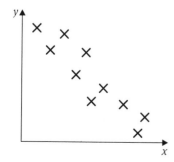

8

Test yourself (continued)	**What to review**

3 For the following data, plot a scatter diagram and evaluate the product moment correlation coefficient.

Section 8.3

x	8	6	5	2	−1	−3	−6
y	−9	−8	−8	0	−5	2	7

4 Explain the meaning of spurious correlation with reference to the following statement:

Section 8.3

'Between 1988 and 1998, the product moment correlation Coefficient between the number of incidents of violent juvenile offences taken to court each year and the average number of hours per week which 16- to 19-year-olds spent watching television was found to be 0.874, indicating a high level of correlation.'

5 The weight losses for 10 females enrolled on the same Watch and Weight course at a local Sports Centre are given below

Section 8.3

Weeks on course	Weight loss (kg)
5	7.6
15	23
12	19.6
3	1.2
10	17.4
8	15.2
20	25.5
10	14
5	2.4
8	9.5

Plot a scatter diagram.

Evaluate the product moment correlation coefficient and comment on its value, referring also to the scatter diagram.

1 $r = 1.2$.

2 (c).

3 $r = -0.904$.

Graph of y against x

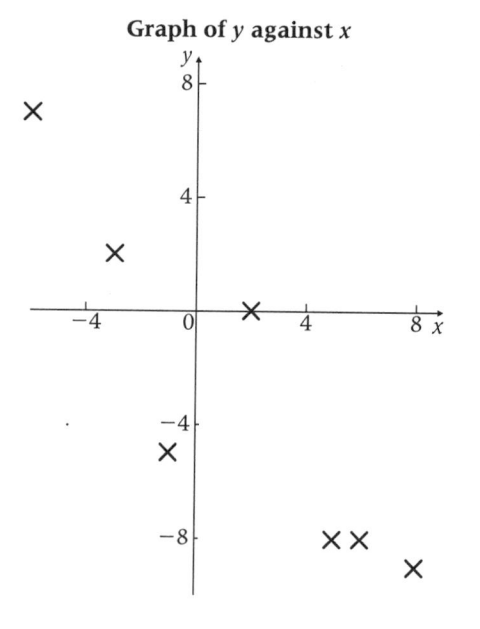

4 Spurious refers to the fact that the link between the two variables may not be causal. They may be two effects from a different cause.

Graph of weight loss against time on course

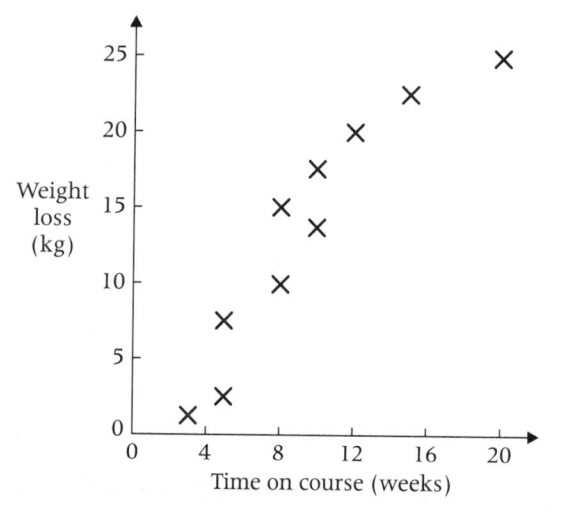

5 $r = 0.936$. Strong positive correlation. Some suggestion from scatter diagram that weight loss is reaching a peak.

CHAPTER 9

Regression

Learning objectives

This chapter continues with the analysis of bivariate data that was started in Chapter 8.

After studying this chapter you should be able to:
- find the equation of regression lines using the method of least squares
- interpret the values obtained for the gradient and intercept of your regression line
- plot a regression line on a scatter diagram and use the line for prediction purposes
- calculate residuals and, when appropriate, use them to check the fit of a regression line and to improve predictions.

9.1 What is regression analysis?

In linear regression analysis, bivariate data is first examined by drawing a scatter diagram in order to determine whether a linear relationship exists (by eye or by finding the product moment correlation coefficient or PMCC). Then the actual equation of the line of best fit is obtained in the form:

$$y = a + bx$$
This is called the
line of y on x

This equation may then be used to predict a value of y from a given value of x.

> The regression line is often called the **line of best fit**.

> Remember that we are still considering linear relationships **(straight lines)** only.

> Look back to Chapter 8, Section 8.1.

> On the scatter diagram, y is plotted on the vertical axis and x and the horizontal.

9.2 Nature of given data

It is always advisable to think about the type of data involved before any regression analysis is started.

For example:

x	y
1. Height of mother	Height of daughter at age 21
2. Load carried by lorry	Fuel consumption of lorry
3. Breadth of skull	Length of skull

> In Pure maths, you may be more familiar with the line equation as
> $$y = mx + c$$

> In cases 1 and 2, x can affect y but y can't affect x. Regression line of y on x is appropriate.

> In case 3, both x and y are influenced by other factors which are not given – correlation is the best analysis.

> If y can, sensibly, be predicted from x, then
> y is called the **dependent** or **response** variable and
> x is called the **independent** or **explanatory** variable.

Consider the two examples mentioned earlier.

The scatter diagrams involved might look like these.

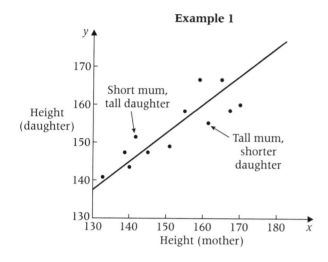

Example 1

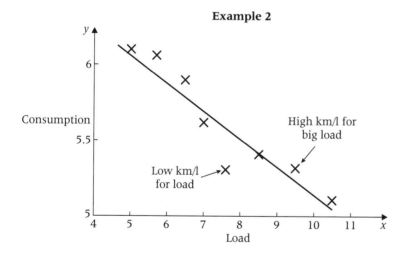

Example 2

In each case, x is the **explanatory** variable and its values are fixed at the start of the experiment.

Clearly, a mother's height is known well before her daughter reaches the age of 21.

The load to be carried by a lorry would be measured before the trial to find fuel consumption.

9

Some questions to consider

- How can the regression line be obtained?
- How good is the fit of the line?
- What do the positions of the individual points mean?

The PMCC can be found. See comments on the scatter diagrams.

9.3 Residuals

If you return to example 2, the data supplied was as follows:

x lorry load (000s kg)	5	5.7	6.5	7	7.6	8.5	9.5	10.5
y fuel consumption (km/l)	6.21	6.12	5.90	5.62	5.25	5.41	5.32	5.11

Note: fuel consumption is given here in km/l. A low value indicates that the lorry is using a lot of fuel, while a high value indicates economical fuel usage.

The product moment correlation coefficient (PMCC)

$r = -0.921$ which indicates a strong negative correlation between fuel consumption and load. The points are all close to a straight line.

How close are they and where should the line be placed?

The vertical distances drawn on the scatter diagram are labelled d_i. These are called the **residuals**.

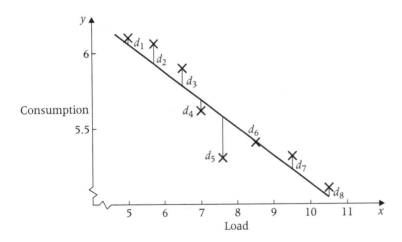

Residuals can be positive (points **above** line) like d_2, d_3, d_7 or negative (points **below** line) like d_4, d_5.

Occasionally, a point might lie exactly on the line.

These distances, labelled d_i, measure how far away, for the y values, each point is from the line of best fit. The sum of the squares of these distances is minimised to find the line of regression of y on x.

For each point, the residual is the difference between the observed value of y and the value of y predicted by the line.

9.4 Finding the regression line

The regression line is obtained using the method of least squares and the line is often called the

$d_1^2 + d_2^2 + d_3^2 + \ldots d_8^2$ or $\sum d_i^2$ is minimised.

least squares regression line

The formula is:

$$(y - \bar{y}) = \frac{S_{XY}}{S_{XX}} (x - \bar{x})$$

From this, you should see that the point $(\bar{x}, \bar{y})$ **always** lies on the regression line.

Written in full:

$$(y - \bar{y}) = \frac{\dfrac{\sum xy}{n} - \overline{xy}}{\dfrac{\sum x^2}{n} - \bar{x}^2} (x - \bar{x})$$

Regression equation can be obtained directly from a calculator. This is quite acceptable in an exam.

Using the formulae

For this data:

$\bar{x} = 7.5375$ $\qquad \bar{y} = 5.6175$ $\qquad$ n = 8

$\sum xy = 333.704$ $\quad \sum x^2 = 479.25$

So the equation of regression of y on x using the method of least squares is:

$$(y - 5.6175) = \frac{(\frac{1}{8} \times 333.704 - 7.5375 \times 5.6175)}{(\frac{1}{8} \times 479.25 - 7.5375^2)} \times (x - 7.5375)$$

Remember that this is an equation connecting x and y
y will remain on the left-hand side and x on the right.

so $y - 5.6175 = -0.20338\,(x - 7.5375)$

and $y = \mathbf{7.15 - 0.203}\,x$ is the regression equation

Be very careful not to round prematurely.

intercept on y axis
at $x = 0$

gradient of line

Equation can be obtained directly from the calculator. Check carefully as some calculators give equation as
$y = ax + b$ rather than
$y = a + bx$

9.5 Interpretation of line

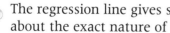

> The regression line gives some important information about the exact nature of the relationship between x and y.

The gradient and intercept values should always be commented upon by reference to the data involved. In this case:

In this case, comments are required referring to fuel consumption and load.

$a = \mathbf{7.15}$

This intercept value gives an estimate of the amount of fuel consumption, y, when the load, x, is zero. This tells you that the fuel consumption of an unladen lorry is 7.15 km/litre.

$b = -0.203$

The gradient indicates, in this case, that y decreases as x increases. Specifically, the fuel consumption, y, decreases by 0.203 km/litre for every extra 1000 kg of load.

9.6 Plotting the regression line

As seen earlier, the point $(\bar{x}, \bar{y})$ always lies on the least squares regression line. This point should be plotted on your scatter diagram.

$(\bar{x}, \bar{y}) \approx (7.54, 5.62)$

To complete plotting the line accurately, one or preferably two other points should be plotted.

Warning! Never assume that any of the given data points will lie on the line.

Any suitable values for x can be chosen but they need to be spread out over the given range. For example:

when $x = 5.5$ $\hat{y} = 6.0$ $(7.15 - 0.203 \times 5.5)$

and $x = 10$ gives $\hat{y} = 5.1$ $(7.15 - 0.203 \times 10)$

$\hat{y}$ means an *estimated* value of y. Many calculators will find $\hat{y}$ directly for a given x.

The three points $(5.5, 6.0)$ $(10, 5.1)$ and $(7.54, 5.62)$ can be joined to draw the regression line.

9.7 Further use of residuals

Consider the data we are examining but imagine that more information has now become available. It has been discovered that three different drivers Ahmed (A), Brian (B) and Carole (C) were involved in the trial. Their individual results were:

Driver	C	B	C	A	A	C	B	B
x load (000s kg)	5	5.7	6.5	7	7.6	8.5	9.5	10.5
y consumption (km/l)	6.21	6.12	5.90	5.62	5.25	5.41	5.32	5.11

The scatter diagram can now be further labelled with this information.

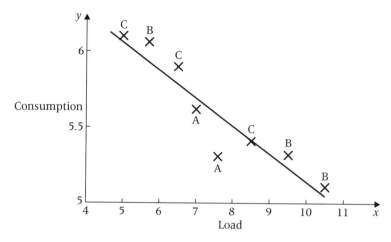

Considering the residual values, further deductions can be made.

It seems that Carole's fuel consumption values lie close to the predicted values given by the line of best fit. However, Ahmed achieves fuel consumption **well below** those predicted by the line and Brian achieves **high** fuel consumption.

Note:
- use commonsense in your interpretations
- always refer to the data given.

This extra information is worth commenting on but always be careful not to make rash judgements, as there may well be other factors involved, for example:

Did all drivers have the same model of lorry?

Did all drivers have the same age of lorry?

Were the journeys of similar length?

Were the journeys over similar types of roads?

You may well think of other factors.

It would be very unfair on Ahmed if it was immediately assumed that he was a 'bad' driver and he was sacked.

9.8 Predictions

How could the transport manager of the freight company that Ahmed, Brian and Carole work for, use the regression line to predict the fuel consumption for the delivery of a specific load?

Several factors need to be considered:

- How close to the line are the points – is the regression line a 'good fit'?

  PMCC measures this, see Chapter 8.

- Is it sensible to predict y from x?

  Look back to Section 9.2.

- What is the range of the x values given from which the line was calculated?

- What is the size of the x value from which a value of y is to be predicted?

  These are the x values given in the table of results.

9

For any regression line where the fit is good, and it is sensible to predict *y* from *x*, a value of *y* can be obtained by substituting a value of *x* into *y* = a + b*x*.

There are **limitations** to these predictions however.

Look at this scatter diagram where the scale on the *x* axis has been extended.

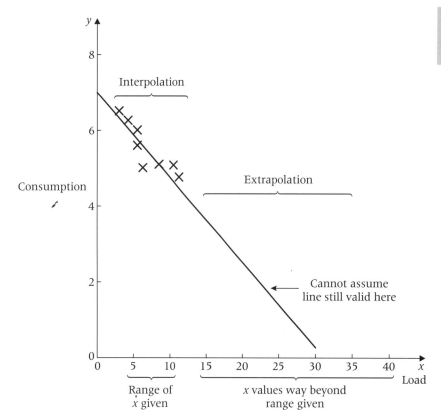

Interpolation

It is perfectly valid to use the least squares regression line *y* = 7.15 − 0.203*x* to predict fuel consumption for loads between 5000 and 10 500 kg.

(5 ≤ *x* ≤ 10.5 is the given range)

This is called *interpolation*.

For example, to find the predicted fuel consumption for a load of 8000 kg.

8000 kg means *x* = 8

$$\hat{y} = 7.15 - 0.203 \times 8 = 5.53 \text{ km/litre.}$$

$\hat{y}$ is the notation for an *estimated* value of *y*, see Section 9.6

Extrapolation

Could the fuel consumption be predicted if the load was 30 000 kg? (*x* = 30)

Clearly, commonsense would indicate that this load is enormous compared to those loads given in the original data. The lorry would probably collapse under the weight!

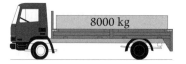

Predicting y from x when x is outside the range of given data is called *extrapolation* and is very dangerous as the y value obtained is likely to be completely inaccurate.

Lorry
collapses

30 000 kg

Examples

This scatter diagram shows the time in seconds to run 100 m against the number of weeks of intensive training undertaken by the athlete.

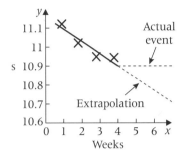

There appears to be a linear relationship but clearly this cannot continue indefinitely. The number of seconds taken to run 100 m will not keep on decreasing but will probably level off when the athlete is fully fit and trained for the event.

The second scatter diagram illustrates a possible relationship between the amount of fertiliser used and the yield from a plot of tomato plants.

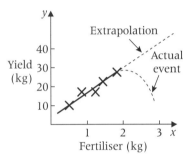

Again, it appears that there is a strong linear relationship between yield and amount of fertiliser but clearly the yield will not continue to increase in this way and, in fact, it will probably decline as too much fertiliser may well lead to a decrease in tomato yield.

Worked example 1

1 An electric fire was turned on in a cold room and the temperature of the room was noted at 5-minute intervals.

Time from switching on fire, x (min)	0	5	10	15	20	25	30	35	40
Temperature, y (°C)	0.4	1.5	3.4	5.5	7.7	9.7	11.7	13.5	15.4

(a) Plot the data on a scatter diagram.

(b) Calculate the line of regression $y = a + bx$ and draw it on your scatter diagram.

(c) Predict the temperature 60 minutes from switching on the fire. Why should this prediction be treated with caution?

(d) Explain why, in (b) the line $y = a + bx$ was calculated.

(e) If, instead of the temperature being measured at 5-minute intervals, the time for the room to reach predetermined temperatures (e.g. 1, 4, 7, 10, 13°C) had been observed what would the appropriate calculation have been?

9

Solution

(a)

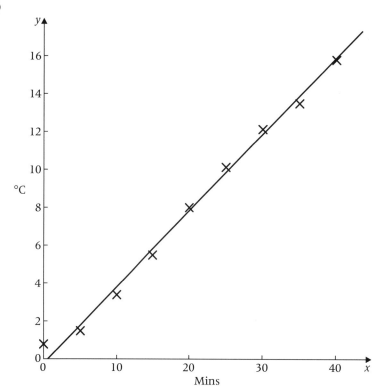

(b) $y = -0.142 + 0.389x$

$\bar{x} = 20, \bar{y} = 7.64,$ plot $(20, 7.64)$

$x = 10, \hat{y} = 3.75,$ plot $(10, 3.75)$

$x = 37.5, \hat{y} = 14.46,$ plot $(37.5, 14.46)$

(c) $x = 60, \hat{y} = 23.2.$

Treat with caution because 60 minutes is outside range of times given. Linear model cannot continue indefinitely as room cannot keep on heating up forever.

(d) The line $y = a + bx$, the equation of temperature on time, was used because y depended on the value of x, the independent variable. y was observed at predetermined values of x.

(e) If the time to reach a temperature was observed, then x would be observed at predetermined values for y. In this case, x would depend on the value of y, so an equation of time on temperature would be appropriate.

> Equation of line of regression can be obtained directly from the calculator.

> $\hat{y}$ can be obtained from the calculator or by substituting into the regression equation, so for $x = 10$.
>
> $\hat{y} = -0.142 + 3.89 = 3.75$

Worked example 2

The following data refer to a particular developed country. The table shows for each year, the annual average temperature $x°C$, and an estimate of the total annual domestic energy consumption, yPJ (peta joules).

Year	x	y
1984	9.6	1664
1985	9.3	1715
1986	9.8	1622
1987	10.3	1624
1988	10.1	1621
1989	10.4	1588
1990	10.8	1577
1991	9.7	1719
1992	10.7	1604
1993	9.2	1811
1994	9.8	1754

(a) Illustrate the relationship between energy consumption and temperature by a scatter diagram. Label the points according to the year.

(b) Calculate the line of regression of y on x and draw the line on your scatter diagram.

(c) Use your equation to estimate the energy consumption in 1995, given that the average temperature in that year was 10.3°C.

(d) Calculate residuals for each of the years 1991, 1992, 1993 and 1994. Comment on their values and interpret the pattern shown by the scatter diagram.

(e) Modify your estimate of energy consumption in 1995 in the light of the residuals you have calculated.

9

Solution

(a)

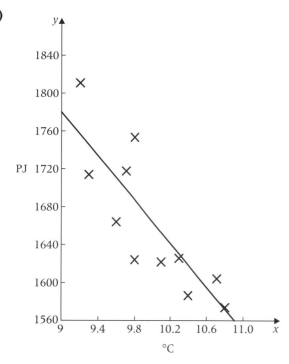

(b) $y = 2849 - 118.9x$

$\bar{x} = 9.97$, $\bar{y} = 1663.5$, plot (9.97, 1663.5)

$x = 9$, $\hat{y} = 1778.9$, plot (9, 1778.9)

$x = 10$, $\hat{y} = 1660$, plot (10, 1660)

(c) Prediction for 1995

$x = 10.3$ $\hat{y} = 1625$

(d) Residuals are obtained in the following way.

Year	y	x	$\hat{y} =$ 2849 − 118.9x	Residual = $y - \hat{y}$
1191	1719	9.7	1695.7	23.3
1992	1604	10.7	1576.8	27.2
1993	1811	9.2	1755.1	55.9
1994	1754	9.8	1683.8	70.2

The residuals seem to be increasing with time. The scatter diagram suggests that fuel consumption decreases as the average temperature increases. There is also an increase in fuel consumption with time.

(e) The modified estimate for 1995 would be
1625 + 85 = 1710.

Regression equation can be obtained directly from the calculator.

$\hat{y}$ from calculator or by substituting into equation as in previous example.

Residuals can be found using the equation or by reading off the vertical difference between the value of y given by the line and the observed value of y.

Clear, commonsense comments needed.

The residuals found in **(d)** clearly indicate a higher value would be expected in 1995. A sensible suggestion would be to add a residual value on to the 1625. This value will be greater than the 70.2 for 1994. Continuing the pattern, approx. 70.2 + 15 = 85 might be the residual in 1995.

EXERCISE 9A

1 The heart and body mass of 14 10-month-old male mice are given in the following table

Body mass (x) grams	Heart mass (y) milligrams
27	118
30	136
37	156
38	150
32	140
36	155
32	157
32	114
38	144
42	159
36	149
44	170
33	131
38	160

(a) Draw a scatter diagram of these data.

(b) Calculate the line of regression of heart mass on body mass (y on x).

2 The systolic blood pressure of 10 men of various ages are given in the following table.

Age, x (years)	Systolic Blood pressure, y (mm mercury)
37	110
35	117
41	125
43	130
42	138
50	146
49	148
54	150
60	154
65	160

(a) Draw a scatter diagram.

(b) Find the line of regression of systolic blood pressure on age.

(c) Use your line to predict the systolic blood pressure for a man who is:

   (i) 20 years old
   (ii) 45 years old.

(d) Comment on the accuracy of your predictions in (i) and (ii).

3 A scientist, working in an agricultural research station, believes that there is a relationship between the hardness of the shells of the eggs laid by chickens and the amount of a certain food supplement put into the diet of the chickens. He selects ten chickens of the same breed and collects the following data.

Chicken	Amount of supplement, x g	Hardness of shell, y
A	7.0	1.2
B	9.8	2.1
C	11.6	3.4
D	17.5	6.1
E	7.6	1.3
F	8.2	1.7
G	12.4	3.4
H	17.5	6.2
I	9.5	2.1
J	19.5	7.1

(Hardness is measured on a scale of 0–10, 10 being the hardest. No units are attached.)

(a) Draw a scatter diagram to illustrate these data.

(b) Calculate the equation of the regression line of hardness on amount of supplement.

(c) Do you believe that this linear model will continue to be appropriate no matter how large or small x becomes? Justify your reply.

4 In an investigation into predictions using the stars, a well-known astrologer, Horace Scope, predicted the ages at which 13 young people would first marry. The completed data, of predicted and actual ages at first marriage, are now available and are summarised in the following table.

Person	Predicted age, x years	Actual age, y years
A	24	23
B	30	31
C	28	28
D	36	35
E	20	20
F	22	25
G	31	45
H	28	30
I	21	22
J	29	27
K	40	40
L	25	27
M	27	26

(a) Draw a scatter diagram of these data.

(b) Calculate the line of regression of y on x.

(c) Plot the regression line on the scatter diagram.

(d) Comment on the results obtained, particularly in view of the data for person G. What further action would you suggest?

5 The given data relate to the price and engine capacity of new cars in January 1982.

Car model	Price (£) y	Capacity (cc) x
A	3900	1000
B	4200	1270
C	5160	1750
D	6980	2230
E	6930	1990
F	2190	600
G	2190	650
H	4160	1500
J	3050	1450
K	6150	1650

(a) Plot a scatter diagram of the data.

(b) Calculate the line of regression of y on x.

(c) Draw the line of regression on the scatter diagram.

(d) A particular customer regards large engine capacity and a low price as the two most important factors in choosing a car. Examine your scatter diagram and the regression line to suggest to him one model which, in January 1982, gave good value for money. Also suggest three models which you would advise the customer not to buy.

9

6 A small firm tries a new approach to negotiating the annual pay rise with each of its 12 employees. In an attempt to simplify the process, it is suggested that each employee should be assigned a score, x, based on his/her level of responsibility. The annual salary will be £$(bx + a)$ and negotiations will only involve the values of a and b.

The following table gives last year's salaries (which were generally regarded as fair) and the proposed scores.

Employee	x	Annual salary (£) y
A	10	5750
B	55	17 300
C	46	14 750
D	27	8200
E	17	6350
F	12	6150
G	85	18 800
H	64	14 850
I	36	9900
J	40	11 000
K	30	9150
L	37	10 400

(a) Plot the data on a scatter diagram.

(b) Estimate the values that could have been used for a and b last year by finding the line of regression of y on x.

(c) Comment on whether the suggested method is likely to prove reasonably satisfactory in practice.

(d) Two employees, B and C, had to work away from for a large part of the year. In the light of this additional information, suggest an improvement to the model.

7 A company specialises in supplying 'stocking fillers' at Christmas time. The company employs several full-time workers all year round but it relies on part-time help at the Christmas rush period.

The time taken to pack orders, together with the packer concerned and the number of items in the order were recorded for orders chosen at random during 3 days just prior to Christmas.

Packer	No. of items x	Time to pack y (mins)
Ada	21	270
Ada	62	420
Betty	30	245
Alice	20	305
Ada	35	320
Ada	57	440
Alice	40	400
Betty	10	180
Ada	48	350
Alice	58	490
Ada	20	285
Betty	45	340

(a) Plot a scatter diagram to illustrate these data. Label clearly which packer was responsible for the order.

(b) Calculate the value of the product moment correlation coefficient and comment on its value.

(c) Find the line of regression of y on x.

(d) Find an estimate for the length of time that it would take to pack an order of 45 items. Comment on how good an estimate you would imagine this to be.

(e) Calculate the residual values for Betty and also for her daughter Alice, who is working in the factory on a temporary basis over the Christmas holiday.

Use these residuals to produce a better estimate of the actual time expected for the next order of 45 items to be assembled if:

(i) Betty is the packer.

(ii) Alice is the packer.

9

8 Over a period of 3 years, a company has been monitoring the number of units of output produced per quarter and the total cost of producing the units. The table below shows the results.

Units of output, x (1000s)	Total cost, y (£1000)
14	35
29	50
55	73
74	93
11	31
23	42
47	65
69	86
18	38
36	54
61	81
79	96

(a) Draw a scatter diagram of these data.

(b) Calculate the equation of the regression line of y on x and draw this line on your scatter diagram.

The selling price of each unit of output is £1.60.

(c) Use your graph to estimate the level of output at which the total income and the total costs are equal.

(d) Give a brief interpretation of this value.

9 In the development of a new plastic material, a variable of interest was its 'deflection' when subjected to a constant force underwater. It was believed that, over a limited range of temperatures, this would be approximately linearly related to the temperature of the water. The 'deflection' was measured at a series of predetermined temperatures with the following results.

Technician	'Deflection' y	Temperature $x(°C)$
A	2.05	15
B	2.45	20
A	2.50	25
C	2.00	30
B	3.25	35
A	3.20	40
C	4.50	45
B	3.85	50
A	3.70	55
C	3.65	60

(a) Illustrate this data with a scatter diagram.

(b) Calculate the equation of the regression line of 'deflection' on temperature and draw this line on your scatter diagram.

(c) Three different technicians A, B and C were involved in the trial. Label your scatter diagram with this information and comment on the performance of each technician.

(d) Suggest what action might be taken before conducting further trials.

10 In addition to its full-time staff, a supermarket employs part-time sales staff on Saturdays. The manager experimented to see if there is a relationship between the takings and the number of part-time staff employed.

He collected data over nine successive Saturdays.

Number of part-time staff employed, x	Takings, £'00 y
10	313
13	320
16	319
19	326
22	333
25	342
28	321
31	361
34	355

(a) Plot a scatter diagram of these data.

(b) Calculate the equation of the regression line of takings on the number of part-time staff employed. Draw the line on your scatter diagram.

(c) If the regression line is denoted by $y = a + bx$, give an interpretation to each of a and b.

(d) On one Saturday, major roadworks blocked a nearby road. Which Saturday do you think this was?

Give a reason for your choice.

(e) The manager had increased the number of part-time staff each week. This was desirable from an organisational point of view but undesirable from a statistical point of view. Comment.

9

Key point summary

1 A scatter diagram should be drawn to judge whether   *p172*
   linear regression analysis is a sensible option.

2 The nature of the data should be considered to   *p173*
   determine which is the *independent* or *explanatory*
   variable (*x*) and which is the *dependent* or *response*
   variable (*y*).

3 The regression line is found using the *method of*   *p175*
   least squares in the form

   $$y = a + bx$$

   This is the regression line of *y* on *x* and may be used
   to predict a value for *y* from a given value of *x*.

   The equations can be found directly from a calculator
   with a linear regression mode

   Be careful to note the form in which your calculator
   presents the equation – it may be as $y = ax + b$

4 *a* estimates the value of *y* when *x* is zero.   *pp175, 176*
   b estimates the rate of change of *y* with *x*.

5 Be very careful when predicting from your line.   *p179*
   Watch out for extrapolation when predictions can be
   wildly inaccurate.

   Look back to Section 9.8

   **Never assume a linear model will keep on going
   forever.**

Test yourself   What to review

1 For each of the following sets of data say which variable is the   *Section 9.2*
   response or dependent variable, and which is the explanatory
   or independent variable.

(a)

Temperature required, *w* (°C)	Time taken to reach required temp, *u* (min)
15	4.3
20	8.7
25	11.9
30	14.8
35	17.1

Test yourself (*continued*)	**What to review**

(b)

Time fire has been switched on, f (min)	Temperature reached g (°C)
5	12.2
10	14.6
15	16.1
20	17.8
25	19.3

2 Which of the following scatter diagrams could illustrate data connected by the given regression equations?

Section 9.4

(a) $y = -6x + 12.3$

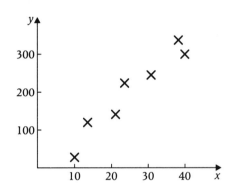

(b) $p = 0.78t - 2.1$

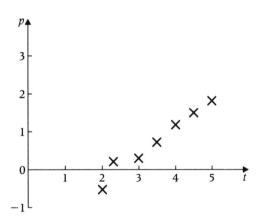

(c) $m = 0.15b - 1.9$

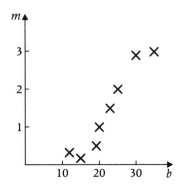

9

Test yourself (continued)	**What to review**

3 The line of regression of mass (y kg) on age (x weeks) for baby giraffes, between 0 and 12 weeks of age, is given below: *Sections 9.2 and 9.5*

$$y = 2.07x + 21.7$$

(a) Is it possible to obtain an estimate of the mass of a baby giraffe at 9 weeks old from this equation?

(b) Is it possible to estimate the age in weeks of a baby giraffe which has mass 42 kg?

(c) Interpret the value of the constant 21.7 in this equation.

4 The table below gives the height of a bean shoot in cm (y) and   *Sections 9.4 and 9.8*
the number of days since it was planted (x)

Number of days, x	Height, y (cm)
40	9.6
45	10.5
50	11.2
55	12.3
60	13.4
65	14.3
70	15.2

Calculate the line of regression of y on x.

Estimate the height of the shoot exactly 8 weeks (56 days) after planting.

Why would it not be sensible to use the regression equation to estimate the height of the shoot 3 months after planting?

Test yourself (continued)

5 As part of his research into the behaviour of the human memory, a leading psychologist asked 15 schoolgirls from years 9, 10 and 11 to talk for 5 minutes on 'my day at school'. The psychologist asked each girl to record how many times she thought she had used the word 'nice' during the talk. The following table gives their replies together with the true values.

Section 9.3

Girl	True value x	Recorded value y
A	12	9
B	20	19
C	1	3
D	8	14
E	0	4
F	12	12
G	12	16
H	17	14
I	6	5
J	5	9
K	24	20
L	23	16
M	10	11
N	18	17
O	16	19

The equation of the regression line of y on x is $y = 4.40 + 0.663x$.

The girls are from three different year groups.

A, C, H, I and L are from year 11

E, F, K, M and N are from year 10

B, D, G, J and O are from year 9.

Find the residuals for the girls in year 9 and for those in year 11. Use these, together with the regression line to estimate

(i) the recorded value for a girl in year 9 whose true value was 15.

(ii) the recorded value for a girl in year 11 whose true value was 10.

1 **(a)** Explanatory: temperature; dependent: time

   (b) Explanatory: time; dependent: temperature

2 **(a)** No,   **(b)** Yes,   **(c)** Yes.

3 **(a)** Yes,

   (b) No (line has y as dependent not x),

   (c) Mass at birth: 21.7 kg.

4 $y = 0.190x + 1.91$.

   $y = 0.190 \times 8 + 1.91 = 12.5$ cm.

   At 3 months, extrapolation would be used and therefore results may be very inaccurate as linear model may not continue.

5 Residuals: B 1.3, D 4.3, G 3.6, J 1.3, O 4.0,
   A −3.4, C −2.1, H −1.7, I −3.4, L −3.7.
   (i) 17, **(ii)** 8.

Exam style practice paper

Time allowed 1 hour 45 minutes

Answer **all** questions

1 As part of a survey on health, a random sample of 50 adolescent boys in the UK are to be asked whether they would prefer to lose weight, gain weight or stay the same. If the proportion of adolescent boys in the UK who would prefer to gain weight is 0.15 find the probability that the number, in the sample, who would prefer to gain weight is

(i) 4 or fewer *(2 marks)*

(ii) 4 or more. *(2 marks)*

2 A secret society records the date on which new members join and the date on which members leave. For members who leave, the length of their membership, in years, is recorded. The lengths of membership of those who left in 1999 are illustrated in the histogram below.

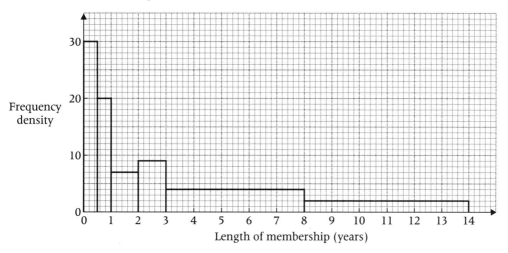

(a) Copy and complete the following table, which summarises the data displayed in the histogram.

Length of membership (years)	Frequency
0–0.5	
–1.0	
–2.0	7
–3.0	
–8.0	
–14.0	

(3 marks)

(b) It is not possible to determine the exact range of the data because it is grouped. State, giving your answers in years to one decimal place,

    (i) the minimum possible range of the data   *(1 mark)*

    (ii) the maximum possible range of the data.   *(1 mark)*

3 The owner of a number of national newspapers bids to buy a famous football club. A large number of the club's supporters write letters to the editors of these newspapers. Of these letters 90% are against the bid, 4% are neutral and 6% are in favour of the bid.

(a) If two letters are selected at random find the probability that

    (i) they will both be against the bid   *(2 marks)*

    (ii) one will be against the bid and one will be neutral.   *(2 marks)*

The probability of a letter being published is

    0.01 if it is against the bid

    0.24 if it is neutral

    0.65 if it is in favour of the bid.

(b) Find the probability that a randomly selected letter is

    (i) against the bid and is published   *(2 marks)*

    (ii) published.   *(3 marks)*

4 The number of telephone calls to a university admissions office during working hours may be modelled by a Poisson distribution with mean 1.4 per minute.

    (a) Find the probability that the number of calls received during a particular

        (i) 1-minute interval is exactly 3   *(3 marks)*

        (ii) 5-minute interval is more than five.   *(3 marks)*

    (b) In a particular 1-minute interval, how many calls will be exceeded with probability just greater than 0.05?

                                            (2 marks)

    (c) Explain why the Poisson distribution is unlikely to be a suitable model for

        (i) the number of calls received by the admissions office per minute over a 24-hour period   *(2 marks)*

        (ii) the number of calls answered per minute during a busy period when the telephone is often engaged.

                                            (2 marks)

5 The lengths of cod caught by a fishing boat may be regarded as a random sample from a normal distribution with mean 74 cm and standard deviation 10 cm.

    (a) Find the probability that

        (i) the length of a randomly selected cod is between 70 cm and 75 cm   *(5 marks)*

        (ii) the mean length of 90 randomly selected cod is more than 73 cm.   *(3 marks)*

    (b) What length is exceeded by the longest 10% of the cod.

                                            (3 marks)

    (c) Would your answer to part (a) (ii) still be valid if it was discovered that

        (i) the sample was not random but the distribution was normal   *(2 marks)*

        (ii) the distribution was not normal but the sample was random?   *(2 marks)*

    Explain your answers.

6 As part of an investigation of sampling methods, 150 plastic rods of varying lengths are placed on a desk by a teacher. A student is invited to view this population of rods. She is asked to estimate the mean length of the rods by choosing a sample of three which she thinks will have a mean length similar to that of the population (i.e. there is no attempt to select a random sample). The three selected rods are then measured and their mean length calculated. This process is repeated by each of the students in the class.

The following eight **mean** lengths, in centimetres, were obtained

$$4.7 \quad 5.3 \quad 4.4 \quad 6.2 \quad 5.2 \quad 4.9 \quad 3.9 \quad 4.8$$

The mean length of the population of rods is 3.4 cm.

(a) Comment on this method of estimating the mean length of the population. *(1 mark)*

(b) Calculate the mean and the standard deviation of the eight mean lengths. *(2 marks)*

The teacher now asks a student to obtain a random sample of size three from the rod population.

(c) Describe how the student could use random number tables to obtain such a sample. *(5 marks)*

Each student then independently obtains a random sample of size three from the population. The rods are measured and their mean lengths calculated as before. The eight **mean** lengths of the random samples are as follows:

$$4.6 \quad 1.9 \quad 7.2 \quad 1.5 \quad 2.2 \quad 2.8 \quad 3.7 \quad 1.4$$

(d) Calculate the mean and the standard deviation of these eight mean lengths. *(2 marks)*

(e) Compare the means of the non-random samples with those of the random samples. Your comments should include reference to the population mean. *(3 marks)*

(f) Use your estimate of the standard deviation of the **mean** lengths of the eight random samples to estimate the standard deviation of the population of rod lengths *(2 marks)*

7 The table on the opposite page shows, for each of a sample of countries, the population, in millions, and the number of medals won at the 1992 Summer Olympic Games plus those won at the 1994 Winter Olympic Games. The final column shows the number of these medals which were won at the 1994 Winter Olympic Games.

Country	Population, x	Total number of medals won at 1992 Summer and 1994 Winter games, y	Number of medals won at 1994 Winter games, z
Britain	58	22	2
Canada	28	31	13
Cuba	11	31	0
Italy	58	39	20
Jamaica	3	4	0
North Korea	23	15	6
Poland	39	19	0
Sweden	9	15	3
Unified Team	232	146	34
United States	261	122	13

(a) Draw a scatter diagram of the population, x, and the total number of medals won, y. *(3 marks)*

(b) Calculate the equation of the regression line of total number of medals won on population. Draw this line on your scatter diagram. *(6 marks)*

The Unified Team was made up of athletes from countries, including Russia, which were formerly part of the USSR.

(c) Use your regression equation to predict how many medals would have been won by Russia (population 150 million) if it had competed separately from the other countries in the Unified Team. *(1 mark)*

(d) State, giving a reason, whether you think the prediction made in part (c) is likely to be an underestimate or an overestimate. *(2 marks)*

(e) Calculate the product moment correlation coefficient between the number of medals won at the 1992 **Summer** Olympic Games and the number of medals won at the 1994 **Winter** Olympic Games. *(4 marks)*

(f) Interpret the correlation coefficient you have calculated in part (e) in the context of this data. *(2 marks)*

(g) Identify **two** features of the data which suggest that the sample is not a random sample of all countries. *(2 marks)*

Appendix

Table 1 Binomial distribution function

The tabulated value is $P(R \leqslant r)$, where R has a binomial distribution with parameters n and p.

r	0.01	0.02	0.03	0.04	0.05	0.06	0.07	0.08	0.09	0.10	0.15	0.20	0.25	0.30	0.35	0.40	0.45	0.50	r
n = 8 0	0.9227	0.8508	0.7837	0.7214	0.6634	0.6096	0.5596	0.5132	0.4703	0.4305	0.2725	0.1678	0.1001	0.0576	0.0319	0.0168	0.0084	0.0039	0
1	0.9973	0.9897	0.9777	0.9619	0.9428	0.9208	0.8965	0.8702	0.8423	0.8131	0.6572	0.5033	0.3671	0.2553	0.1691	0.1064	0.0632	0.0352	1
2	0.9999	0.9996	0.9987	0.9969	0.9942	0.9904	0.9853	0.9789	0.9711	0.9619	0.8948	0.7969	0.6785	0.5518	0.4278	0.3154	0.2201	0.1445	2
3	1.000	1.000	0.9999	0.9998	0.9996	0.9993	0.9987	0.9978	0.9966	0.9950	0.9786	0.9437	0.8862	0.8059	0.7064	0.5941	0.4770	0.3633	3
4			1.000	1.000	1.000	1.000	0.9999	0.9999	0.9997	0.9996	0.9971	0.9896	0.9727	0.9420	0.8939	0.8263	0.7396	0.6367	4
5							1.000	1.000	1.000	1.000	0.9998	0.9988	0.9958	0.9887	0.9747	0.9502	0.9115	0.8555	5
6											1.000	0.9999	0.9996	0.9987	0.9964	0.9915	0.9819	0.9648	6
7												1.000	1.000	0.9999	0.9998	0.9993	0.9983	0.9961	7
8														1.000	1.000	1.000	1.000	1.000	8
n = 12 0	0.8864	0.7847	0.6938	0.6127	0.5404	0.4759	0.4186	0.3677	0.3225	0.2824	0.1422	0.0687	0.0317	0.0138	0.0057	0.0022	0.0008	0.0002	0
1	0.9938	0.9769	0.9514	0.9191	0.8816	0.8405	0.7967	0.7513	0.7052	0.6590	0.4435	0.2749	0.1584	0.0850	0.0424	0.0196	0.0083	0.0032	1
2	0.9998	0.9985	0.9952	0.9893	0.9804	0.9684	0.9532	0.9348	0.9134	0.8891	0.7358	0.5583	0.3907	0.2528	0.1513	0.0834	0.0421	0.0193	2
3	1.000	0.9999	0.9997	0.9990	0.9978	0.9957	0.9925	0.9880	0.9820	0.9744	0.9078	0.7946	0.6488	0.4925	0.3467	0.2253	0.1345	0.0730	3
4		1.000	1.000	0.9999	0.9998	0.9996	0.9991	0.9984	0.9973	0.9957	0.9761	0.9274	0.8424	0.7237	0.5833	0.4382	0.3044	0.1938	4
5				1.000	1.000	1.000	0.9999	0.9998	0.9997	0.9995	0.9954	0.9806	0.9456	0.8822	0.7873	0.6652	0.5269	0.3872	5
6							1.000	1.000	1.000	0.9999	0.9993	0.9961	0.9857	0.9614	0.9154	0.8418	0.7393	0.6128	6
7										1.000	0.9999	0.9994	0.9972	0.9905	0.9745	0.9427	0.8883	0.8062	7
8											1.000	0.9999	0.9996	0.9983	0.9944	0.9847	0.9644	0.9270	8
9												1.000	1.000	0.9998	0.9992	0.9972	0.9921	0.9807	9
10														1.000	0.9999	0.9997	0.9989	0.9968	10
11															1.000	1.000	0.9999	0.9998	11
12																	1.000	1.000	12
n = 15 0	0.8601	0.7386	0.6333	0.5421	0.4633	0.3953	0.3367	0.2863	0.2430	0.2059	0.0874	0.0352	0.0134	0.0047	0.0016	0.0005	0.0001	0.0000	0
1	0.9904	0.9647	0.9270	0.8809	0.8290	0.7738	0.7168	0.6597	0.6035	0.5490	0.3186	0.1671	0.0802	0.0353	0.0142	0.0052	0.0017	0.0005	1
2	0.9996	0.9970	0.9906	0.9797	0.9638	0.9429	0.9171	0.8870	0.8531	0.8159	0.6042	0.3980	0.2361	0.1268	0.0617	0.0271	0.0107	0.0037	2
3	1.000	0.9998	0.9992	0.9976	0.9945	0.9896	0.9825	0.9727	0.9601	0.9444	0.8227	0.6482	0.4613	0.2969	0.1727	0.0905	0.0424	0.0176	3
4		1.000	0.9999	0.9998	0.9994	0.9986	0.9972	0.9950	0.9918	0.9873	0.9383	0.8358	0.6865	0.5155	0.3519	0.2173	0.1204	0.0592	4
5			1.000	1.000	0.9999	0.9999	0.9997	0.9993	0.9987	0.9978	0.9832	0.9389	0.8516	0.7216	0.5643	0.4032	0.2608	0.1509	5
6					1.000	1.000	1.000	0.9999	0.9998	0.9997	0.9964	0.9819	0.9434	0.8689	0.7548	0.6098	0.4522	0.3036	6
7								1.000	1.000	1.000	0.9994	0.9958	0.9827	0.9500	0.8868	0.7869	0.6535	0.5000	7
8											0.9999	0.9992	0.9958	0.9848	0.9578	0.9050	0.8182	0.6964	8
9											1.000	0.9999	0.9992	0.9963	0.9876	0.9662	0.9231	0.8491	9
10												1.000	0.9999	0.9993	0.9972	0.9907	0.9745	0.9408	10
11													1.000	0.9999	0.9995	0.9981	0.9937	0.9824	11
12														1.000	0.9999	0.9997	0.9989	0.9963	12
13															1.000	1.000	0.9999	0.9995	13
14																	1.000	1.000	14

Table 1 Binomial distribution function (continued)

r	0.01	0.02	0.03	0.04	0.05	0.06	0.07	0.08	0.09	0.10	0.15	0.20	0.25	0.30	0.35	0.40	0.45	0.50	r
$n=20$ 0	0.8179	0.6676	0.5438	0.4420	0.3585	0.2901	0.2342	0.1887	0.1516	0.1216	0.0388	0.0115	0.0032	0.0008	0.0002	0.0000	0.0000	0.0000	0
1	0.9831	0.9401	0.8802	0.8103	0.7358	0.6605	0.5869	0.5169	0.4516	0.3917	0.1756	0.0692	0.0243	0.0076	0.0021	0.0005	0.0001	0.0000	1
2	0.9990	0.9929	0.9790	0.9561	0.9245	0.8850	0.8390	0.7879	0.7334	0.6769	0.4049	0.2061	0.0913	0.0355	0.0121	0.0036	0.0009	0.0002	2
3	1.000	0.9994	0.9973	0.9926	0.9841	0.9710	0.9529	0.9294	0.9007	0.8670	0.6477	0.4114	0.2252	0.1071	0.0444	0.0160	0.0049	0.0013	3
4		1.000	0.9997	0.9990	0.9974	0.9944	0.9893	0.9817	0.9710	0.9568	0.8298	0.6296	0.4148	0.2375	0.1182	0.0510	0.0189	0.0059	4
5			1.000	0.9999	0.9997	0.9991	0.9981	0.9962	0.9932	0.9887	0.9327	0.8042	0.6172	0.4164	0.2454	0.1256	0.0553	0.0207	5
6				1.000	1.000	0.9999	0.9997	0.9994	0.9987	0.9976	0.9781	0.9133	0.7858	0.6080	0.4166	0.2500	0.1299	0.0577	6
7						1.000	1.000	0.9999	0.9998	0.9996	0.9941	0.9679	0.8982	0.7723	0.6010	0.4159	0.2520	0.1316	7
8								1.000	1.000	0.9999	0.9987	0.9900	0.9591	0.8867	0.7624	0.5956	0.4143	0.2517	8
9										1.000	0.9998	0.9974	0.9861	0.9520	0.8782	0.7553	0.5914	0.4119	9
10											1.000	0.9994	0.9961	0.9829	0.9468	0.8725	0.7507	0.5881	10
11												0.9999	0.9991	0.9949	0.9804	0.9435	0.8692	0.7483	11
12												1.000	0.9998	0.9987	0.9940	0.9790	0.9420	0.8684	12
13													1.000	0.9997	0.9985	0.9935	0.9786	0.9423	13
14														1.000	0.9997	0.9984	0.9936	0.9793	14
15															1.000	0.9997	0.9985	0.9941	15
16																1.000	0.9997	0.9987	16
17																	1.000	0.9998	17
18																		1.000	18
$n=25$ 0	0.7778	0.6035	0.4670	0.3604	0.2774	0.2129	0.1630	0.1244	0.0946	0.0718	0.0172	0.0038	0.0008	0.0001	0.0000	0.0000	0.0000	0.0000	0
1	0.9742	0.9114	0.8280	0.7358	0.6424	0.5527	0.4696	0.3947	0.3286	0.2712	0.0931	0.0274	0.0070	0.0016	0.0003	0.0001	0.0000	0.0000	1
2	0.9980	0.9868	0.9620	0.9235	0.8729	0.8129	0.7466	0.6768	0.6063	0.5371	0.2537	0.0982	0.0321	0.0090	0.0021	0.0004	0.0001	0.0000	2
3	0.9999	0.9986	0.9938	0.9835	0.9659	0.9402	0.9064	0.8649	0.8169	0.7636	0.4711	0.2340	0.0962	0.0332	0.0097	0.0024	0.0005	0.0001	3
4	1.000	0.9999	0.9992	0.9972	0.9928	0.9850	0.9726	0.9549	0.9314	0.9020	0.6821	0.4207	0.2137	0.0905	0.0320	0.0095	0.0023	0.0005	4
5		1.000	0.9999	0.9996	0.9988	0.9969	0.9935	0.9877	0.9790	0.9666	0.8385	0.6167	0.3783	0.1935	0.0826	0.0294	0.0086	0.0020	5
6			1.000	1.000	0.9998	0.9995	0.9987	0.9972	0.9946	0.9905	0.9305	0.7800	0.5611	0.3407	0.1734	0.0736	0.0258	0.0073	6
7					1.000	0.9999	0.9998	0.9995	0.9989	0.9977	0.9745	0.8909	0.7265	0.5118	0.3061	0.1536	0.0639	0.0216	7
8						1.000	1.000	0.9999	0.9998	0.9995	0.9920	0.9532	0.8506	0.6769	0.4668	0.2735	0.1340	0.0539	8
9								1.000	0.9999	0.9998	0.9979	0.9827	0.9287	0.8106	0.6303	0.4246	0.2424	0.1148	9
10									1.000	1.000	0.9995	0.9944	0.9703	0.9022	0.7712	0.5858	0.3843	0.2122	10
11											0.9999	0.9985	0.9893	0.9558	0.8476	0.7323	0.5426	0.3450	11
12											1.000	0.9996	0.9966	0.9825	0.9396	0.8462	0.6937	0.5000	12
13												0.9999	0.9991	0.9940	0.9745	0.9222	0.8173	0.6550	13
14												1.000	0.9998	0.9982	0.9907	0.9656	0.9040	0.7878	14
15													1.000	0.9995	0.9971	0.9868	0.9560	0.8852	15
16														0.9999	0.9992	0.9957	0.9826	0.9461	16
17														1.000	0.9998	0.9988	0.9942	0.9784	17
18															1.000	0.9997	0.9984	0.9927	18
19																0.9999	0.9996	0.9980	19
20																1.000	0.9999	0.9995	20
21																	1.000	0.9999	21
22																		1.000	22
$n=30$ 0	0.7397	0.5455	0.4010	0.2939	0.2146	0.1563	0.1134	0.0820	0.0591	0.0424	0.0076	0.0012	0.0002	0.0000	0.0000	0.0000	0.0000	0.0000	0
1	0.9639	0.8795	0.7731	0.6612	0.5535	0.4555	0.3694	0.2958	0.2343	0.1837	0.0480	0.0105	0.0020	0.0003	0.0000	0.0000	0.0000	0.0000	1
2	0.9967	0.9783	0.9399	0.8831	0.8122	0.7324	0.6487	0.5654	0.4855	0.4114	0.1514	0.0442	0.0106	0.0021	0.0003	0.0000	0.0000	0.0000	2
3	0.9998	0.9971	0.9881	0.9694	0.9392	0.8974	0.8450	0.7842	0.7175	0.6474	0.3217	0.1227	0.0374	0.0093	0.0019	0.0003	0.0000	0.0000	3
4	1.000	0.9997	0.9982	0.9937	0.9844	0.9685	0.9447	0.9126	0.8723	0.8245	0.5245	0.2552	0.0979	0.0302	0.0075	0.0015	0.0002	0.0000	4
5		1.000	0.9998	0.9989	0.9967	0.9921	0.9838	0.9707	0.9519	0.9268	0.7106	0.4275	0.2026	0.0766	0.0233	0.0057	0.0011	0.0002	5
6			1.000	0.9999	0.9994	0.9983	0.9960	0.9918	0.9848	0.9742	0.8474	0.6070	0.3481	0.1595	0.0586	0.0172	0.0040	0.0007	6
7				1.000	0.9999	0.9997	0.9992	0.9980	0.9959	0.9922	0.9302	0.7608	0.5143	0.2814	0.1238	0.0435	0.0121	0.0026	7
8						1.000	0.9999	0.9996	0.9990	0.9980	0.9722	0.8713	0.6736	0.4315	0.2247	0.0940	0.0312	0.0081	8
9								1.000	0.9999	0.9996	0.9903	0.9389	0.8034	0.5888	0.3575	0.1763	0.0694	0.0214	9
10									1.000	0.9999	0.9971	0.9744	0.8943	0.7304	0.5078	0.2915	0.1350	0.0494	10
11										1.000	0.9992	0.9905	0.9493	0.8407	0.6548	0.4311	0.2327	0.1002	11
12											0.9998	0.9969	0.9784	0.9155	0.7802	0.5785	0.3592	0.1808	12
13											1.000	0.9991	0.9918	0.9599	0.8737	0.7145	0.5025	0.2923	13
14												0.9998	0.9973	0.9831	0.9348	0.8246	0.6448	0.4278	14
15												0.9999	0.9992	0.9936	0.9699	0.9029	0.7691	0.5722	15
16												1.000	0.9998	0.9979	0.9876	0.9519	0.8644	0.7077	16
17													0.9999	0.9994	0.9955	0.9788	0.9286	0.8192	17
18													1.000	0.9998	0.9986	0.9917	0.9666	0.8998	18
19														1.000	0.9996	0.9971	0.9682	0.9506	19
20															0.9999	0.9991	0.9950	0.9786	20
21															1.000	0.9998	0.9984	0.9919	21
22																1.000	0.9996	0.9974	22
23																	0.9999	0.9993	23
24																	1.000	0.9998	24
25																		1.000	25

Table 1 Binomial distribution function (continued)

n = 40

r \\ p	0.01	0.02	0.03	0.04	0.05	0.06	0.07	0.08	0.09	0.10	0.15	0.20	0.25	0.30	0.35	0.40	0.45	0.50	p \\ r
0	0.6690	0.4457	0.2957	0.1954	0.1285	0.0842	0.0549	0.0356	0.0230	0.0148	0.0015	0.0002	0.0000	0.0000	0.0000	0.0000	0.0000	0.0000	0
1	0.9393	0.8095	0.6615	0.5210	0.3991	0.2990	0.2201	0.1594	0.1140	0.0805	0.0121	0.0015	0.0001	0.0000	0.0000	0.0000	0.0000	0.0000	1
2	0.9925	0.9543	0.8822	0.7855	0.6767	0.5665	0.4625	0.3694	0.2894	0.2228	0.0486	0.0079	0.0010	0.0001	0.0000	0.0000	0.0000	0.0000	2
3	0.9993	0.9918	0.9686	0.9252	0.8619	0.7827	0.6937	0.6007	0.5092	0.4231	0.1302	0.0285	0.0047	0.0006	0.0001	0.0000	0.0000	0.0000	3
4	1.000	0.9988	0.9933	0.9790	0.9520	0.9104	0.8546	0.7868	0.7103	0.6290	0.2633	0.0759	0.0160	0.0026	0.0003	0.0000	0.0000	0.0000	4
5		0.9999	0.9988	0.9951	0.9861	0.9691	0.9419	0.9033	0.8535	0.7937	0.4325	0.1613	0.0433	0.0086	0.0013	0.0001	0.0000	0.0000	5
6		1.000	0.9998	0.9990	0.9966	0.9909	0.9801	0.9624	0.9361	0.9005	0.6067	0.2859	0.0962	0.0238	0.0044	0.0006	0.0001	0.0000	6
7			1.000	0.9998	0.9993	0.9977	0.9942	0.9873	0.9758	0.9581	0.7559	0.4371	0.1820	0.0553	0.0124	0.0021	0.0002	0.0000	7
8				1.000	0.9999	0.9995	0.9985	0.9963	0.9919	0.9845	0.8646	0.5931	0.2998	0.1110	0.0303	0.0061	0.0009	0.0001	8
9					1.000	0.9999	0.9997	0.9990	0.9976	0.9949	0.9328	0.7318	0.4395	0.1959	0.0644	0.0156	0.0027	0.0003	9
10						1.000	0.9999	0.9998	0.9994	0.9985	0.9701	0.8392	0.5839	0.3087	0.1215	0.0352	0.0074	0.0011	10
11							1.000	1.000	0.9999	0.9996	0.9880	0.9125	0.7151	0.4406	0.2053	0.0709	0.0179	0.0032	11
12									1.000	0.9999	0.9957	0.9568	0.8209	0.5772	0.3143	0.1285	0.0386	0.0083	12
13										1.000	0.9986	0.9806	0.8968	0.7032	0.4408	0.2112	0.0751	0.0192	13
14											0.9996	0.9921	0.9456	0.8074	0.5721	0.3174	0.1326	0.0403	14
15											0.9999	0.9971	0.9738	0.8849	0.6946	0.4402	0.2142	0.0769	15
16											1.000	0.9990	0.9884	0.9367	0.7978	0.5681	0.3185	0.1341	16
17												0.9997	0.9953	0.9680	0.8761	0.6885	0.4391	0.2148	17
18												0.9999	0.9983	0.9852	0.9301	0.7911	0.5651	0.3179	18
19												1.000	0.9994	0.9937	0.9637	0.8702	0.6844	0.4373	19
20													0.9998	0.9976	0.9827	0.9256	0.7870	0.5627	20
21													1.000	0.9991	0.9925	0.9608	0.8669	0.6821	21
22														0.9997	0.9970	0.9811	0.9233	0.7852	22
23														0.9999	0.9989	0.9917	0.9595	0.8659	23
24														1.000	0.9996	0.9966	0.9804	0.9231	24
25															0.9999	0.9988	0.9914	0.9597	25
26															1.000	0.9996	0.9966	0.9808	26
27																0.9999	0.9988	0.9917	27
28																1.000	0.9996	0.9968	28
29																	0.9999	0.9989	29
30																	1.000	0.9997	30
31																		0.9999	31
32																		1.000	32

n = 50

r \\ p	0.01	0.02	0.03	0.04	0.05	0.06	0.07	0.08	0.09	0.10	0.15	0.20	0.25	0.30	0.35	0.40	0.45	0.50	p \\ r
0	0.6050	0.3642	0.2181	0.1299	0.0769	0.0453	0.0266	0.0155	0.0090	0.0052	0.0003	0.0000	0.0000	0.0000	0.0000	0.0000	0.0000	0.0000	0
1	0.9106	0.7358	0.5553	0.4005	0.2794	0.1900	0.1265	0.0827	0.0532	0.0338	0.0029	0.0002	0.0000	0.0000	0.0000	0.0000	0.0000	0.0000	1
2	0.9862	0.9216	0.8108	0.6767	0.5405	0.4162	0.3108	0.2260	0.1605	0.1117	0.0142	0.0013	0.0001	0.0000	0.0000	0.0000	0.0000	0.0000	2
3	0.9984	0.9822	0.9372	0.8609	0.7604	0.6473	0.5327	0.4253	0.3303	0.2503	0.0460	0.0057	0.0005	0.0000	0.0000	0.0000	0.0000	0.0000	3
4	0.9999	0.9968	0.9832	0.9510	0.8964	0.8206	0.7290	0.6290	0.5277	0.4312	0.1121	0.0185	0.0021	0.0002	0.0000	0.0000	0.0000	0.0000	4
5	1.000	0.9995	0.9963	0.9856	0.9622	0.9224	0.8650	0.7919	0.7072	0.6161	0.2194	0.0480	0.0070	0.0007	0.0001	0.0000	0.0000	0.0000	5
6		0.9999	0.9993	0.9964	0.9882	0.9711	0.9417	0.8981	0.8404	0.7702	0.3613	0.1034	0.0194	0.0025	0.0002	0.0000	0.0000	0.0000	6
7		1.000	0.9999	0.9992	0.9968	0.9906	0.9780	0.9562	0.9232	0.8779	0.5188	0.1904	0.0453	0.0073	0.0008	0.0001	0.0000	0.0000	7
8			1.000	0.9999	0.9992	0.9973	0.9927	0.9833	0.9672	0.9421	0.6681	0.3073	0.0916	0.0183	0.0025	0.0002	0.0000	0.0000	8
9				1.000	0.9998	0.9993	0.9978	0.9944	0.9875	0.9755	0.7911	0.4437	0.1637	0.0402	0.0067	0.0008	0.0001	0.0000	9
10					1.000	0.9998	0.9994	0.9983	0.9957	0.9906	0.8801	0.5836	0.2622	0.0789	0.0160	0.0022	0.0002	0.0000	10
11						1.000	0.9999	0.9995	0.9987	0.9968	0.9372	0.7107	0.3816	0.1390	0.0342	0.0057	0.0006	0.0000	11
12							1.000	0.9999	0.9996	0.9990	0.9699	0.8139	0.5110	0.2229	0.0661	0.0133	0.0018	0.0002	12
13								1.000	0.9999	0.9997	0.9868	0.8894	0.6370	0.3279	0.1163	0.0280	0.0045	0.0005	13
14									1.000	0.9999	0.9947	0.9393	0.7481	0.4468	0.1878	0.0540	0.0104	0.0013	14
15										1.000	0.9981	0.9692	0.8369	0.5692	0.2801	0.0955	0.0220	0.0033	15
16											0.9993	0.9856	0.9017	0.6839	0.3889	0.1561	0.0427	0.0077	16
17											0.9998	0.9937	0.9449	0.7822	0.5060	0.2369	0.0765	0.0164	17
18											0.9999	0.9975	0.9713	0.8594	0.6216	0.3356	0.1273	0.0325	18
19											1.000	0.9991	0.9861	0.9152	0.7264	0.4465	0.12974	0.0595	19
20												0.9997	0.9937	0.9522	0.8139	0.5610	0.2862	0.1013	20
21												0.9999	0.9974	0.9749	0.8813	0.6701	0.3900	0.1611	21
22												1.000	0.9990	0.9877	0.9290	0.7660	0.5019	0.2399	22
23													0.9996	0.9944	0.9604	0.8438	0.6134	0.3359	23
24													0.9999	0.9976	0.9793	0.9022	0.7160	0.4439	24
25													1.000	0.9991	0.9900	0.9427	0.8034	0.5561	25
26														0.9997	0.9955	0.9686	0.8721	0.6641	26
27														0.9999	0.9981	0.9840	0.9220	0.7601	27
28														1.000	0.9993	0.9924	0.9556	0.8389	28
29															0.9997	0.9966	0.9765	0.8987	29
30															0.9999	0.9986	0.9884	0.9405	30
31															1.000	0.9995	0.9947	0.9675	31
32																0.9998	0.9978	0.9836	32
33																0.9999	0.9991	0.9923	33
34																1.000	0.9997	0.9967	34
35																	0.9999	0.9987	35
36																	1.000	0.9995	36
37																		0.9998	37
38																		1.000	38

Table 2 Poisson distribution function

The tabulated value is $P(R \leqslant r)$, where R has a Poisson distribution with mean λ.

r \ λ	0.1	0.2	0.3	0.4	0.5	0.6	0.7	0.8	0.9	1.0	1.2	1.4	1.6	1.8	λ \ r
0	0.9048	0.8187	0.7408	0.6703	0.6065	0.5488	0.4966	0.4493	0.4066	0.3679	0.3012	0.2466	0.2019	0.1653	0
1	0.9953	0.9825	0.9631	0.9384	0.9098	0.8781	0.8442	0.8088	0.7725	0.7358	0.6626	0.5918	0.5249	0.4628	1
2	0.9998	0.9989	0.9964	0.9921	0.9856	0.9769	0.9659	0.9526	0.9371	0.9197	0.8795	0.8335	0.7834	0.7306	2
3	1.000	0.9999	0.9997	0.9992	0.9982	0.9966	0.9942	0.9909	0.9865	0.9810	0.9662	0.9463	0.9212	0.8913	3
4		1.000	1.000	0.9999	0.9998	0.9996	0.9992	0.9986	0.9977	0.9963	0.9923	0.9857	0.9763	0.9636	4
5				1.000	1.000	1.000	0.9999	0.9998	0.9997	0.9994	0.9985	0.9968	0.9940	0.9896	5
6							1.000	1.000	1.000	0.9999	0.9997	0.9994	0.9987	0.9974	6
7										1.000	1.000	0.9999	0.9997	0.9994	7
8												1.000	1.000	0.9999	8
9														1.000	9

r \ λ	2.0	2.2	2.4	2.6	2.8	3.0	3.2	3.4	3.6	3.8	4.0	4.5	5.0	5.5	λ \ r
0	0.1353	0.1108	0.0907	0.0743	0.0608	0.0498	0.0408	0.0334	0.0273	0.0224	0.0183	0.0111	0.0067	0.0041	0
1	0.4060	0.3546	0.3084	0.2674	0.2311	0.1991	0.1712	0.1468	0.1257	0.1074	0.0916	0.0611	0.0404	0.0266	1
2	0.6767	0.6227	0.5697	0.5184	0.4695	0.4232	0.3799	0.3397	0.3027	0.2689	0.2381	0.1736	0.1247	0.0884	2
3	0.8571	0.8194	0.7787	0.7360	0.6919	0.6472	0.6025	0.5584	0.5152	0.4735	0.4335	0.3423	0.2650	0.2017	3
4	0.9473	0.9275	0.9041	0.8774	0.8477	0.8153	0.7806	0.7442	0.7064	0.6678	0.6288	0.5321	0.4405	0.3575	4
5	0.9834	0.9751	0.9643	0.9510	0.9349	0.9161	0.8946	0.8705	0.8441	0.8156	0.7851	0.7029	0.6160	0.5289	5
6	0.9955	0.9925	0.9884	0.9828	0.9756	0.9665	0.9554	0.9421	0.9267	0.9091	0.8893	0.8311	0.7622	0.6860	6
7	0.9989	0.9980	0.9967	0.9947	0.9919	0.9881	0.9832	0.9769	0.9692	0.9599	0.9489	0.9134	0.8666	0.8095	7
8	0.9998	0.9995	0.9991	0.9985	0.9976	0.9962	0.9943	0.9917	0.9883	0.9840	0.9786	0.9597	0.9319	0.8944	8
9	1.000	0.9999	0.9998	0.9996	0.9993	0.9989	0.9982	0.9973	0.9960	0.9942	0.9919	0.9829	0.9682	0.9462	9
10		1.000	1.000	0.9999	0.9998	0.9997	0.9995	0.9992	0.9987	0.9981	0.9972	0.9933	0.9863	0.9747	10
11				1.000	1.000	0.9999	0.9999	0.9998	0.9996	0.9994	0.9991	0.9976	0.9945	0.9890	11
12						1.000	1.000	0.9999	0.9999	0.9998	0.9997	0.9992	0.9980	0.9955	12
13								1.000	1.000	1.000	0.9999	0.9997	0.9993	0.9983	13
14										1.000	1.000	0.9999	0.9998	0.9994	14
15												1.000	0.9999	0.9998	15
16													1.000	0.9999	16
17														1.0000	17

r \ λ	6.0	6.5	7.0	7.5	8.0	8.5	9.0	9.5	10.0	11.0	12.0	13.0	14.0	15.0	λ \ r
0	0.0025	0.0015	0.0009	0.0006	0.0003	0.0002	0.0001	0.0001	0.0000	0.0000	0.0000	0.0000	0.0000	0.0000	0
1	0.0174	0.0113	0.0073	0.0047	0.0030	0.0019	0.0012	0.0008	0.0005	0.0002	0.0001	0.0000	0.0000	0.0000	1
2	0.0620	0.0430	0.0296	0.0203	0.0138	0.0093	0.0062	0.0042	0.0028	0.0012	0.0005	0.0002	0.0001	0.0000	2
3	0.1512	0.1118	0.0818	0.0591	0.0424	0.0301	0.0212	0.0149	0.0103	0.0049	0.0023	0.0011	0.0005	0.0002	3
4	0.2851	0.2237	0.1730	0.1321	0.0996	0.0744	0.0550	0.0403	0.0293	0.0151	0.0076	0.0037	0.0018	0.0009	4
5	0.4457	0.3690	0.3007	0.2414	0.1912	0.1496	0.1157	0.0885	0.0671	0.0375	0.0203	0.0107	0.0055	0.0028	5
6	0.6063	0.5265	0.4497	0.3782	0.3134	0.2562	0.2068	0.1649	0.1301	0.0786	0.0458	0.0259	0.0142	0.0076	6
7	0.7440	0.6728	0.5987	0.5246	0.4530	0.3856	0.3239	0.2687	0.2202	0.1432	0.0895	0.0540	0.0316	0.0180	7
8	0.8472	0.7916	0.7291	0.6620	0.5925	0.5231	0.4557	0.3918	0.3328	0.2320	0.1550	0.0998	0.0621	0.0374	8
9	0.9161	0.8774	0.8305	0.7764	0.7166	0.6530	0.5874	0.5218	0.4579	0.3405	0.2424	0.1658	0.1094	0.0699	9
10	0.9574	0.9332	0.9015	0.8622	0.8159	0.7634	0.7060	0.6453	0.5830	0.4599	0.3472	0.2517	0.1757	0.1185	10
11	0.9799	0.9661	0.9467	0.9208	0.8881	0.8487	0.8030	0.7520	0.6968	0.5793	0.4616	0.3532	0.2500	0.1848	11
12	0.9912	0.9840	0.9730	0.9573	0.9362	0.9091	0.8758	0.8364	0.7916	0.6887	0.5760	0.4631	0.3585	0.2676	12
13	0.9964	0.9929	0.9872	0.9784	0.9658	0.9486	0.9261	0.8981	0.8645	0.7813	0.6815	0.5730	0.4644	0.3632	13
14	0.9986	0.9970	0.9943	0.9897	0.9827	0.9726	0.9585	0.9400	0.9165	0.8540	0.7720	0.6751	0.5704	0.4657	14
15	0.9995	0.9988	0.9976	0.9954	0.9918	0.9862	0.9780	0.9665	0.9513	0.9074	0.8444	0.7636	0.6694	0.5681	15
16	0.9998	0.9996	0.9990	0.9980	0.9963	0.9934	0.9889	0.9823	0.9730	0.9441	0.8987	0.8355	0.7559	0.6641	16
17	0.9999	0.9998	0.9996	0.9992	0.9984	0.9970	0.9947	0.9911	0.9857	0.9678	0.9370	0.8905	0.8272	0.7489	17
18	1.000	0.9999	0.9999	0.9997	0.9993	0.9987	0.9976	0.9957	0.9928	0.9823	0.9626	0.9302	0.8826	0.8195	18
19		1.000	1.000	0.9999	0.9997	0.9995	0.9989	0.9980	0.9965	0.9907	0.9787	0.9573	0.9235	0.8752	19
20				1.000	0.9999	0.9998	0.9996	0.9991	0.9984	0.9953	0.9884	0.9750	0.9521	0.9170	20
21					1.000	0.9999	0.9998	0.9996	0.9993	0.9977	0.9939	0.9859	0.9712	0.9469	21
22						1.000	0.9999	0.9999	0.9997	0.9990	0.9970	0.9924	0.9833	0.9673	22
23							1.000	0.9999	0.9999	0.9995	0.9985	0.9960	0.9907	0.9805	23
24								1.000	1.000	0.9998	0.9993	0.9980	0.9950	0.9888	24
25										0.9999	0.9997	0.9990	0.9974	0.9938	25
26										1.000	0.9999	0.9995	0.9987	0.9967	26
27											0.9999	0.9998	0.9994	0.9983	27
28											1.000	0.9999	0.9997	0.9991	28
29												1.000	0.9999	0.9996	29
30													0.9999	0.9998	30
31													1.000	0.9999	31
32														1.000	32

Table 3 Normal distribution function

The tabulated value is $\Phi(z) = P(Z \leq z)$,
where Z is the standardised normal random variable, $N(0, 1)$.

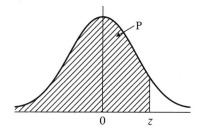

z	0.00	0.01	0.02	0.03	0.04	0.05	0.06	0.07	0.08	0.09	z
0.0	0.50000	0.50399	0.50798	0.51197	0.51595	0.51994	0.52392	0.52790	0.53188	0.53586	0.0
0.1	0.53983	0.54380	0.54776	0.55172	0.55567	0.55962	0.56356	0.56749	0.57142	0.57535	0.1
0.2	0.57926	0.58317	0.58706	0.59095	0.59483	0.59871	0.60257	0.60642	0.61026	0.61409	0.2
0.3	0.61791	0.62172	0.62552	0.62930	0.63307	0.63683	0.64058	0.64431	0.64803	0.65173	0.3
0.4	0.65542	0.65910	0.66276	0.66640	0.67003	0.67364	0.67724	0.68082	0.68439	0.68793	0.4
0.5	0.69146	0.69497	0.69847	0.70194	0.70540	0.70884	0.71226	0.71566	0.71904	0.72240	0.5
0.6	0.72575	0.72907	0.73237	0.73565	0.73891	0.74215	0.74537	0.74857	0.75175	0.75490	0.6
0.7	0.75804	0.76115	0.76424	0.76730	0.77035	0.77337	0.77637	0.77935	0.78230	0.78524	0.7
0.8	0.78814	0.79103	0.79389	0.79673	0.79955	0.80234	0.80511	0.80785	0.81057	0.81327	0.8
0.9	0.81594	0.81859	0.82121	0.82381	0.82639	0.82894	0.83147	0.83398	0.83646	0.83891	0.9
1.0	0.84134	0.84375	0.84614	0.84849	0.85083	0.85314	0.85543	0.85769	0.85993	0.86214	1.0
1.1	0.86433	0.86650	0.86864	0.87076	0.87286	0.87493	0.87698	0.87900	0.88100	0.88298	1.1
1.2	0.88493	0.88686	0.88877	0.89065	0.89251	0.89435	0.89617	0.89796	0.89973	0.90147	1.2
1.3	0.90320	0.90490	0.90658	0.90824	0.90988	0.91149	0.91309	0.91466	0.91621	0.91774	1.3
1.4	0.91924	0.92073	0.92220	0.92364	0.92507	0.92647	0.92785	0.92922	0.93056	0.93189	1.4
1.5	0.93319	0.93448	0.93574	0.93699	0.93822	0.93943	0.94062	0.94179	0.94295	0.94408	1.5
1.6	0.94520	0.94630	0.94738	0.94845	0.94950	0.95053	0.95154	0.95254	0.95352	0.95449	1.6
1.7	0.95543	0.95637	0.95728	0.95818	0.95907	0.95994	0.96080	0.96164	0.96246	0.96327	1.7
1.8	0.96407	0.96485	0.96562	0.96638	0.96712	0.96784	0.96856	0.96926	0.96995	0.97062	1.8
1.9	0.97128	0.97193	0.97257	0.97320	0.97381	0.97441	0.97500	0.97558	0.97615	0.97670	1.9
2.0	0.97725	0.97778	0.97831	0.97882	0.97932	0.97982	0.98030	0.98077	0.98124	0.98169	2.0
2.1	0.98214	0.98257	0.98300	0.98341	0.98382	0.98422	0.98461	0.98500	0.98537	0.98574	2.1
2.2	0.98610	0.98645	0.98679	0.98679	0.98713	0.98745	0.98778	0.98809	0.98840	0.98899	2.2
2.3	0.98928	0.98956	0.98983	0.99010	0.99036	0.99061	0.99086	0.99111	0.99134	0.99158	2.3
2.4	0.99180	0.99202	0.99224	0.99245	0.99266	0.99286	0.99305	0.99324	0.99343	0.99361	2.4
2.5	0.99379	0.99396	0.99413	0.99430	0.99446	0.99461	0.99477	0.99492	0.99506	0.99520	2.5
2.6	0.99534	0.99547	0.99560	0.99573	0.99585	0.99598	0.99609	0.99621	0.99632	0.99643	2.6
2.7	0.99653	0.99664	0.99674	0.99683	0.99693	0.99702	0.99711	0.99720	0.99728	0.99736	2.7
2.8	0.99744	0.99752	0.99760	0.99767	0.99774	0.99781	0.99788	0.99795	0.99801	0.99807	2.8
2.9	0.99813	0.99819	0.99825	0.99831	0.99836	0.99841	0.99846	0.99851	0.99856	0.99861	2.9
3.0	0.99865	0.99869	0.99874	0.99878	0.99882	0.99886	0.99889	0.99893	0.99896	0.99900	3.0
3.1	0.99903	0.99906	0.99910	0.99913	0.99916	0.99918	0.99921	0.99924	0.99926	0.99929	3.1
3.2	0.99931	0.99934	0.99936	0.99938	0.99940	0.99942	0.99944	0.99946	0.99948	0.99950	3.2
3.3	0.99952	0.99953	0.99955	0.99957	0.99958	0.99960	0.99961	0.99962	0.99964	0.99965	3.3
3.4	0.99966	0.99968	0.99969	0.99970	0.99971	0.99972	0.99973	0.99974	0.99975	0.99976	3.4
3.5	0.99977	0.99978	0.99978	0.99979	0.99980	0.99981	0.9981	0.99982	0.99983	0.99983	3.5
3.6	0.99984	0.99985	0.99985	0.99986	0.99986	0.99987	0.99987	0.99988	0.99988	0.99989	3.6
3.7	0.99989	0.99990	0.99990	0.99990	0.99991	0.99991	0.99992	0.99992	0.99992	0.99992	3.7
3.8	0.99993	0.99993	0.99993	0.99994	0.99994	0.99994	0.99994	0.99995	0.99995	0.99995	3.8
3.9	0.99995	0.99995	0.99996	0.99996	0.99996	0.99996	0.99996	0.99996	0.99997	0.99997	3.9

Table 4 Percentage points of the normal distribution

The table gives the values of z satisfying $P(Z \leq z) = p$,
where Z is the standardised normal random variable, $N(0, 1)$.

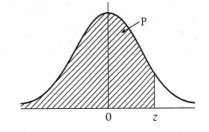

p	0.00	0.01	0.02	0.03	0.04	0.05	0.06	0.07	0.08	0.09	p
0.5	0.0000	0.0251	0.0502	0.0753	0.1004	0.1257	0.1510	0.1764	0.2019	0.2275	0.5
0.6	0.2533	0.2793	0.3055	0.3319	0.3585	0.3853	0.4125	0.4399	0.4677	0.4958	0.6
0.7	0.5244	0.5534	0.5828	0.6128	0.6433	0.6745	0.7063	0.7388	0.7722	0.8064	0.7
0.8	0.8416	0.8779	0.9154	0.9542	0.9945	1.0364	1.0803	1.1264	1.1750	1.2265	0.8
0.9	1.2816	1.3408	1.4051	1.4758	1.5548	1.6449	1.7507	1.8808	2.0537	2.3263	0.9

p	0.000	0.001	0.002	0.003	0.004	0.005	0.006	0.007	0.008	0.009	p
0.95	1.6449	1.6546	1.6646	1.6747	1.6849	1.6954	1.7060	1.7169	1.7279	1.7392	0.95
0.96	1.7507	1.7624	1.7744	1.7866	1.7991	1.8119	1.8250	1.8384	1.8522	1.8663	0.96
0.97	1.8808	1.8957	1.9110	1.9268	1.9431	1.9600	1.9774	1.9954	2.0141	2.0335	0.97
0.98	2.0537	2.0749	2.0969	2.1201	2.1444	2.1701	2.1973	2.2262	2.2571	2.2904	0.98
0.99	2.3263	2.3656	2.4089	2.4573	2.5121	2.5758	2.6521	2.7478	2.8782	3.0902	0.99

Answers

1 Collection of data

EXERCISE 1A

1 (a) Qualitative
  (b) Discrete quantitative
  (c) Continuous quantitative (but age in years is discrete)
  (d) Continuous quantitative
  (e) Qualitative
  (f) Discrete quantitative
  (g) Discrete quantitative
  (h) Continuous quantitative
  (i) Discrete quantitative
  (j) Qualitative.

EXERCISE 1B

1 In this question more than one answer is possible. You may find answers in addition to those given below.

  (a) The populations mentioned in the passage will relate to all first division matches in 1999/2000 and are either the results, the total number of goals scored or the amounts of time played before a goal is scored.

  (b) The total numbers of goals scored in each match played on the first Saturday of the season.

  (c) Mean number of goals per match for the 1999/2000 season.

  (d) Mean number of goals per match on the first Saturday of the season.

  (e) The result of matches (home, away or draw).

  (f) Number of goals scored in each match (the mean number of goals scored in each match is also discrete. For example if 100 matches were played the only possible outcomes are 0.00, 0.01, 0.02 ... . However, the steps will be so small that this could also be treated as a continuous variable).

  (g) The amounts of time played before a goal is scored.

  (h) The data the journalist collected in the 1999/2000 season.

  (i) The mean number of goals per game in the previous season.

EXERCISE 1C

1 **(a)** Place of birth; sex.

(b) Height, weight.

(c) Number of pupils weighed (age in years and months is also discrete although exact age is continuous).

(d) The data collected at the medical examination.

(e) The data collected by the class.

(f) The weights of all second year pupils.

(g) The weights of those second year pupils who were weighed.

(h) Mean weight of a sample of pupils.

EXERCISE 1D

1 Number books 0000 to 2124. Select four-digit random numbers. Ignore repeats and >2124. Continue until 20 numbers obtained. Select corresponding books.

2 Obtain list of employees names and number 000 to 711. Select three-digit random numbers. Ignore repeats and >711. Continue until six numbers obtained. Select corresponding employees.

3 Number the plants 00 to 27. Select two-digit random numbers. Ignore repeats and >27. Continue until eight numbers obtained. Select corresponding plants.

4 **(a)** There are 36 students ages. Allocate the number 00 to the first age (19), the number 01 to the second age (20 ... allocate the number 35 to the last age (27).

Select two digit random numbers ignoring >35

62 50 62 27 80 30 72 07 93 38 68 35 86 27 65 33
        27   38   19   27   27   41

The ages selected are 27, 38, 19, 27, 27, 41 (answers will vary according to your starting point in the random number tables).

(b) As in part (a) except that now repeats of random numbers are ignored.

62 50 62 27 80 30 72 07 93 38 68 35 86 27 65 33 40 18
        27   38   19   27   41   20

The ages selected are 27, 38, 19, 27, 41, 20.

5 Number rods 000 to 499. Select 3-digit random numbers. Ignore repeats and >499. Continue until 20 numbers selected. Choose corresponding rods.

6 **(a)** No, because not all sets of 40 customers can be chosen.

(b) Number names 0000 to 8949. Select 4-digit random numbers. Ignore repeats and >8949. Continue until 40 numbers selected. Choose corresponding names.

7 No, because not all sets of 128 electors can be selected.

2 Numerical measures

EXERCISE 2A

1 Mode 6, median 9, mean 10.

2 Mean 11.7, mode 9, median 10.

3 96 kg.

4 Mode 1, median 2, mean 2.02.

5 (a) 4   (b) 4   (c) 3.85.

6 (a) 10   (b) 10   (c) 8.42.

The highest mark is 10 (although also by far the most common). It would be more realistic if your measure of 'average' reflected the fact that no marks are greater than 10 but a substantial number of marks are less than 10. Mean is preferred.

7 {3, 3, 4, 5, 10}, {3, 3, 4, 6, 9}, {3, 3, 4, 7, 8}.

EXERCISE 2B

1 (a) 93.75 g   (b) 93.70 g.

2 (a) 62–63 s   (b) 62.5 s   (c) 62.2 s.

3 (a) 100–110   (b) 106.3 cm   (c) 105.8 cm not within tolerance.

4 (a) £176   (b) £183.

5 65.7 s.

EXERCISE 2C

1 9, 17.

2 33.5.

3 Median 19, lower quartile 16, upper quartile 21.

4 Lower quartile 9, upper quartile 16, median 13.

5 Lower quartile 9, upper quartile 15.5, median 13.

6 (a) 3.63 min   (b) 2.21 min, 5.66 min   (c) 3.45 min.

7 (a) £313,   (b) £203.

8 (a) $6 \leqslant x < 7$,   (b) £6.16,   (c) £1.56.

9 Mode 6, median 7, interquartile range 2.

10 {0, 1, 1, 1, 1, 1, 9} {1, 1, 1, 1, 1, 1, 8}.

EXERCISE 2D

1 3.63.

2 **A** mean 5, s.d. 1.58.   **B** mean 5, s.d. 3.16.

3 Mean 80, s.d. 4.63.

4 3.63 same as question 1 since variability of both samples is the same.

5 8.66 kg.

6 Mean 60.2, s.d. 18.8.

7 Mean 54.6 s, s.d. 8.33 s.

EXERCISE 2E

1 Mean 3.51, s.d. 1.73.

2 Mean 1.70, s.d. 1.61.

3 Mean 1.32, s.d. 1.83.

4 Mean 78.25, s.d. 7.66.

5 Mean 13.25, s.d. 5.18.

EXERCISE 2F

1 Mean 23, s.d. 4.

2 Mean 3.3 cm, s.d. 0.4 cm.

3 **(i)**   Mean £51, s.d. £18.

  (ii) Mean £31.50, s.d. £9.
       Mean £30, s.d. £12.

4 Median 0.235, interquartile range 0.063.

5 **(i)**   Mean 230 g, s.d. 63 g.

  (ii) Mean 223.8 g, s.d. 60 g.

6 **(i)**   Mean £12 400, s.d. £1000.

  (ii) Mean £12 535, s.d. £1090.

7 Mode 4, range 4.

EXERCISE 2G

1 A's batteries are to be preferred as they last longer and are less variable than B's.

2 **(a)** Line 1: mean 221, s.d. 104.2.
       Line 2: mean 206, s.d. 23.9.

  (b) Production line 1 has been going slightly longer on average between stoppages than production line 2. The intervals are much more variable for line 1.

3 Line 1: median 205, interquartile range 176.
Line 2: median 209, interquartile range 27.
Average as measured by median longer for line 2 but, as for the mean, the difference is small. Intervals much more variable for line 1 as in 2(b).

4 (a) A's ropes are strongest on average but are much more variable than B's or C's. C's ropes are much weaker than A's or B's on average. They are the least variable.

(b) High mean and low standard deviation is desirable. B is the best option.

5 (a) Moira: mean £3182, s.d £1843.
Everton: mean £3522, s.d. £637.
Syra: mean £2592, s.d. £280.

(b) Syra has lowest average sales with low variability. Moira has higher average sales but is very erratic. Everton is most satisfactory with highest average sales and less variability than Moira.

6 Moira: median £2750, interquartile range £2810.
Everton: median £3435, interquartile range £1000.
Syra: median £2595, interquartile range £460.
Comparison as for 5(b).

3 Pictorial representation of data

EXERCISE 3A

1
Bungalow	10
Detached house	19
Semi-detached house	31
Terraced house	31
Purpose built flat	7
Converted flat	3

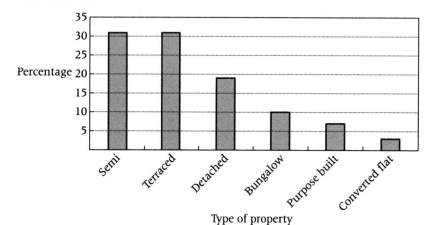

Type of property

2
Drink	Frequency	Angle
Coffee	8	125
Orange	5	78
Tea	10	157
Total	23	

Pie chart to show types of drinks sold from 11:00 to 12:00 hours

Drink	Frequency	Angle
Coffee	24	122
Orange	38	193
Tea	9	46
Total	71	

Drink sales from 12:00 to 13:00 hours

Note: radius for 11.00–12.00 is 0.7 cm

so radius for 12.00–13.00 is $\sqrt{\dfrac{71}{23}} \times 0.7 = 1.2$ cm

3 (a)

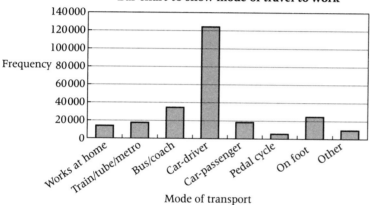

(b)

Works at home	10980
Train/tube/metro	13456
Bus/coach	22910
Car-driver	124293
Car-passenger	18106
Pedal cycle	6924
On foot	27056
Other	9129
Total	232854

Pie chart to show mode of transport

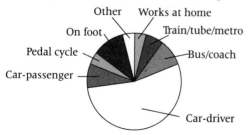

Pie chart illustrates the **proportion** of people in each category.

Bar chart illustrates the **number** of people in each category.

EXERCISE 3B

1

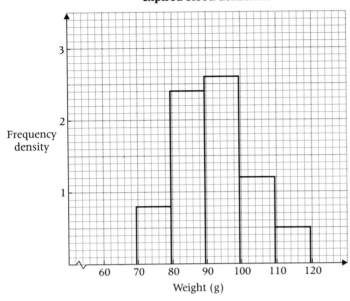

Histogram to show the weight of a sample of expired blood donations

Weight (g)	70–79	80–89	90–99	100–109	110–119
Frequency	8	24	26	12	5
Interval width	10	10	10	10	10
Frequency density	0.8	2.4	2.6	1.2	0.5

As all classes are of equal width the shape would be the same if frequency had been plotted on the vertical axis.

2

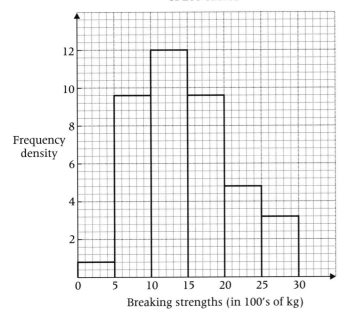

Histogram to show the breaking strain
of 200 cables

Breaking strengths (in 100's of kg)

Breaking strength	0–	5–	10–	15–	20–	25–30
Frequency	4	48	60	48	24	16
Interval width	5	5	5	5	5	5
Frequency density	0.8	9.6	12	9.6	4.8	3.2

All classes of equal width as in question 1.

3

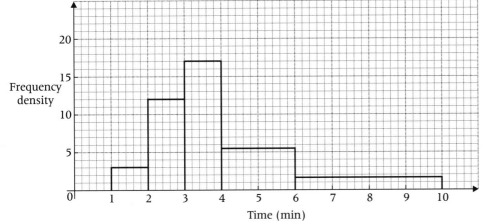

Histogram to show time taken to complete a jigsaw puzzle

Time (min)

Time in (min)	1–2	2–3	3–4	4–6	6–10
Frequency	3	12	17	11	7
Interval width	1	1	1	2	4
Frequency density	3	12	17	5.5	1.75

4

Age	0–4	5–15	16–24	25–44	45–74	75 and over•
Frequency	4462	12 214	10 898	19 309	22 820	3364
Interval width	5	11	9	20	30	25
Frequency density	892.4	1110.4	1210.9	965.45	760.6	134.56

• Assuming an upper age limit of 100 years.

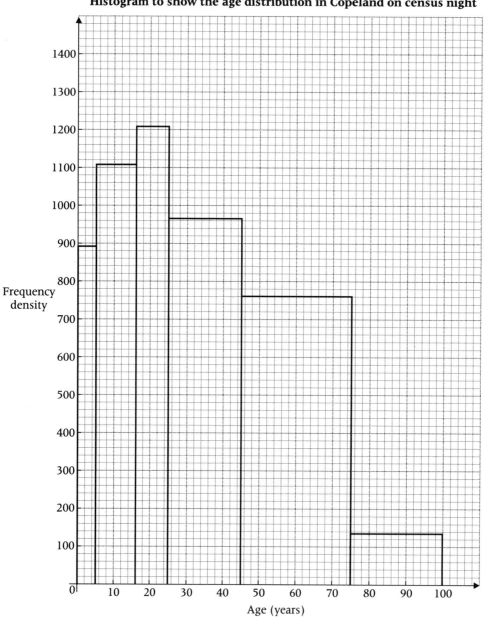

Histogram to show the age distribution in Copeland on census night

5 (a) A pie chart.

(b)

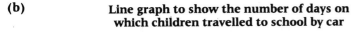

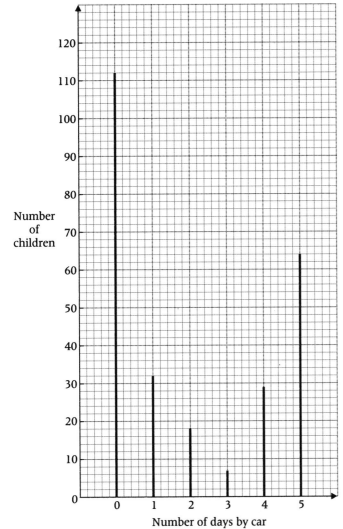

Note: in order to see the line for 0 days it has been moved across from where the origin usually is.

Distribution is U-shaped, shows children tend to travel by car either every day or not at all.

(c)

Time (min)	0.5–15.5	15.5–25.5	25.5–35.5	35.5–55.5	55.5–90.5
Frequency	129	52	34	26	21
Interval width	15	10	10	20	35
Frequency density	8.6	5.2	3.4	1.3	0.6

Histogram to show the journey times

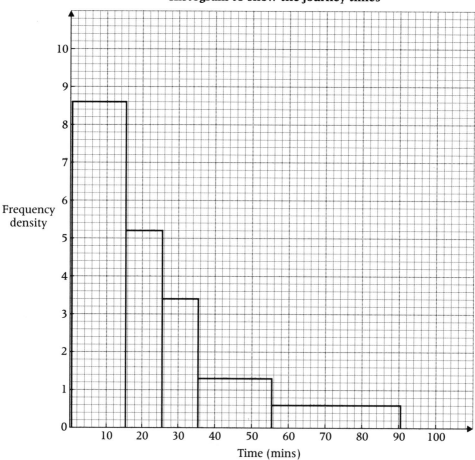

EXERCISE 3C

1 When in order the data read

48 49 59 59 61 63 66 67 70 72

74 74 77 81 82 86 102 165 229

(a) the median is 72

(b) the lower quartile is 61, the upper quartile is 82

(c) boundaries for outliers are $61 - 1.5 \times (82 - 61) = 29.5$ and
$82 + 1.5 \times (82 - 61) = 113.5$, so 165 and 229 are outliers.

(d)

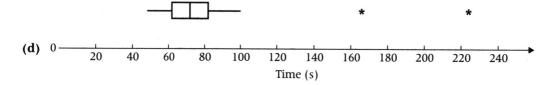

2 When sorted the data read

> 57.7 58.1 58.2 58.4 58.7 58.8 58.9 59.3
>
> 59.4 59.4 59.8 60.1 60.3 60.4 61.0

(a) For Brand A, smallest value 57.7, lower quartile 58.4, median 59.3, upper quartile 60.1, largest value 61.0.

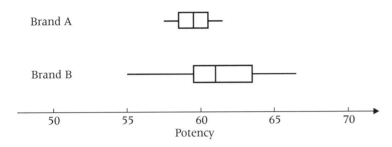

(b) The median potency for Brand B is greater than for Brand A, i.e. on average Brand B is more potent.

The variability of the potency for Brand A is smaller than that for Brand B.

3 (a) Median waiting time is the same for both offices.

B has three large outliers.

Ignoring these B has lower mean and less variability.

A is positive skew.

B is negative skew.

(b) (i) The outliers were due to a cause outside post office's control – choose B for quicker service.

(ii) Outliers post office's responsibility, may recur. B generally quicker but there may be some very long waits. A avoids the very long waits.

4 (a) C's range (variability) is greater than that of D.

C's median time is greater than that of D.

C's times have positive skew, D's times have negative skew.

D will always beat C in a race on the basis of times in the box-and-whisker plot.

(b) (i) Choose A, since C's times are almost always longer than A's.

(ii) Choose B, since B is more likely to produce a very short time than A. A will hardly ever have a time overlapping the times taken by D.

(c) A.

EXERCISE 3D

1

Upper boundary	19.5	22.5	25.5	28.5	31.5	34.5
Cumulative frequency	0	3	9	21	30	32

(a)

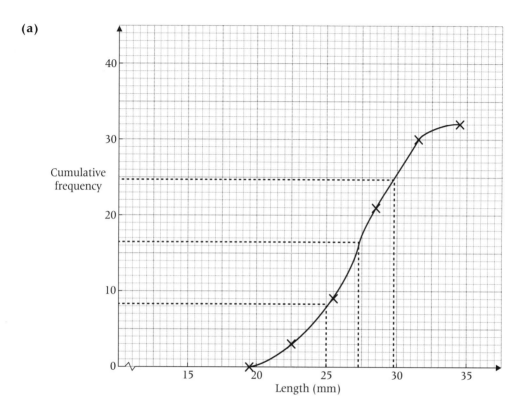

(b) median $= \dfrac{32 + 1}{2}$th $=$ 16.5th reading $=$ **27.2** mm

lower quartile $= \dfrac{32 + 1}{4}$th $=$ 8.25th $=$ **25.0** mm

upper quartile $= \dfrac{3(32 + 1)}{4}$th $=$ 24.75th $=$ **29.8** mm

Answers estimated from graph, there may be disagreement about the third significant figure.

2

upper boundary	399.5	900.5	1500.5	3500.5	8000.5	20000.5
cumulative frequency	0	5	14	54	99	159

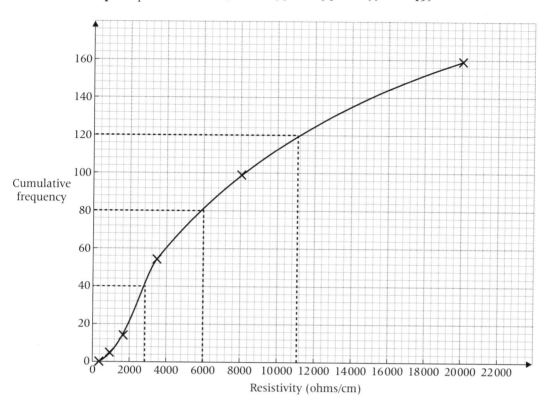

median = $\dfrac{159 + 1}{2}$th = 80th = **6000** ohms/cm

lower quartile = $\dfrac{159 + 1}{4}$th = 40th = **2800** ohms/cm

upper quartile = $\dfrac{3(159 + 1)}{4}$th = 120th = **11100** ohms/cm

3

upper boundary	0	400	800	1200	1600	2000	3000	4000	5000	6000	8000
cumulative frequency	0	25	56	100	157	231	389	444	470	488	500

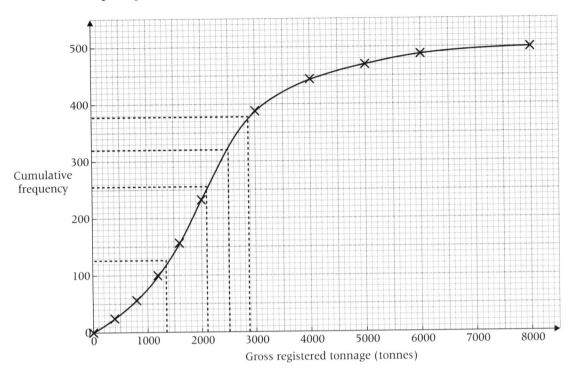

Gross registered tonnage (tonnes)

(a) median = 500 + 1\2th = 250.5th = **2100** tonnes

(b) lower quartile = 125.25th = **1380** tonnes

upper quartile = 375.75th = **2880** tonnes

∴ interquartile range = 2880 − 1380
= **1500** tonnes

(c) % exceeding 2500 tonnes = $\dfrac{(500 - 320)}{500} \times 100 = \textbf{36\%}$

EXERCISE 3E

1

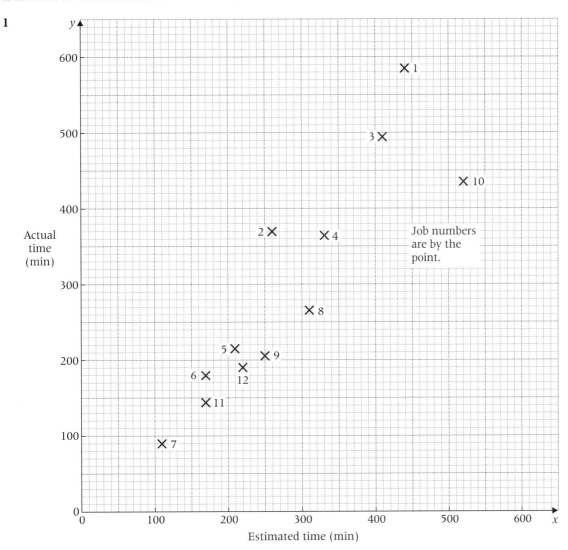

Job numbers
are by the
point.

2

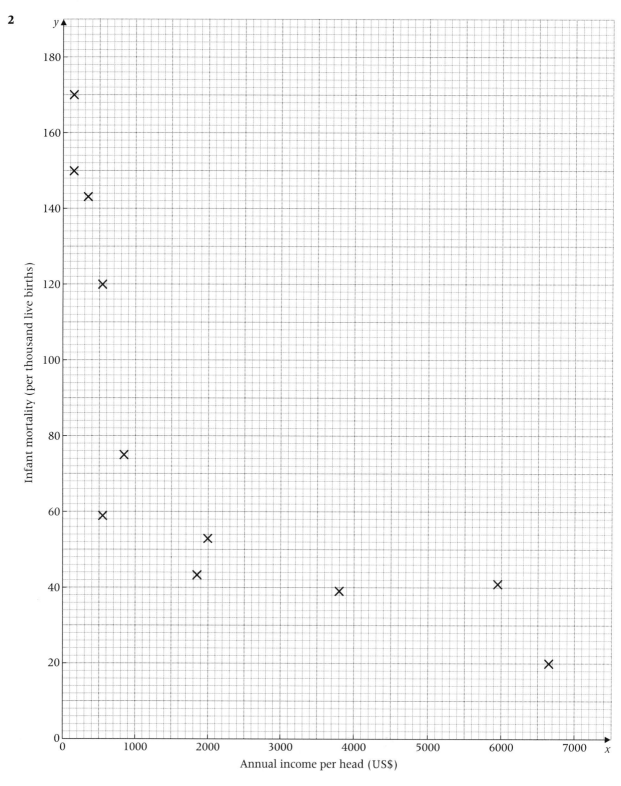

Infant mortality appears to decline as income per head increases.
However, this tendency is much more marked in the low income than
in the high income group of countries.

MIXED EXERCISE

1

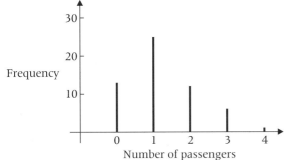

2

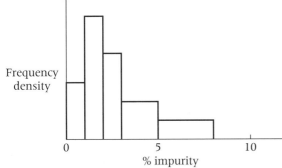

Poorest 10% eat more white bread and potatoes and less fruit and vegetables than the richest 10%.

3

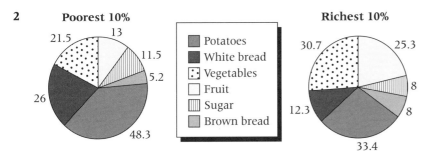

4 (a) (i) 122 seconds,

(ii) 132 and 109 seconds,

(b) 16, 255 and 298 are outliers.

(c)

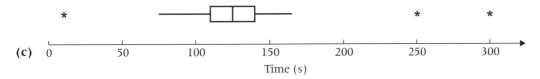

5

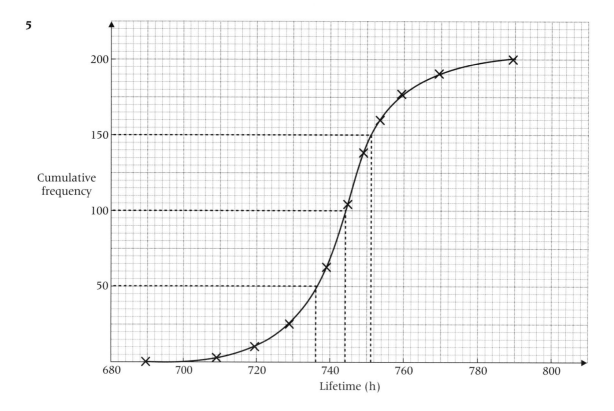

Estimated median 744 hours, lower quartile 736 hours, upper quartile
752 hours.

6

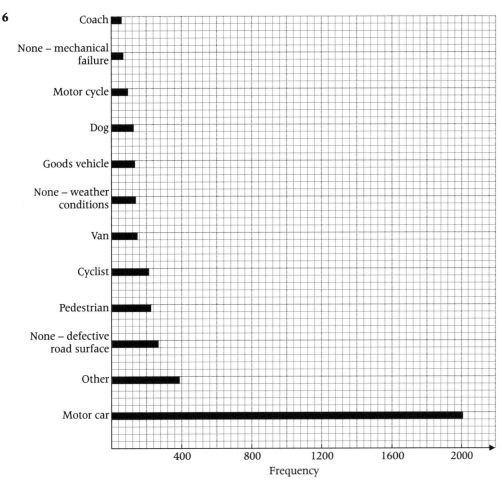

7 (a)

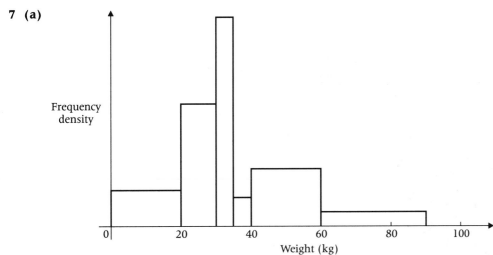

(b) Bimodal distribution, probably because passengers who would have taken just over 35 kg of luggage have taken less to avoid excess charge.

(c)

(d) The box-and-whisker plot does not illustrate the feature described in **(b)**. The histogram is a better diagram for this data.

8 (a)

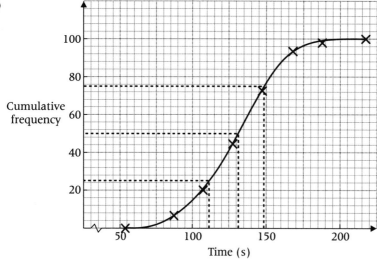

(b) Estimated median 131 seconds, interquartile range 38 seconds.

(c) Second jigsaw takes longer on average so more difficult, also times taken are more variable.

(d) 137 seconds.

It is possible to estimate the median of the times of the 116 children. It is not possible to calculate the arithmetic mean as the times for the slowest 16 children are unknown.

9 (a) A has lowest variability, median just over 5, apart from 4 outliers B has low variability and lowest median, C has large variability and median close to 6, it is negative skew.

(b) Choose A as it has low variability and no outliers. The mean can be adjusted to bring it to the required value.

10 (a)

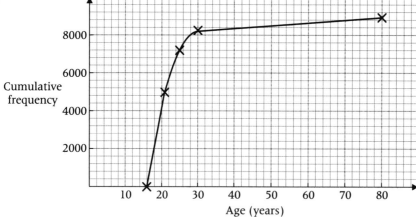

For the diagram it has been assumed that the oldest age of marriage is 80 years.

(b) For this data it is easiest to estimate the median and interquartile numerically rather than using the diagram. Estimated median 20.3 years, interquartile range 5.3 years.

(c) Age of wife at marriage for marriages ending in divorce in 1990 is slightly higher on average, and more variable than in 1977. Median and interquartile range can be found without knowing the ages of '30/over' group.

(d) Average age at marriage of wife for marriage that ended in divorce in 1990 is much lower than for all marriages in 1990.

11

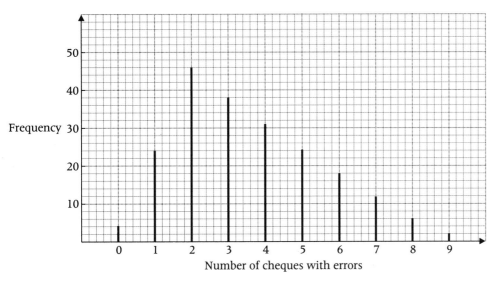

Modal value 2, median 3, mean 3.53, standard deviation 1.99.
0.799 0.769 similar values, both positive.
long tail to the right.

12

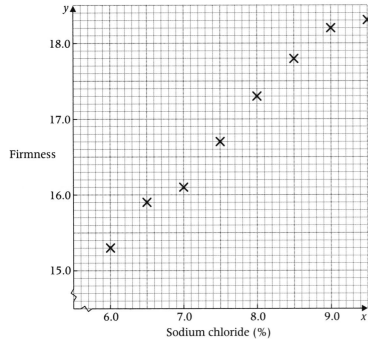

13

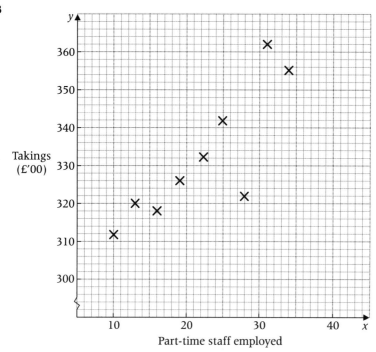

Part-time staff employed

14 (a) 190 seconds, 379 and 82 seconds.

(b)

(c)

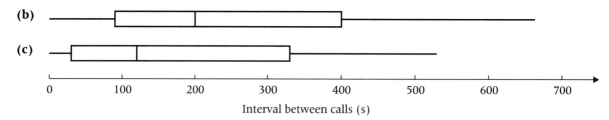

Interval between calls (s)

(d) First school has more variable and, on average, longer intervals between calls. Both distributions are positive skew.

4 Probability

EXERCISE 4A

1 (a) 0.05, **(b)** 0.25, **(c)** 0.3, **(d)** 0.1.

2 (a) $\frac{1}{7}$, **(b)** $\frac{2}{7}$, **(c)** $\frac{4}{7}$.

3 (a) $\frac{1}{7}$, **(b)** $\frac{4}{7}$, **(c)** $\frac{5}{7}$.

4 (a) $\frac{7}{15}$, **(b)** $\frac{1}{3}$, **(c)** $\frac{4}{5}$, **(d)** 0. **(e)** $\frac{1}{3}$.

5 (a) $\frac{1}{11}$, **(b)** $\frac{3}{11}$, **(c)** $\frac{9}{11}$, **(d)** $\frac{3}{11}$.

EXERCISE 4B

1 0.4.

2 0.78.

3 **(a)** 0.6, **(b)** 0.5, **(c)** 0.9.

4 **(a)** 0.7, **(b)** 0.4, **(c)** 0.8, **(d)** 0.7. **(e)** 0.2.

5 **(a)** $\frac{27}{35}$, **(b)** $\frac{32}{35}$, **(c)** $\frac{3}{35}$, **(d)** $\frac{23}{35}$.

6 **(a)** **(i)** A,B, **(ii)** A,C or B,C

  (b) the event that the baby will not have blue eyes.

7 **(a)** A, **(b)** yes, **(c)** B,C.

EXERCISE 4C

1 0.42.

2 0.022.

3 0.25.

4 **(a)** 0.01, **(b)** 0.81.

5 0.125.

EXERCISE 4D

Answers to three significant figures.

1 **(a)** 0.165, **(b)** 0.48, **(c)** 0.615.

2 **(a)** **(i)** 0.846, **(ii)** 0.147, **(iii)** 0.154.

  (b) **(i)** 0.779, **(ii)** 0.203, **(iii)** 0.0182.

3 **(a)** **(i)** 0.0625, **(ii)** 0.375.

  (b) **(i)** 0.422, **(ii)** 0.141, **(iii)** 0.156,
  (iv) 0.844.

  (c) 0.316.

4 **(a)** **(i)** 0.64, **(ii)** 0.24, **(iii)** 0.665,
  (iv) 0.9025, **(v)** 0.335.

  (b) **(i)** 0.512, **(ii)** 0.288, **(iii)** 0.008,
  (iv) 0.5155, **(v)** 0.036.

EXERCISE 4E

1 **(a)** $\frac{5}{8}$, **(b)** $\frac{2}{3}$, **(c)** $\frac{3}{8}$, **(d)** $\frac{47}{120}$, **(e)** $\frac{9}{10}$,

  (f) $\frac{47}{80}$, **(g)** $\frac{28}{75}$, **(h)** $\frac{7}{10}$, **(i)** $\frac{33}{80}$, **(j)** $\frac{7}{30}$.

2 (a) $\frac{23}{30}$,   (b) $\frac{121}{150}$,   (c) $\frac{25}{29}$,   (d) $\frac{119}{150}$,   (e) $\frac{1}{6}$,

  (f) $\frac{3}{5}$,   (g) $\frac{2}{5}$,   (h) $\frac{90}{121}$,   (i) $\frac{31}{35}$.

3 (a) $\frac{4}{9}$,   (b) $\frac{2}{3}$,   (c) $\frac{5}{9}$,   (d) $\frac{2}{15}$,   (e) $\frac{4}{5}$,

  (f) $\frac{13}{23}$,   (g) $\frac{1}{5}$,   (h) $\frac{7}{10}$,   (i) 0.

A and C not independent.

EXERCISE 4F

(All answers to three significant figures.)

1 (a) 0.195,   (b) 0.499.

2 (i) 0.357,   (ii) 0.536.

3 (a) (i) 0.0152,   (ii) 0.182,   (iii) 0.227.
  (b) (i) 0.0909,   (ii) 0.136,   (iii) 0.409,   (iv) 0.218.

4 (a) 0.0480, (b) 0.506,   (c) 0.305.

5 (i) 0.196,   (ii) 0.0240,   (iii) 0.0840,   (iv) 0.0960,
  (v) 0.240,   (vi) 0.228,   (vii) 0.192.

6 (i) 0.0461,   (ii) 0.233,   (iii) 0.0121,   (iv) 0.279,
  (v) 0.0101,   (vi) 0.266,   (vii) 0.152.

MIXED EXERCISE

1 (a) $\frac{1}{343}$,   (b) $\frac{1}{49}$,   (c) $\frac{30}{49}$,   (d) $\frac{8}{343}$,   (e) 6.

2 (a) (i) 0.576,   (ii) 0.932,   (b) 0.912.

3 (i) 0.0429,   (ii) 0.142,   (iii) 0.1215,   (iv) 0.189,
  (v) 0.334.

4 (a) (i) 0.36,   (ii) 0.09,   (iii) 0.89,   (iv) 0.36
  (b) $R' \cap T'$ [or $(R \cup T)'$].

5 (a) (i) 0.343,   (ii) 0.441,
  (b) (i) 0.063,   (ii) 0.09,   (c) 0.141.

6 (a) (i) 0.12,   (ii) 0.0455,   (iii) 0.318,   (iv) 0.0133,
      (v) 0.893.
  (b) 0.0827

7 (a) (i) 0.462,   (ii) 0.223,   (iii) 0.808,   (iv) 0.517.
  (b) (i) 0.1575,   (ii) 0.153,
  (c) 0.224.

5 Binomial distribution

EXERCISE 5A

1

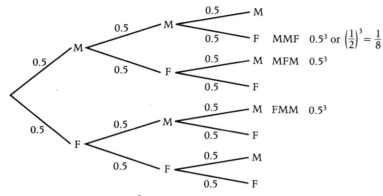

$P(2 \text{ boys}) = 0.5^3 + 0.5^3 + 0.5^3 \text{ or } \frac{3}{8}.$

2

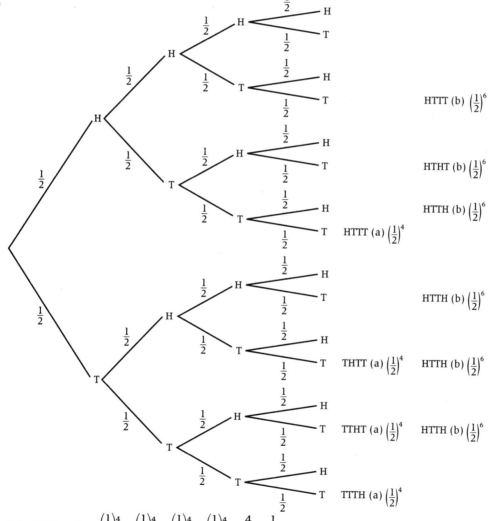

(a) $P(1 \text{ head}) = \left(\frac{1}{2}\right)^4 + \left(\frac{1}{2}\right)^4 + \left(\frac{1}{2}\right)^4 + \left(\frac{1}{2}\right)^4 = \frac{4}{16} = \frac{1}{4}$

(b) $P(2 \text{ heads}) = \left(\frac{1}{2}\right)^4 + \left(\frac{1}{2}\right)^4 + \left(\frac{1}{2}\right)^4 + \left(\frac{1}{2}\right)^4 + \left(\frac{1}{2}\right)^4 + \left(\frac{1}{2}\right)^4 = \frac{6}{16} = \frac{3}{8}$

...

3 $0.4 \times 0.4 \times 0.4 = 0.064$
not   not   not
light light light

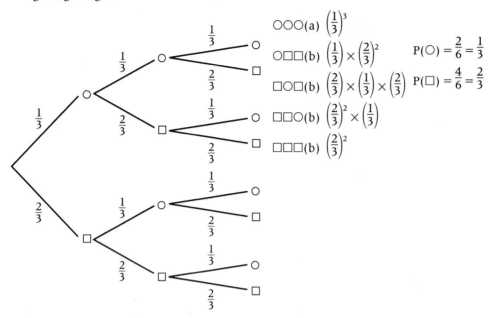

$$\text{OOO(a)} \ \left(\tfrac{1}{3}\right)^3$$
$$\text{O}\square\square\text{(b)} \ \left(\tfrac{1}{3}\right) \times \left(\tfrac{2}{3}\right)^2 \qquad P(\text{O}) = \tfrac{2}{6} = \tfrac{1}{3}$$
$$\square\text{OO(b)} \ \left(\tfrac{2}{3}\right) \times \left(\tfrac{1}{3}\right) \times \left(\tfrac{2}{3}\right) \quad P(\square) = \tfrac{4}{6} = \tfrac{2}{3}$$
$$\square\square\text{O(b)} \ \left(\tfrac{2}{3}\right)^2 \times \left(\tfrac{1}{3}\right)$$
$$\square\square\square\text{(b)} \ \left(\tfrac{2}{3}\right)^2$$

4 (a) $P(\text{no squares}) = \tfrac{1}{3} \times \tfrac{1}{3} \times \tfrac{1}{3} = \tfrac{1}{27}$

(b) $P(\text{2 or 3 squares}) = \tfrac{1}{3} \times \left(\tfrac{2}{3}\right)^2 + \tfrac{1}{3} \times \left(\tfrac{2}{3}\right)^2 + \tfrac{1}{3} \times \left(\tfrac{2}{3}\right)^2 + \left(\tfrac{2}{3}\right)^3$

$$= \tfrac{4}{27} + \tfrac{4}{27} + \tfrac{4}{27} + \tfrac{8}{27}$$

$$= \tfrac{20}{27}$$

(At least two squares means two or three.)

EXERCISE 5B

1 $n = 4, p = \tfrac{1}{4}$, $P(X = 2) = \binom{4}{2}\left(\tfrac{1}{4}\right)^2\left(\tfrac{3}{4}\right)^2 = 6 \times \tfrac{1}{16} \times \tfrac{9}{16} = \tfrac{27}{128}$

2 $n = 5, p = \tfrac{3}{5}$, $P(X = 4) = \binom{5}{4}\left(\tfrac{3}{5}\right)^4\left(\tfrac{2}{5}\right)^1 = 5 \times \tfrac{81}{625} \times \tfrac{2}{5} = \tfrac{162}{625}$

3 $n = 10, p = 0.4$, $P(X = 3) = \binom{10}{3}\left(0.4\right)^3\left(0.6\right)^7 = 120 \times 0.064 \times 0.6^7$

$= 0.215$

4 $n = 10, p = 0.2$, $P(X = 3) = \binom{10}{3}\left(0.2\right)^3\left(0.8\right)^7 = 120 \times 0.008 \times 0.8^7$

$= 0.201$

5 $n = 10, p = 0.3$, $P(X = 4) = \binom{10}{4}\left(0.3\right)^4\left(0.7\right)^6 = 210 \times 0.3^4 \times 0.7^6$

$= 0.200$

6 $n = 20$, $p = 0.153$, $P(X = 2) = \binom{20}{2}(0.15)^2(0.85)^{18}$

$= 190 \times 0.15^2 \times 0.85^{18} = 0.229$

7 $n = 30$, $p = 0.2$, $P(X = 8) = \binom{30}{8}(0.2)^8(0.8)^{22} = 5852925 \times 0.2^8 \times 0.8^{22}$

$= 0.111$

8 $n = 25$, $p = 0.1$, $P(X = 2) = \binom{25}{2}(0.1)^2(0.9)^{23} = 300 \times 0.01 \times 0.9^{23}$

$= 0.266$

EXERCISE 5C

Answers from tables have been given to four decimal places. However three significant figures is sufficient.

1 $n = 20$, $p = 0.2$, $X \sim B(20, 0.2)$

    (a) $P(X \leq 3) = 0.4114$

    (b) $P(X < 3) = P(X \leq 2) = 0.2061$

    (c) $P(X > 1) = 1 - P(X \leq 1) = 1 - 0.0692 = 0.9308$

0, 1, 2, 3, |4 ...
0, 1, 2,| 3, 4 ...
0, 1,|2, 3, 4 ...
X ≤ 1   X > 1

2 $n = 8$, $p = \frac{2}{5}$, $X \sim B(8, 0.4)$

    (a) $P(X < 3) = P(X \leq 2) = 0.3154$

    (b) $P(X \geq 2) = 1 - P(X \leq 1) = 1 - 0.1064 = 0.8936$

    (c) $P(X = 0) = 0.0168$

0, 1, 2,|3, 4 ...
0, 1,|2, 3, 4 ...
X ≤ 1   X ≥ 2

3 $n = 25$, $p = \frac{1}{5} = 0.2$, $X \sim B(25, 0.2)$

    (a) $P(X > 5) = 1 - P(X \leq 5) = 1 - 0.6167 = 0.3833$

    (b) $P(X \geq 6) = 1 - P(X \leq 5) = 0.3833$

    at least 6 = 6 or more = more than 5 see (a)

    (c) $P(X < 4) = P(X \leq 3) = 0.2340$

0, 1, 2, 3, 4, 5,|6, 7 ...
X ≤ 5   X > 5

0, 1, 2, 3,|4, 5, 6, 7 ...

4 $n = 25$, $p = 0.3$, $X \sim B(25, 0.3)$

    (a) $P(X < 5) = P(X \leq 4) = 0.0905$

    (b) $P(X \leq 8) = 0.6769$
        no more than 8 = 8 or less

    (c) $P(X > 3) = 1 - P(X \leq 3) = 1 - 0.0332 = 0.9668$

0, 1, 2, 3, 4,|5, 6, 7, 8

0, 1, 2, 3, 4, 5, 6, 7, 8,|9

0, 1, 2, 3,|4, 5, 6, 7, 8, 9 ...
X ≤ 3   X > 3

5 $n = 20$, $p = \frac{3}{100} = 0.03$, $X \sim B(20, 0.03)$

    (a) $P(X = 0) = 0.5438$

    (b) $P(X \geq 2) = 1 - P(X \leq 1) = 1 - 0.8802 = 0.1198$

    (c) $P(X < 3) = P(X \leq 2) = 0.9790$

    (d) $P(X = 1) = P(X \leq 1) = P(X = 0) = 0.8802 - 0.5438 = 0.3364$

        or $\binom{20}{1}(0.03)^1(0.97)^{19} = 0.336$ (three significant figures)

0, 1,|2, 3, 4

0, 1, 2,|3, 4

0, 1,|2, 3, 4

6 $n = 25$, $p = 0.15$, $X \sim B(25, 0.15)$

    (a) $P(X \geq 4) = 1 - P(X \leq 3) = 1 - 0.4711 = 0.5289$

    (b) $P(X \leq 5) = 0.8385$
         no more than $5 = 5$ or less

    (c) $P(5 \leq X \leq 10) = P(X \leq 10) - P(X \leq 4) = 0.9995 - 0.6821 = 0.3174$

```
0, 1, 2, 3,|4, 5, 6, 7, 8, 9, 10 ...
X ≤ 3    X ≥ 4
```

```
0, 1, 2, 3, 4,|5, 6, 7, 8, 9, 10,|11 ...
   X ≤ 4         5 ≤ X ≤ 10
```

7 $n = 12$, $p = 0.2$, $X \sim B(12, 0.2)$

    (a) $P(X \leq 3) = 0.7946$

    (b) $P(X = 3) = 0.2362 = P(X \leq 3) - P(X \leq 2)$

    (c) $P(X \leq 1) = 0.2749$
         no more than $1 = 1$ or less

    (d) $P(\geq 10 \text{ agree}) = P(10, 11, 12 \text{ agree}) = P(0, 1, 2 \text{ refuse})$
         $P(X \leq 2) = 0.5583$

```
0, 1, 2,|3,|4, 5
```

8 $n = 40$, $p = 0.15$, $X \sim B(40, 0.15)$

    (a) $P(X \leq 5) = 0.4325$

    (b) $P(X = 7) = P(X \leq 7) - P(X \leq 6) = 0.7359 - 0.6067 = 0.1492$

    (c) $P(4 \leq X \leq 10) = P(X \leq 10) - P(X \leq 3) = 0.9701 - 0.1302 = 0.8399$

    (d) $P(36, 37, 38, 39, 40 \text{ agree}) = P(0, 1, 2, 3, 4 \text{ decline})$
         $P(X \leq 4) = 0.2633$

```
0, 1, 2, 3, 4, 5, 6,|7,|8 ...
```

```
0, 1, 2, 3,|4, 5, 6, 7, 8, 9, 10,|11
   X ≤ 3        4 ≤ X ≤ 10
```

EXERCISE 5D

1 **(a)** $W \sim B(20, 0.08)$

        (i) $P(W = 0) = 0.1887$

        (ii) $P(W \geq 2) = 1 - P(W \leq 1) = 1 - 0.5169 = 0.4831$

        (iii) $P(W = 2) = P(W \leq 2) - P(W \leq 1) = 0.7879 - 0.5169 = 0.2710$

    (b) $R \sim B(22, 0.08)$

$$P(R \geq 2) = 1 - P(R = 1) - P(R = 0)$$
$$= 1 - \binom{22}{1}(0.08)(0.92)^{21} - (0.92)^{22}$$
$$= 1 - 0.3055 - 0.1597 = 0.5348$$

2 **(a)** $n = 40$, $p = 0.15$, $X \sim B(40, 0.15)$

        (i) $P(X \leq 5) = 0.4325$

        (ii) $P(X = 7) = P(X \leq 7) - P(X \leq 6) = 0.7559 - 0.6067 = 0.1492$

        (iii) $P(X > 4) = 1 - P(X \leq 4) = 1 - 0.2633 = 0.7367$

    (b) $n = 25$, $p = 0.2$, $X \sim B(25, 0.2)$

        (i) $P(X \geq 3) = 1 - P(X \leq 2) = 1 - 0.0982 = 0.9018$

        (ii) $P(X \leq 5) = 0.6167$

    (c) X is not binomial, since the total number of trials is not fixed.

```
0, 1, 2, 3, 4,|5, 6, ...
   X ≤ 4    X > 4
```

```
0, 1, 2,|3, 4 ...
X ≤ 2   X ≥ 3
```

3 $n = 25$, $p = \dfrac{1}{5} = 0.2$, $X \sim B(25, 0.2)$

    (a) **(i)** $P(\text{marks} \leq 8) = P(X \leq 8) = 0.9532$

  (ii) P(marks > 12) = P(X > 12) = 1 − P($X \le$ 12)

             = 1 − 0.9996 = 0.0004

  (iii) P(10 marks) = P(X = 10) = P($X \le$ 10) − P($X \le$ 9)

           = 0.9944 − 0.9827 = 0.0117 (direct calculation gives 0.0118)

(b) Mean mark = np = 25 × 0.2 = 5

  (i) 0

  (ii) 75

(c) 20

4 $X \sim B(20, 0.4)$

(a) P($X \ge$ 10) = 1 − P($X \le$ 9) = 1 − 0.7553 = 0.2447

(b) P(yes) = 0.6 too big for tables

P(no) = 0.4 use p = 0.4

P($\ge$ 10 say 'yes')

= P($\le$ 10 say 'no') $X \sim B(20, 0.4)$ for 'no'

= 0.8725

(c) Union meeting is likely to influence opinions and

  (i) probability of voting 'Yes' may be different for those attending meeting.

  (iii) Trials are not independent as a show of hands is used. Drivers may be influenced by how friends vote.

6 Poisson distribution

Answers have been given to four decimal places. However to three significant figures is sufficient.

EXERCISE 6A

1 (a) 0.8472, **(b)** 0.8488, **(c)** 0.4457,
  (d) 0.5928, **(e)** 0.1377.

2 (a) 0.2381, **(b)** 0.8893, **(c)** 0.1954,
  (d) 0.7108, **(e)** 0.3712.

3 (a) 0.1048, **(b)** 0.0895, **(c)** 0.1013,
  (d) 0.6894, **(e)** 0.7720.

4 (a) 0.0403, **(b)** 0.7479, **(c)** 0.7313,
  (d) 0.1067, **(e)** 0.2480.

EXERCISE 6B

1 3.

2 (a) 13, **(b)** 15, **(c)** 17.

3 (a) 17, **(b)** 21.

4 (a) 20, **(b)** 23, **(c)** 24.

EXERCISE 6C

1 (a) 0.00499,   (b) 0.0265,   (c) 0.0701,
   (d) 0.124,   (e) 0.775,   (f) 0.220.

2 (a) 0.0523,   (b) 0.154,   (c) 0.228,
   (d) 0.224,   (e) 0.793,   (f) 0.606.

3 (a) 0.432,   (b) 0.363,   (c) 0.152,
   (d) 0.0426,   (e) 0.0533,   (f) 0.558.

EXERCISE 6D

1 (a) 0.3374,   (b) 0.2560,   (c) 0.1377,
   (d) 0.5928.

2 (a) 0.1665,   (b) 0.0985,   (c) 0.6575,
   (d) 0.0479,   (e) 0.1757.

3 (a) 0.9921,   (b) 0.1429,   (c) 0.6512,
   (d) 0.2424.

4 (a) 0.9909,   (b) 0.5940,   (c) 0.6919,
   (d) 0.2224,   (e) 0.0651.

5 (a) 0.2090,   (b) 0.1378,   (c) 0.3712,
   (d) 0.7668,   (e) 0.8444,   (f) 0.4075.

EXERCISE 6E

(a) Yes, Poisson likely to be valid.

(b) Where there is congestion lorries won't 'flow' independently so Poisson won't be valid.

(c) Unlikely as cars won't pass the point independently.

(d) Not Poisson, since there is an upper limit on the number of components.

(e) Yes, Poisson likely to be valid.

(f) Likely to be Poisson (although near Christmas the average rate is likely to change).

(g) Poisson likely.

(h) Not Poisson, mean not constant.

(i) Poisson likely.

(j) Poisson likely.

(k) If more than one person injured in an accident, injuries not independent, probably not Poisson.

MIXED EXERCISE

1 (a) 0.1653,   (b) 0.2694.

2 (a) 0.7787,   (b) 0.1254.

3 0.2213.

4 (a) (i) 0.5768, **(ii)** 0.9881, **(iii)** 0.0116

(b) 18.

5 (a) 0.2419, **(b)** 0.0424

Rate 1.6 per hour.

6 (a) The rate of arrival will vary – probably higher near 'mealtimes', lower at night. Not Poisson.

(b) Not Poisson, calls can't arrive independently and at random.

(c) Not Poisson since there is an upper limit of 150.

7 (a) (i) 0.3027, **(ii)** 0.6665, **(iii)** 0.0273

(b) 0.0290

(c) Demand may vary its rate with the seasons or for different days of the week.

8 (a) 0.5305,

(b) The average rate will vary e.g. more on birthdays or near Christmas.

9 (a) (i) 0.7306, **(ii)** 5.

(b) (i) Poisson. Conditions fulfilled.
(ii) Not Poisson. Calls interfere with each other. Not random.
(iii) Not Poisson. Mean not constant.

7 Normal distribution

EXERCISE 7A

1 (a) 0.891, **(b)** 0.834, **(c)** 0.968,
(d) 0.663, **(e)** 0.536, **(f)** 0.942,
(g) 0.974, **(h)** 0.726, **(i)** 0.991,
(j) 0.853.

EXERCISE 7B

1 (a) 0.0869, **(b)** 0.281, **(c)** 0.109,
(d) 0.195, **(e)** 0.374, **(f)** 0.0262,
(g) 0.00889, **(h)** 0.258, **(i)** 0.464,
(j) 0.0885.

EXERCISE 7C

1 (a) 0.823, **(b)** 0.281, **(c)** 0.862,
(d) 0.681, **(e)** 0.326, **(f)** 0.626,
(g) 0.261, **(h)** 0.802, **(i)** 0.773,
(j) 0.330.

EXERCISE 7D

1. (a) 0.209,   (b) 0.0948,   (c) 0.516,

   (d) 0.877,   (e) 0.112,   (f) 0.0214,

   (g) 0.888,   (h) 0.00361,   (i) 0.0792,

   (j) 0.968.

EXERCISE 7E

1. (a) 1.4,   (b) 0.6,   (c) −0.8,

   (d) −1.6,   (e) 2.1.

2. (a) 0.652,

   (b) −1.370,

   (c) 1.348,

   (d) −1.804.

3. (a) 1.167,

   (b) −0.167,

   (c) 0.667,

   (d) −1.167.

EXERCISE 7F

1. (a) 0.663,   (b) 0.104,   (c) 0.134,

   (d) 0.943,   (e) 0.396,   (f) 0.256.

2. (a) 0.779,   (b) 0.663,   (c) 0.0336,

   (d) 0.0367,   (e) 0.913,   (f) 0.295.

3. (a) 0.245,   (b) 0.755,   (c) 0.832,

   (d) 0.152,   (e) 0.659,   (f) 0.603.

4. (a) 0.637,   (b) 0.0838,   (c) 0.0455,

   (d) 0.705,   (e) 0.179,   (f) 0.395.

5. (a) 0.230,   (b) 0.152,   (c) 0.858.

EXERCISE 7G

1. (a) +1.960,   (b) −1.282,   (c) −1.645,

   (d) +1.44 (using interpolation),   (e) −1.960,

   (f) +1.036,   (g) −0.842,   (h) +1.282,

   (i) +2.326.

2. (a) −1.645 and +1.645,

   (b) −2.576 and +2.576,

   (c) −3.090 and +3.090.

EXERCISE 7H _____

1 **(a)** 85.5,   **(b)** 80.1,   **(c)** 69.3,

   (d) 88.8,   **(e)** 59.2 – 88.8,   **(f)** 66.4 – 81.6.

2 **(a)** 421,   **(b)** 370,   **(c)** 355,

   (d) 321,   **(e)** 231. The limits are 277–433.

3 **(a)** 2.35 (35 minutes past 2 – answer to nearest minute to ensure arriving **before** 3.00),

   (b) 2.30,

   (c) 2.26,

   (d) 2.46,

   (e) 2.40 (nearest minute to arrive **after** 3.00),

   (f) 2.47.

EXERCISE 7I _____

1 26.78 to 31.62 cm.

2 **(a) (i)** 0.894,   **(ii)** 0.493.

   (b) Longest possible stay is 60 minutes. For proposed model about 60% of times will exceed 60 minutes. Model could not apply.

   (c) 99.9% of normal distribution less than $\mu + 3\sigma$, i.e. $65 + 3 \times 20 = 125$ minutes. Model could be plausible for users entering 125 minutes or more before closing time, i.e. 6.55 pm. [A]

   Note: this answer is very cautious, you could argue that 95% of the distribution is sufficient.

3 **(a)** 0.405.

   (b) £761.

   (c) 0.0269

   (d) Cannot be exact because money is a discrete variable and also because negative takings impossible.   [A]

EXERCISE 7J _____

(Interpolation has been used, your answers may be slightly different if you have not used interpolation.)

1 **(a)** 0.909,   **(b)** 0.0710,   **(c)** 0.838.

2 **(a)** 45.75 – 46.65 cm.

   (b) 46.58 cm.

   (c) 128.

3 **(a) (i)** 0.122,   **(ii)** 0.661,   **(iii)** 0.488.

   (b) 15.6 – 20.4 s.

4 129. Large sample → sample mean normally distributed, whatever the population distribution. Might be invalid if sample size small and population not normal (or sample not random).

MIXED EXERCISE

1 (a) 0.291 or 29.1%,   (b) 403.

2 0.841.

3 (a) 0.159,   (b) 0.801,   (c) 60.2 g.

4 (a) 0.919,   (b) 0.274,   (c) 8.11 am.

5 (a) 0.02275,

   (b) 0.821,

   (c) 0.0886 (answers may be slightly different without interpolation). Large sample in (c) so answer unchanged if weights not normally distributed.

6 0.0475 or 4.75%.

7 0.910.

8 (a) 0.401,   (b) 0.691,   (c) 0.494, unaffected.

9 (a) 0.212 or 21.2%,   (b) 22.6 g.

10 (a) 0.386,   (b) 0.0644.
   Money is discrete variable normal is continuous; cannot carry a negative amount of change.

11 (a) 0.115,   (b) 33.2 g.

12 (a) 0.685,   (b) 40.5 m,   (c) 40 m, 4.9 m

   (d) Gwen.

13 (a) (i) 0.0495, (ii) 0.00005,
   I and II aren't satisfied.

   (b) (i) 105.3 ml,   (ii) 106.5 ml,
   mean at least 106.5 ml.

   (c) (i) 103.3 ml (mean), 3.98 ml (sd).
     (ii) Yes, conditions just met, but if sd reduced, conditions can be met with smaller mean content.

8 Correlation

EXERCISE 8A

1 (a) (i) yes,   (ii) yes,   (iii) no.
   (b) (i) No – all points do not lie on the same line.
     (ii) Yes – weak, negative correlation is evident.
     (iii) No – $-1 \leq r \leq 1$ so $r = 1.2$ is impossible.

2 (i) 0.9,   (ii) −0.3,   (iii) 0.85,   (iv) 0.

3 (a) and **(b)** **(i)**

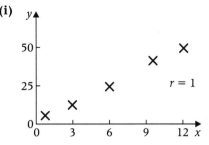

(ii)

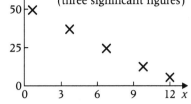

r = −0.994
(three significant figures)

(iii)

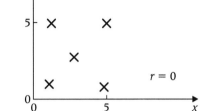

(iv)

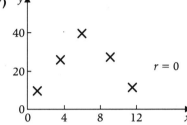

4 $\bar{x} = 56.9$, $\bar{y} = 27.7$

$S_{XX} = 16570.9$, $S_{YY} = 3568.9$

$r = 0.880$.

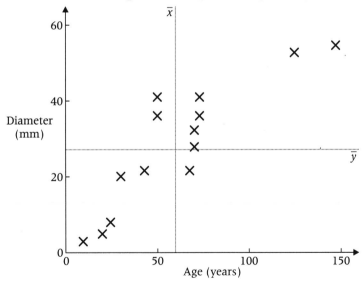

Graph of lichen diameter against age

5 (i)

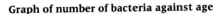

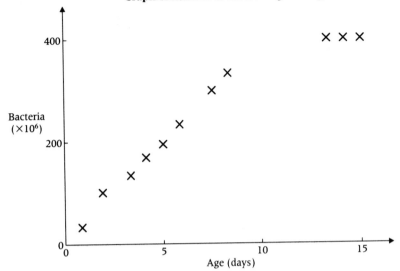

(ii) $r = 0.989$.

(iii) Although a very strong correlation was found in (ii), it appears that the rate of growth is decreasing, i.e. the linear relationship will probably not continue.

6

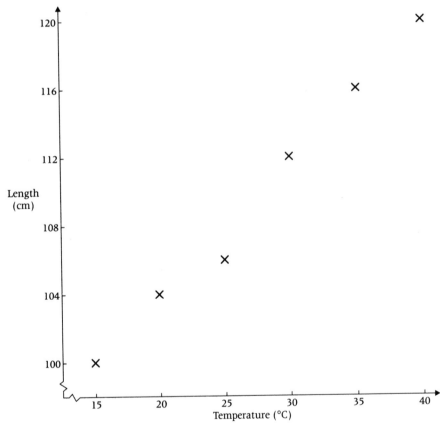

$r = 0.995$.

Discard $(25, 106.1) \rightarrow$ new $r = 0.99991$, $r \approx 1$.

It appears there is an exact linear relationship once $(25, 106.1)$ is removed. However, even when including this point the fit was very good.

7 (a)

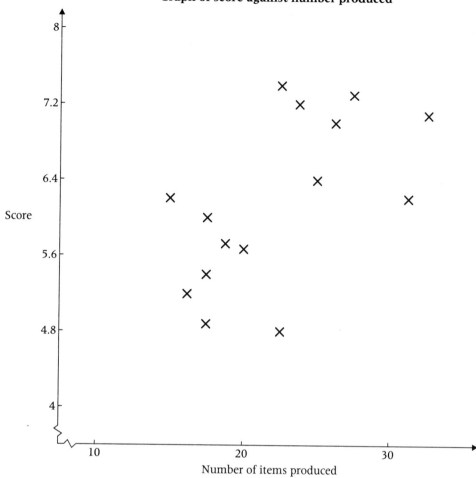

Graph of score against number produced

(b) $r = 0.610$.

(c) The data appear to show that the owner's belief is incorrect as
there is weak positive correlation. However, if the data were
divided into two groups, the owner's belief may be true as the
experienced craftsmen (2, 4, 8, 9, 10, 13, 14 perhaps) may produce
higher quality goods, but this quality may deteriorate if rushed.

8 (a)

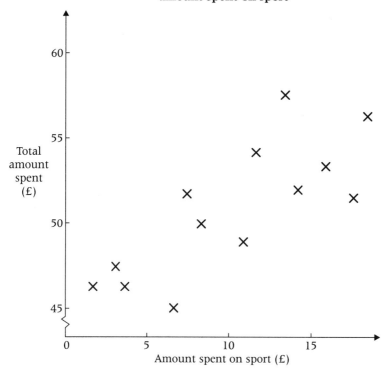

Graph of total amount spent against amount spent on sport

(b) $r = 0.824$.

(c) It appears appropriate since the data seem to follow a linear relationship. Since x is part of y, it might be better to examine relationship of x with $y - x$.

9 (b) $r = 0.937$.

(c) Calculations seem inappropriate as a clear non-linear relationship is seen – despite high value of r.

10 (a) $r = -0.800$.

(b) $r = -0.817$.

(c) Both values for r show fairly strong negative correlation indicating (a) higher heart value function links to lower baldness and (b) higher hours of TV links to lower heart function.

(d) Data does not provide evidence for a causal link between watching TV and any effect on heart function. There may be a separate factor which is linked to both number of hours watching TV and heart function.

9 Regression

EXERCISE 9A

1 **(a)**

Graph of heart mass against body mass for 14 mice

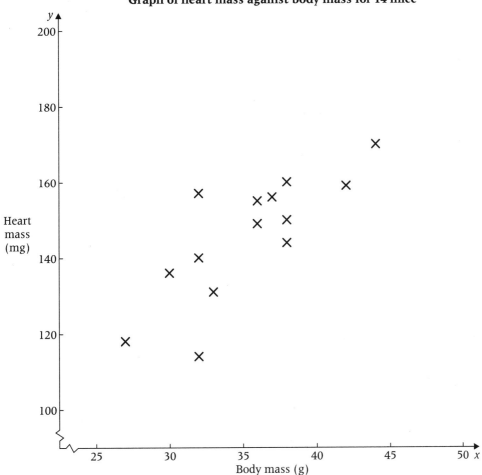

(b) $y = 48.4 + 2.75x$

2 (a)

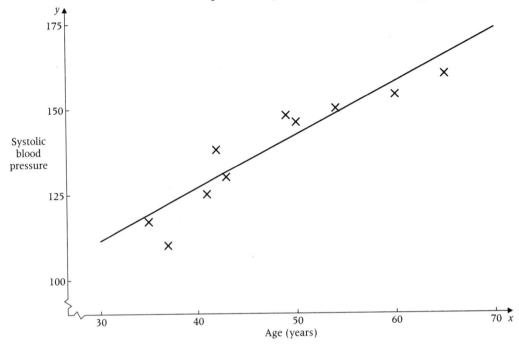

Graph of blood pressure against age

(b) $y = 62.8 + 1.58x$

(c) (i) $y = 1.5763 \times 20 + 62.766 = 94.3$
(ii) $y = 1.5763 \times 45 + 62.766 = 133.7$

(d) (i) Extrapolation – not accurate, linear model may not continue
(ii) Interpolation – likely to be reasonably accurate

3 (a)

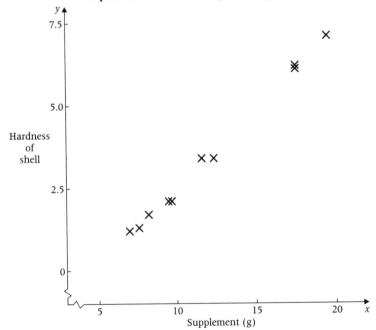

Graph of hardness of shell against supplement amount

(b) $y = 0.486x - 2.40$

(c) y on scale 0–10; model cannot extend to values of x outside range 5 to 25 (approximately).

4 (a) and **(c)**

Graph of predicted age against and actual age

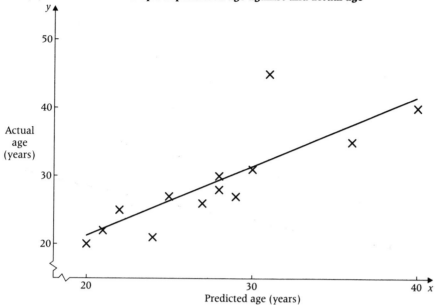

(b) $y = 1.03x + 0.533$.

(d) With the exception of *G*, predictions seem fairly accurate – the points all lie close to the line. It would be advisable to investigate person G to see if they should be excluded (been ill/in prison?).

5 (a) and **(c)**

Graph of price against capacity

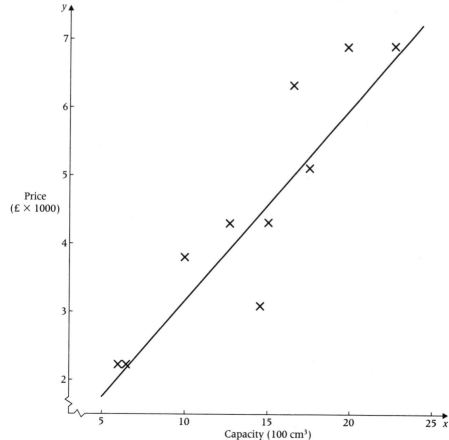

(b) $y = 3.02x + 237$.

(d) Model J is recommended (well below line – very low price).
Discourage models A, E and K (above line – high price)

6 (a)

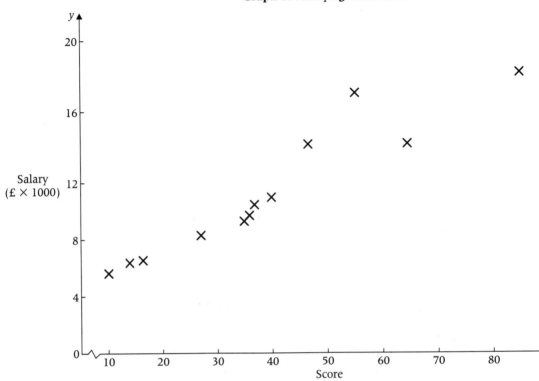

Graph of salary against score

(b) $y = 192x + 3713$

(c) Points close to straight line, apart from B and C. Method should be
reasonably satisfactory.

(d) Salary $= a + bx + t$, where t is an additional payment for
employees who have to work away from home.

7 **(a)**

Graph of time to pack against number of items

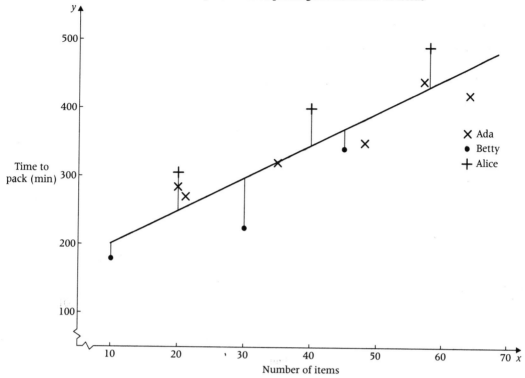

(b) $r = 0.897$

(c) $y = 166 + 4.62x$.

(d) $y = 4.6161 \times 45 + 165.52 = 373$, should be fairly accurate but would depend on packer

(e) Betty $\simeq -59.0, -31.7, -33.2$, average -41.3
Alice $\simeq +47.2, +49.8, +56.7$, average $+51.2$

   (i) Betty $373.2 - 41.3 = 332$
   (ii) Alice $373.2 + 51.2 = 424$.

8 **(a)**

Graph of cost against output

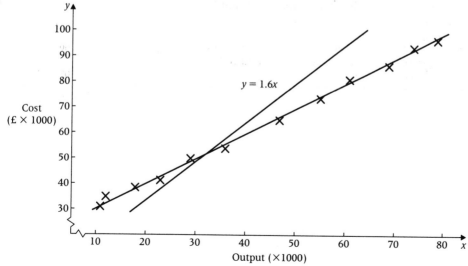

(b) $y = 0.961x + 20.7$

(c) Approximately 32 000 output

(d) If output above 32 000 a quarter, profit will be made

9 (a)

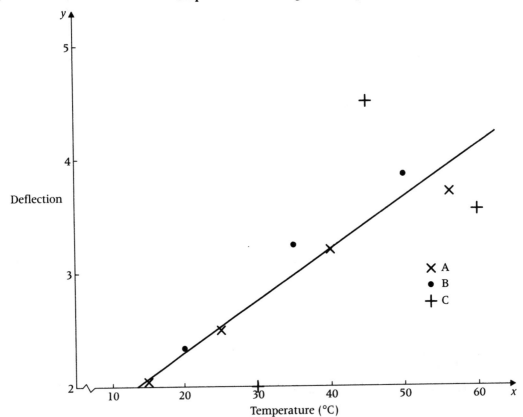

Graph of deflection against temperature

(b) $y = 0.0453x + 1.42.$

(c) Technician B seems to give higher results than A. A and B are both consistent, however, C's results are very erratic.

(d) Check which of A and B is 'accurate'. Try to find and eliminate cause of small systematic difference between A and B. Check C's measurements: C needs retraining.

10 (a)

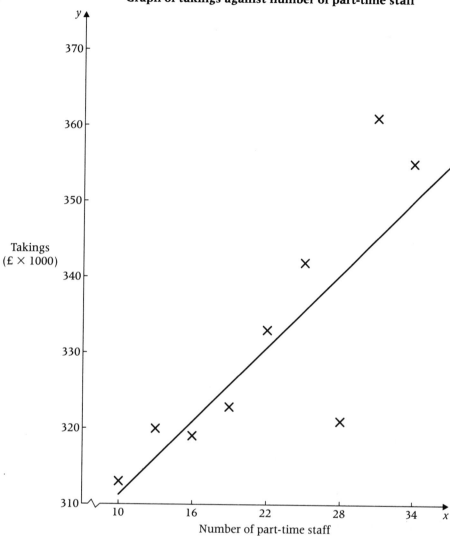

Graph of takings against number of part-time staff

(b) $y = 294 + 1.73x$

(c) £29 400, estimate of takings when no part-time staff employed.
£173 extra taken per extra part-time member of staff.

(d) Week with 28 staff – abnormally low takings relative to pattern.

(e) Might be run-up to Christmas and takings would increase
anyway. There may be other outside factors affecting the
experiment. Better to choose random levels of part-time staff.

Practice exam paper

1 (i) 0.112, **(ii)** 0.954.

2 (a) frequencies 15, 10, 7, 9, 20, 12,

   (b) (i) 7.5 years, **(ii)** 14.0 years.

3 (a) (i) 0.81, **(ii)** 0.072,

   (b) (i) 0.009, **(ii)** 0.0576.

4 (a) (i) 0.113, **(ii)** 0.699,

   (b) 3,

   (c) (i) mean unlikely to be constant,
      (ii) not independent.

5 (a) (i) 0.195, **(ii)** 0.829,

   (b) 86.8 cm,

   (c) (i) Not valid – sample likely to be biased,
      (ii) still valid. May assume mean of large sample is normally distributed.

6 (a) Appears to be biased – all sample means exceed population mean.

   (b) 4.925, 0.680 (allow 0.636),

   (c) Number rods 000 to 149; select three digit random numbers; ignore > 149 and repeats; when 3 obtained select the corresponding rods,

   (d) 3.16, 1.97 (allow 1.84),

   (e) some random sample means above population mean some below – non-random sample means all above. Mean of random sample means closer to population mean than mean of non-random samples. Random sample means more variable than non-random sample means,

   (f) 3.41 (allow 3.19).

7 (a)

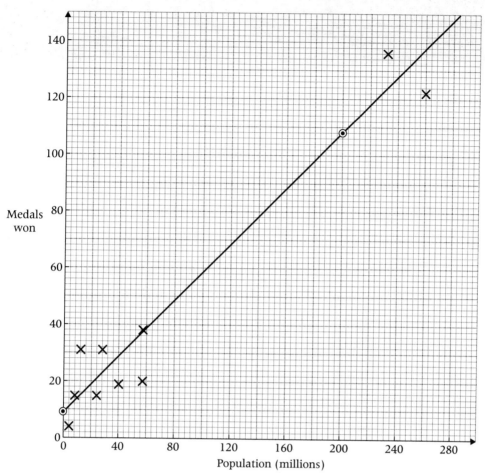

(b) $y = 8.44 + 0.498x$

(c) 83

(d) underestimate – unified team won more medals than predicted by line, Russia a large proportion of the population of countries making up the unified team,

(e) 0.683,

(f) fairly large, positive correlation coefficient offers some support for suggestion that those countries which win a large number of medals at the Summer games also tend to win a large number of medals at the Winter games

(g) only countries which won at least four medals included, unified team made up of several countries, (other comments, e.g. no African countries, also acceptable).